Sylvia Wynne Jones was born in 1929, a time of hardship and poverty, to a working class family in Plaistow, East London. Her early life was disrupted, as she was shuttled between Catholic and state schools at the whim of her parents.

When war broke out she was just ten and was evacuated to rural Carmarthenshire in west Wales for two years. For the first time she found stability in a Catholic convent school. Returning to London at the height of the bombing, she was pitchforked into a rough elementary school, constantly truanting, until she passed the Scholarship examination to Grammar school, gaining the School Certificate in 1944. She then had to work to help with the family finances; insurance clerk, trainee Marks and Spencer assistant and even time in the Women's Auxiliary Air Force. Dissatisfied, she insisted on returning to school to take the Higher School Certificate and from there went to Teacher Training College.

Her first teaching post was in a deprived area of East Ham and then a post in Germany. Fleeing a married man there, she spent a year in Paris studying French. Back in England, she was caught up in the change to comprehensive education. This career was brutally interupted when her husband decided they should emigrate to New Zealand. It was a disaster and she returned to England after three months without a job or husband. She became a Deputy Head in Brynmawr Comprehensive school in South Wales, at the same time studying for an M.A. in Education. Her children, now grown up, she returned to London as Deputy Head of a large comprehensive school. She remained there for seven years until she retired in 1989. Now at leisure, her interests are travel, writing, reading and learning languages.

Breaking Free

A Memoir

Sylvia Wynne-Jones

Breaking Free

A Memoir

Olympia Publishers
London

www.olympiapublishers.com
OLYMPIA PAPERBACK EDITION

Copyright © Sylvia Wynne-Jones 2013

The right of Sylvia Wynne-Jones to be identified as author of
this work has been asserted in accordance with sections 77 and 78 of the
Copyright, Designs and Patents Act 1988.

All Rights Reserved

No reproduction, copy or transmission of this publication
may be made without written permission.
No paragraph of this publication may be reproduced,
copied or transmitted save with the written permission of the publisher, or in
accordance with the provisions
of the Copyright Act 1956 (as amended).

Any person who commits any unauthorised act in relation to
this publication may be liable to criminal
prosecution and civil claims for damage.

A CIP catalogue record for this title is
available from the British Library.

ISBN: 978-1-84897-261 2

This is a work of fiction.
Names, characters, places and incidents originate from the writer's
imagination. Any resemblance to actual persons, living or dead, is purely
coincidental.

First Published in 2013

Olympia Publishers
60 Cannon Street
London
EC4N 6NP

Printed in Great Britain

To my grandson, Leigh Hyder, who has helped me with any problems; and the use of the computer!

Contents

Preface	13
Chapter 1 *The Past is Mine*	17
CHAPTER 2 *Rumblings of War*	29
Chapter 3 *Images of War*	38
Chapter 4 *Opening Vistas*	46
Chapter 5 *Adolescence*	54
Chapter 6 *The World of Work*	65
Chapter 7 *College Life*	79
Chapter 8 *Initiations*	90
Chapter 9 *Foreign Climes*	105
Chapter 10 *Paris*	120

Chapter 11 *Love and Marriage*	132
Chapter 12 *Songs of Innocence*	152
Chaper 13 *Marriage in Free-fall*	170
Chapter 14 *Stalemate*	186
Chapter 15 *Vistas new*	200
Chapter 16 *Country Life*	215
Chapter 17 *Changing Times*	241
Chapter 18 *Retiring Pleasures*	260
Conclusion	274

Preface

Is it the Zeitgeist? This desire, need, compulsion – call it what you will – to write memoirs and autobiographies? So many people are doing it – even thirty-year-olds who, one would think, are too busy living their lives to take time out to write about themselves, when they haven't yet reached the uplands to see themselves properly. But they all key in to the breast-baring, breast-beating confessional of our times. And what vicarious pleasure, pain, prurience, horror, shock we feel when we read of all the abuses these writers have suffered – abuse from Mums, Dads and even siblings. The more outrageous and shocking the story, the more it sells.

Once upon a time in the 40s and 50s, the stiff upper lip still existed – it was considered unseemly to share one's innermost thoughts with strangers. It was just not British! But here am I now, tapping into this *Zeitgeist,* going with the flow. It's taken a long time to come, this freedom to write and now that I'm coasting along in the cool, ever-more shallow waters of life, I have to hurry to record it. It's a new venture, but I agree with Browning in his poem *Andrea del Sarto*:

> *A man's reach should exceed his grasp*
> *Or what's a heaven for?*

Why do I have the temerity to think that anyone would be interested in *my* story? Am I seeking enlightenment through my past? Two contrasting feelings have dogged me all my life and maybe writing about them may help me to understand the paradox. One seems to be a very *modern* feeling, a sense of 'otherness', of exclusion from society – Camus' philosophy of alienation. So I feel like *L'Étranger*, only from a female point of view. I suppose this feeling came from my status in society, a dirt-poor working-class girl. Could it also be part of my temperament? According to my French horoscope, *L'Enfant Capricorne fait bande à part* (if one can believe horoscopes.) Could it have been because I was a Roman Catholic? The Catholics were a beleaguered sect in a Protestant enclave in East London. Or could it have been genetic? My father was a very antisocial character. Whatever. But the feeling is not a comfortable one. I have wished with all my heart that I could feel 'included' in society. But I don't. And now, I have resigned myself to the role of outsider, embarrassed among the working class where I started and uncomfortable in the presence of the educated middle class where I rightly belong. In one sense, this enforced detachment from society is a boon. I can see more clearly the foibles, the posturings, some of the weaknesses of society, but deep down I envy those who display supreme self-confidence, beset as I am with constant fears and misgivings.

The other feeling is the peculiar sense of superiority that I used to have, without any reason for it. This perception may be linked to the previous one, *faute de mieux*, as the French say. Because I felt excluded, I made a virtue of it by considering myself above some people. I can't have got it from my mother, a slapdash but loquacious Irish woman, happiest when gossiping with the neighbours. Did it come from my intelligent, unschooled father? He had a very jaundiced view of all his workmates and allowed no one but his brothers into the house. Did it come from the grammar school, where we had inculcated into us the fact that we were the top ten per cent of the population? This was quite ridiculous really, since Plaistow Grammar School was a poor school, on the edge of the London docklands. Whatever the reason for my sense of superiority, it dissipated quite quickly when I became an adolescent. I was suddenly and shockingly aware that I was the daughter of the lowest form of life, a casual dockworker. The word 'casual', innocent as it may seem, was the crux of the problem. It meant that sometimes my father had work and sometimes he didn't, depending on the work available. The 'casuals' were given the work that was left over after the regular stevedores had jobs allocated to them. So sometimes he brought home some wages and sometimes he didn't…

When I was at college, I read Durkheim, the sociologist. He quoted some interesting statistics about the working class. Apparently, the son of a casual labourer was very unlikely to succeed in life, but the daughter of the aforesaid labourer had no chance at all! So there was I, a lower-working-class girl, Class V in the statistics, dressed in frumpish garments run up by my mother on the sewing machine, excruciatingly shy and awkward, a washout socially and sexually even worse. What with my mother's repressive Irish Catholicism and my father's violent temper, I was frightened of the whole of the opposite sex. But I did have a keen curiosity about life, a lively intelligence, a wide vocabulary because I escaped from the life at home into books, and a strong work ethic, inculcated in me by my mother. Later in life I discovered that people, especially men, (well, some at least) thought that I had a sense of humour and a vivacious personality. And it is with these attributes that I sallied forth to begin the journey round my life.

Chapter 1
The Past is Mine

It was an inauspicious beginning, the day that I was born the 28 December 1929. My father was lying in bed in the next room fighting smallpox, never having been vaccinated against the dread disease. My mother was giving birth to me, her sixth child in the next room, aided manfully by a midwife. I had come as a complete surprise, two months too early. I was puny, but obviously just as eager to face the world as I still am. "What'll I call her, nurse?" After four previous children, my mother had exhausted her stock of names. She was weary of giving birth now, worried and anxious as to how she would feed another mouth. The nurse cast her mind around, equally weary after the ordeal. "Well, Sylvia Sims is very popular now. So why don't you call her 'Sylvia'?" And Sylvia, it was, although I have always hated the name...

This momentous event took place in a flat in West Ham, an area near Epping Forest, which had been very wealthy in the eighteenth and early nineteenth century. Merchant bankers and city magnates had built their large and important country houses there. But by the end of the nineteenth century with the arrival of the docks, the railways and other industrial enterprises, and the phenomenal rise in the population (from 18,000 in 1851 to 205.000 in 1891) the other side of industrialization was clearly to be seen. West Ham's main claims to fame by the end of the century was to elect Keir Hardie as the very first Labour MP to sit in the House of Commons, and to have provided the newspapers with some excitement when a factory manufacturing TNT in Silvertown blew up in 1917 killing sixty-nine employees. Now, the grand houses still remaining are very popular with the large Asian families who have moved into the area. They appreciate their spacious rooms.

By 1929 the area had improved considerably, but was still highly impoverished, with much substandard housing. We lived in what was colloquially known as 'The Buildings', those solid blocks of flats, five storeys high, reminiscent of the substantial blocks still part of the cityscape in Europe. I've often wondered why most of them have disappeared; some were obviously bombed, but others were torn down in the manic rebuilding of London after the Second World War, to be replaced by the hated high-rise flats. These pre-war blocks were built on a human scale, still low enough to be friendly and welcoming. They could have been as successful as the European ones except that, in our part of London, the poorest and the lowest of society inhabited them. I'm told we lived on the third floor. Each flat consisted of a living room, a small kitchen and three bedrooms, which may sound fairly spacious, but one of the bedrooms was let out to a lodger to help pay the rent. The rest of the family, ten in all, slept in the other two. For me, only the street outside was real. The street was our playground and our battlefield. Unlike the carefully cosseted and protected middle-class girls who played in the security of their gardens, we had no gardens. We played on the pavements outside, shouting and giggling raucously at each other, unconsciously developing useful aggressive instincts as we vied with each other to dominate whatever game was in progress. We also played in the street, since most of the traffic consisted of horse-and-carts and proved to be of little danger. We were more likely to run the danger of being sprayed with horse manure and thus be exposed to the wrath of our parents. We liked to watch these old carthorses horses when they were stationed outside a house or shop; we had to scatter from their vicinity when they snuffled in their nosebags and sent up showers of chaff. We also had to be wary of their urine as they sprayed what seemed like oceans of piss onto the road. We would play 'Whippy', a game where you hung onto the tailboard of the carts, much to the fury of the driver. We ran after the ice-cream tricycle, pursuing the hapless vendor, shouting coarse expressions at him as he was perched high on the tricycle trilling, "Stop me and buy one!" With no money to buy an ice-cream, we weren't too kindly disposed towards him. We also ran after the rag-and-bone man whose raucous calls advertising his presence echoed down the streets. We were more careful of the coalman who could land a hefty blow on us with his empty, dust-laden sack if we bothered him too much. We would stand watching him respectfully as he hoisted the heavy sack filled with coals onto his head and shoulders, protected by a canvas hat with huge flaps at the back of it. He shovelled the black shiny coal into the small coal-holes outside the houses with consummate skill. Some of these manholes were brightly polished and with intricate designs on their cast-iron lids. Our games consisted of playing marbles in the gutters, (I loved the way the colours were refracted through the glass of the marbles), and five-stones, at which I was an unexpected expert. Somewhat more energetic was the game of hopscotch. Someone would find a piece of chalk from somewhere and draw the squares on the pavement and we would hop skilfully from one to the other. The girls also liked skipping, when we could find a skipping rope, and liked to show off that we were more agile than the boys. They in turn, when there was a craze for spinning tops, would demonstrate their prowess as they whipped the tops savagely, making them spin faster and faster in a myriad of colours. The boys also indulged in 'Knocking Down Ginger', knocking on front doors and running away. They had the sense to get away fast and left us girls gawping at the furious owner who would scream obscenities at us until we scattered. More adventurously, we visited the blacksmith at the end of the street and peered into the black cavernous interior, with its glowing fire and bellows showering sparks around the walls. I would watch with fascinated horror as he pressed the red-hot iron onto the horse's foot and heard the hissing as heat made contact with flesh. Then I would transfer my gaze to the horse's face and marvel at its stoicism.

Our favourite pastime was swinging on the lamp-posts, always at night, when the gas lamps flared, shedding a circular pool of light on the pavement around. We sat on the railings of the houses nearby, like small birds in a row, waiting our turn for the rope. The night seemed always to be dark and cold, studded with stars, creating a magical atmosphere, enhanced by our breath freezing in a white cloud around us. I was focussed on the flying figure creating arabesques around the lamp-post. And when my turn came, the exhilaration of swinging out widely and rhythmically, kicking out at the post as I came dangerously near to smacking into it, filled me with delight. I stayed out as long as I could, usually after the rest of the girls had disappeared, until I reluctantly dragged myself home through the darkness. My mother never called me in until Dad arrived back home. Then there was a great scurry to get in just after him or there would be trouble. My mother was quite happy to have us outside all day long, so that we weren't 'under her feet'. The living room was the communal room. There, surrounded by all the rest of the family, I would read and read voraciously. I had discovered the local library at the age of about eight and borrowed such delights as the 'Milly, Molly, Mandy' series, and Elinor Brent-Dyers' stories of the Chalet School and its boarding-school inmates in Switzerland. The books had the occasional French word scattered throughout the text which really intrigued me. Perhaps these books were the beginning with my love affair with France. I loved *Little Women* by Louisa M. Alcott, and the Angela Brazil's stories of middle-class boarding school life; they were all permeated with middle-class values and morals. Fortunately we did not possess a wireless at that time to distract my attention, so I was able to read for hours when in enforced seclusion in the flat. Occasionally my mother would become exasperated at the sight of me sitting in the corner, oblivious to everything except my storybook. She would come up to me, wrench the book from my hand and say angrily, "Will you leave that book alone? I'll tear it up if you don't watch out!" It was an empty threat since she would have to pay the library for a replacement, but the warning was enough for me and I would escape upstairs to the bedroom, clutching my beloved book with me.

I did sometimes help out with the 'chores'. Often it was to try to get the fire started on the range. I would have to hold a newspaper over the weak, flickering flame to provide a draft and coax it to become more courageous. My heart would be in my mouth waiting for the newspaper suddenly to catch light. One had to judge the moment when the brown scorch marks appearing on the newspaper would suddenly ignite and then hastily push it onto the fire, trying not to get burned. I was never very good at this ploy. I hated the job and hated it even more after one momentous event. I was ordered to 'black the stove', to put blacklead on it to keep it from rusting. I removed the flat irons and in order to polish the stove more vigorously, I leaned my arm on it, only to discover that it was still very hot. The ensuing sizzling of my flesh was very similar to that suffered by the horse in the blacksmith's. I don't remember the aftermath of this unfortunate incident, but I still bear the fairly large scar and noted the description of it most proudly and meticulously on my first passport.

My parents were a curiously ill-matched couple. My mother was the third born of eleven surviving children, issue of a feckless, immigrant, Catholic family, which left Cork in the 1840s, to escape the grinding poverty and the strong possibility of starvation during the potato famine. They settled in the St Katharine's dock area as wharf labourers living in overcrowded, unsanitary blocks of flats near Tower Bridge. Ironically, they would not recognise the area now; those grim blocks, leaching misery and hopelessness have been transformed into desirable residences; the docks transmuted into a Mediterranean-like marina, complete with large, gleaming-white yachts and motorboats. But in spite of the poverty, they were a happy family, fond of Guinness and singing. I remember seeing my grandmother, years later, dressed in funereal black and sitting upright in a high-backed chair, as she sipped her daily ration of stout and licked the foaming head from her lips. Every day, whoever was available, would have to run to the off-licence with a jug to fetch her ration.

My father, David George, was the first-born of an equally large family. The atmosphere in his family must have been one of poverty, bitterness and repression. His mother Emmeline had known better days and she could not come to terms with her changed circumstances. Her grandfather had been a wealthy builder in Chelmsford who left much money and property to his son Arthur. But Arthur disappeared in mysterious circumstances after moving his family to West Ham in London, presumably taking the money with him. She had tried to reclaim some of the missing family money but with little success. All we have of her past is a letter from a solicitor stating that he would give her five pounds and would try to pursue the matter, but nothing more was said. She married a dock labourer, Henry, at eighteen and had eleven children, thus setting the seal on *her* fate. My father was born a year after her marriage and bore the brunt of his mother's resentment at what life had brought her to; his early years must have been ones of extreme hardship. He inherited her sternness, her almost obsessive cleanliness, and her temper. Her husband Henry was a casual dock labourer, more out of work than in. He must have been of less stalwart stock than Emmeline; he committed suicide when he was fifty-five, because of cancer, but my grandmother lived on until she was ninety-three. I remember her visiting us occasionally, filling the cramped living room with her tall presence and frightening us with her deep voice and severe demeanour. My parents met soon after the 1914-1918 war. In fact my mother was engaged to an Italian Roman Catholic when she met my father for the first time. It was a *coup de foudre*; he was over six feet tall, handsome, with regular features and a mop of curly brown hair. He had emerged from the war comparatively unscathed, with only slight shell shock, which may or may not have explained his violent rages later on. Whenever he felt frustrated and angry, he would shout, "I should have stayed in Europe. Radermacher offered me a job! I could have had a good life. But I had to come back here, didn't I? And look what you and your kids have brought me to!" Although how and where he met this man he never condescended to tell us. Perhaps he was a figment of his imagination, a convenient story to beat us with. He would glare at my mother, willing her to admit that she was the cause of all his misery.

My father followed his father into the docks, upholding a long-standing tradition. The London Docks were popular until the early 1920s because they offered plenty of work; so sons 'got their card' and joined their fathers in the docks. During the First World War they were kept very busy, but afterwards, they suffered the same unemployment problems as the mining, steel and shipbuilding industries which no longer had a market for their goods. The General Strike in May 1926, which brought the country to a standstill, meant that my father was almost permanently unemployed and our normal poverty became deprivation. Baldwin, the Prime Minister, availed himself of the latest invention, 'the wireless' to broadcast avuncular and reassuring words to those members of the population who could afford a wireless. He called in the army to help, and the police managed to arrest 5,000 people during the nine days stoppage. Class divisions showed up starkly during this fraught time. Many of the middle class were eager to help maintain skeleton services and stories abounded of Oxbridge students manning the buses and entrepreneurs taking advantage of the crisis. It ended in a humiliating and historic defeat for the Labour movement. The Wall Street crash of 1929 made matters worse. There was no let-up in the misery in our family. My father never blamed the unions or the Labour Party for all our troubles; working-class solidarity was alive and strong. Only my mother retained bitter memories of the strike and the pressing problem of feeding all her family. She became dismissive of all political figures and continued to speak darkly of Baldwin and his economic policies which prolonged the Depression. His stock went down even further during the Abdication crisis in 1936 because she was very much a royalist. My father must have suffered grievously during those dark times. He had to drag himself down to the docks every day to see if there was any work. Every day he went off carrying the bale-hook handed down to him by his father, a docker's tool with a vicious-looking curve in it. He would join the hundreds of other day labourers impatiently crowding around the port official as he climbed onto his box. Then the wait and the hope that his name would be called and he could have work for the day and some money to take home. Unlike many of the dockers, my father, a lonely man and a teetotaller, would go straight home to face my mother's recriminations. Sometimes he had a job working on the boats for a week or more, sometimes he didn't. How my mother managed this hand-to-mouth existence, I cannot imagine. I still find it a mystery that my father did not try later to escape from this penal servitude which affected our family so grievously. He had some sort of perverted pride in the fact that he was following an ancient tradition.

These dreadful times continued until 1937 when the government started on a policy of re-armament, in the light of the dangerous events unfolding in Europe. Suddenly my father was in work again and life became easier, although still hard. Shoes were the biggest problem. I remember my father having a black iron last, on which our shoes and boots were placed to have new soles hammered inexpertly onto them. As for our clothes, I could never decide whether one was more unfortunate having 'new' clothes that my mother made on her sewing machine, which invariably turned out to be ill-fitting, or suffer the ignominy of the 'hand-me-downs'. There was never any money to buy new ones. She paid into a weekly club for clothes from Granditer's, a local dress shop, and whenever enough money was collected, one of us had the luck (or not so lucky in some cases) of being kitted out with what my mother thought was plain and enduring. My sister Irene grieved over her appearance and compensates today by wearing elegant, expensive clothes, most of which remain in the wardrobe. We wore liberty bodices in the winter, smeared with goose-fat to keep out the cold and ward off diseases such as measles, chickenpox and the dreaded whooping cough. Like most poor people, we were not vaccinated against any of these deadly diseases, but were regularly dosed with cod-liver oil and malt, courtesy of the government. But the worst problem for my mother was to try to feed all of the family on the meagre amount given to her by the Unemployment Assistance Board. She had to be 'means-tested' to get this money and the experience of strangers wanting to know all the 'ins and outs' of our family life engendered in her a hatred both of means-testing and of Baldwin. We were always hungry, but my mother would say to us firmly as we reluctantly left the table, "It's good for you to leave the table wanting more!" We would scowl at such remarks, which seemed to add insult to injury. She would occasionally rebel against the hardship and violent rages between them, and would try to leave my father, dragging us in tow. But where to go? She had short shrift from my Irish grandmother, who was of the school, 'You've made your bed, now lie on it'. The Irish family had been implacably opposed to the mixed marriage and had never accepted my father. My grandmother would listen to my mother's tale of woe, but was mainly indifferent to her sufferings, probably believing that it was God's punishment for entering into such a sinful union.

The peculiarly joyless rigour of Irish Catholicism, as opposed to the European form, was very much in evidence here. Although they were married in a Catholic church (how did he get dispensation from 'an unlawful and pernicious' mixed marriage?) and my father had agreed that the children should be brought up in the 'real' faith, he soon reneged on this deal and endless were the arguments every Sunday when we stood by fearfully in our best clothes waiting to see whether we would be going to Mass, for not to do so was a mortal sin and we would go to Hell. Sometimes my mother won the day, sometimes my father's violent, jealous rage would prevent us leaving the house. The most amusing incidents, with hindsight, were when he had gone out on a Sunday morning to play cards with his brothers, but would return just as we were putting on our Sunday best. The scenario would be, "Quick, your father's got his key in the door! Get out the back way!" And we would rush out with fear in our hearts, to have more fear instilled in us in church as the priest fulminated against the congregation's wicked practices. Then there would be the inevitable visit from the priest on Mondays when we hadn't managed to get to church, demanding to know why we had not gone to Mass and threatening eternal hellfire if we missed the next Sunday. This tirade would be followed with more frightening strictures at the convent school the next day. Instilling fear in us was an ongoing ritual which never let up.

In the Roman Catholic faith, the Bible was not at the centre of the liturgy. Many priests did not read it and most parishioners in our area never opened it. Consequently, when I reached the sixth form and needed this biblical heritage to understand Milton's 'Samson Agonistes', I was totally ignorant and had to rush to read the relevant passages in a bible which I found in the library. The catechism took pride of place in our convent school and Friday afternoons were reserved for it. We would sit together on our long benches, handling small, scruffy, dog-eared books, a dirty shade of red, which smelled faintly of sweat and anxiety. Inside the booklet, the question and response format looked innocent enough, but make no mistake, this was indoctrination of the most intense kind. The nun would ask the questions and, in a sing-song voice, we would chant the responses:

What is actual sin? Actual sin is every sin which we ourselves commit.

How is actual sin divided? Actual sin is divided into mortal sin and venal sin

What is mortal sin? Mortal sin is a grievous offence against God.

Why is it called mortal sin? It is called mortal sin because it kills the soul and deserves hell.

And so on. These eternal truths, repeated so mechanically yet insistently, permeated our consciousness, sank deep into our subconscious minds and formed part of our living personalities. They would presumably remain with us until the Day of Judgement, when, if I had been good, I would be among the Chosen Ones and would ascend into the ethereal blue of heaven. The dreaded thought would occasionally occur to me that these catechism sessions might even continue when we were in heaven, with our ageing nun transformed into a shining, but equally repressive God.

Every week, we were 'crocodiled' to attend the interminable masses, with only the holy days as a break in the routine. Holy days were the highlight of our lives; they meant a day off school. Not that we were completely free of the heavy hand of the priest. Attendance at a Mass was *de rigueur* some time during the day, usually in the morning, as we had to fast beforehand to mortify our flesh. This was quite a trial for me. My last meal would have been in the early evening of the day before and it was never sufficient. If I complained, my mother would repeat the old mantra, "It's good for you to leave the table still hungry". What could one say in the face of this logic? But to have to wait until eleven o'clock the next day for my two Shredded Wheat was a true punishment for any supposed sins I had committed. These holy days were a celebration of the 'joyful mysteries' of the Roman Catholic faith; on Palm Sunday we had a free gift of a palm in the shape of a cross, an item to be treasured and put up in the bedroom or stuck into the frame of a holy painting; on Good Friday, the church was draped all in black and we were almost suffocated by the heavy incense swirling around us; on Passion Sunday, the church would be in mourning for the anticipated death of Jesus Christ and purple palls were thrown over the statues, creating an atmosphere of intense gloom. One holy day I remember with great clarity was Ash Wednesday. For some reason I was in the church by myself – an excess of zeal on my part? I duly went up to the altar rail, had my forehead marked with the sign of the cross from the ash of previous year's burnt palms and heard the words, *"Remember, man, that thou art dust and unto dust thou shalt return"*, which sent a chill round my heart. I returned not yet to dust but to my pew, swooning almost sensuously with the intense emotion of the scene, the pungent incense and the soaring ethereal voices of the choir. The bell pealed urgently three times, the moment of transubstantiation and the prayers of the congregation increased in fervour. I tried to join in but my religious euphoria had begun to subside and I became aware of earthly discomforts – the hard pew digging into my flesh, the intense cold in the church and the urgent need to go to the toilet. After what seemed an eternity of prayers and hymns, with my bodily discomforts taking precedence over my spiritual needs, I suddenly noticed that people were queuing up again for their mark of penitence. Were they sinners who needed even more penitence? Had a new service started while I had been communing with God? Taking my courage in my hands, I looked around wildly, and chose the least prostrate person in the pew to whisper to her:

"Excuse me, how much longer does the Mass go on for?" Regarding me with irritation and suspicion, an unkempt slip of a girl daring to drag her from her meditations, the lady replied shortly, 'It's Ash Wednesday! It goes on for twenty-four hours continuously'. When I digested this momentous piece of information, I was appalled and then asked, "Can you please tell me the time?" When she replied, "It's half-past eleven", I realised that I had been sitting in the church for over two hours. No wonder I was beginning to 'seize up'.

Up to this time in my life, I had never considered myself a lucky person. But there was one momentous day when God must have decided that I had been particularly good (perhaps extra-diligent in my catechismal responses?) and had decided to reward me. It was the day when the nuns and priests of St Margaret's Convent decided to have a spring-clean. A large over-life-size statue of the Virgin Mary and Child was suddenly surplus to requirements and it was to be raffled to the unsuspecting pupils. Well, there are no prizes for guessing who won it. I was euphoric! There she stood, the Virgin Mary, fully six feet tall, serene, smiling, in pale-blue drapery, her hand raised in benediction to me. Even the chubby baby Jesus was gazing down indulgently on me. I could not wait to get home to tell the good news to my family. Gasping and hiccuping in my rush to get home, with a stitch developing painfully in my side, finally seeing my mother standing at the front door, I shouted, "Mum! Mum! I've won a prize! I've won a statue of the Virgin Mary." While my mother looked at me trying to take in the enormity of what I was saying, arrangements were already being made to transport the statue to our cramped flat in 'The Buildings'. The euphoria was short-lived. Obviously, I hadn't been sufficiently devotional in my catechismal responses. Reality broke through when I looked at my mother's face, gazing horrified at the statue which filled all the available space in our cluttered overcrowded living room. The speed with which she managed to divest herself of this apparition before my father returned from work, was nothing short of miraculous itself. And that was the first and last prize I ever won.

The East End of London has always been a Mecca for immigrants. Huguenots in the eighteenth century, Jews and Irish in the nineteenth. In the 1930s, there was a large and flourishing Catholic community around Wapping and, on the Catholic holy days, the streets of the East End came to life with the Catholic processions. For many years, my uncle led the processions through the grimy streets, wearing the brightly-coloured sash of St Margaret over his Sunday-best suit and wielding with consummate skill the golden mace over his head – twirling it audaciously, spinning it up in the air and deftly catching it again, to the bold, ear-splitting rhythm of the brass band accompanying the procession. It was a gloriously multi-coloured spectacle lighting up the mean, dank streets and culminating in a march past St Margaret's church. Sometimes the procession fanned out on to the main road, astonishingly free of traffic for the occasion, and ended at the convent garden for an open-air service. One of the most important processions celebrated Confirmation and First Communion. So when I was nine years old, there was I with my younger sister, (how she managed to get into the act so young, I never found out) about to take First Communion.

We had been preparing at school for months for this important occasion, not that I had any conception of what it meant. The Catholic Church grabs its children young, to initiate them as full members of the Holy Church. We were mystified and uncomprehending, but were aware of the joy to come, marching along with this excited throng. The joy was made deeper by the knowledge that we would have new white satin dresses, new white shoes and socks especially for the occasion. How my mother managed to get the shining fabric to make into dresses, I don't know. We were the poorest of the poor, given meal tickets for school dinners, but presumably the imperative to rise up to the memorable event brought the whole of the Catholic congregation to her aid. We had already been warned in our regular Catechism lessons that the round circular wafer that would be placed on our tongues at the first communion was not bread, but the living Christ transmogrified. Any attempt to chew it, move it around in the mouth or even, horror of horrors! swallow it would be a mortal sin and could lead to eternal damnation. Mortal sins could never be washed away by prayer; they stayed with you until the Day of Judgement, until God himself decided your fate. I would suffer regular paroxysms of fear and terror as the Host lay on my tongue, inert but potent, and the fear could not be assuaged until it had melted in my mouth. Such was the power of the Catholic Church. And its heavy hand lies on me still, in spite of the beneficial vestiges; the sense of morality and duty inculcated in me, the love of language and the appreciation of artistic beauty. I am now a non-believer, yet not a day goes by without intimations of death intruding on my thoughts. Memento mori!

Chapter 2
Rumblings of War

Poverty continued to dog us in the 1930s – what Alan Bennett called, 'a muddy and grubby time'. My sisters, Irene the eldest, Doreen the youngest and I slept three to a bed and I remember the indignities of being pee-ed upon by my younger sister during the night and the wet warm urine seeping up my back. We were given meal tokens for school dinner, which we threw away in disgust when presented with the terrible food on offer and assuaged our hunger with sweets and cakes. At home, my mother would rant on about Baldwin, "What's he doing for the poor? Where's the help for the likes of us?" My father would listen to her in a sullen, uncharacteristic silence, presumably brought down by his inability to do anything. Like most of the working class, in their cloth caps and collarless shirts, he accepted his lot fatalistically. Why didn't he attempt to find other work? I suppose the ancient pride of the docker and the acceptance of the social hierarchies kept him in his place. But not everyone was suffering in the 1930s. My father would come home after walking the streets of Wanstead for something to do and talk of the washing machines, electric irons, fridges and vacuum cleaners displayed in the shops for the middle classes. Only a few miles from us, it was like another world.

Of course, not all was doom and gloom. There were minor excitements; occasionally having some cherries which my sister Doreen and I used as earrings. We would prance around and preen ourselves in the mirror, admiring the deep-red, glossy balls which we thought made us look so attractive, although we had to make sure that my mother wasn't in the vicinity. She would have made some caustic comment and ordered us to take them off. I also loved going to Rathbone Market in the evenings. It was usually a Friday evening when my father brought some wages home. The market was so mysterious, with its gas lamps flaring in the darkness, creating pools of light over the stalls. The noise of the vendors was deafening and the large throng of people making their way down the narrow path between the stalls added to the noise. They always seemed to be in a good humour, shouting ribald comments to each other. My mother would meet a neighbour and spend what seemed to me to be hours happily gossiping, while I stood dancing impatiently around them. Sometimes I would be included in the conversation, "My! Hasn't she grown! You are a big girl now, aren't you?" And I would squirm with embarrassment. My mother loved fish, one of the cheapest forms of food and she, being an East Ender, was very partial to eels. I hated standing at the fish stall. The fishy smell was overpowering, but what was worse, the eels were alive in a bucket, squirming and wriggling slowly around in the confined space. My mother would ask for a pound and the fishmonger would plunge his huge fist into the bucket and bring out a handful of writhing silver and black eels and, slapping them on the counter, deftly cut off their heads. I would gaze in fascinated horror at the spectacle, but became even more alarmed as the eels continued to writhe convulsively. I imagined them sliding headless off the counter and slithering towards me. Opposite the fish stall was the Pie and Mash shop, my favourite, where we were often sent to have a meat pie, mashed potatoes and what was called 'liquor', a bright green glutinous sauce. We loved it. There were also moments I remember of pure fear when I would be sent to buy a gas mantle for the gas lamp. They came in very small square boxes and were exceedingly fragile. One knock against the box and the mantle would crumble into dust. That happened to me only once. I was so frightened that I couldn't go home. I wandered around for some time until my elder sister, Irene who had been sent to find me, came across me dragging my feet disconsolately along the pavement. With her beside me, I gathered up the courage to face the inevitable scolding. I was also whisked into hospital once to have my tonsils taken out, a very fashionable operation in the 1930s, thousands of tonsils and their owner were parted. I remember waking up from the anaesthetic to discover that my pillow was covered with bright red blood. Terrified that I would be scolded for such carelessness, I turned the pillow over. It worked for a while, until the nurse came to make the bed and found the telltale bloodstain which was even bigger now, staining the sheet as well. She was not too pleased. I disliked her intensely, mainly because when my mother brought me a bag of sweets, she decided that I would have to share it with the other unfortunates in the ward.

But then it was 1939 and the quiet routine of my life, the close triangle of school, church and library, was suddenly to change. Almost imperceptibly at first, unusual incidents began to occur around us. One day, playing in the streets as usual, we noticed groups of workers systematically moving along the road digging up all the railings fronting the terraced houses, leaving them with a naked, defenceless look. We stared at these men curiously, tacitly accepting this vandalism. Mum said that the railings were being removed for the 'War effort', although many years later I noticed that the great urban houses of London had either retained their fine, wrought-iron railings or had had them replaced. We had no such luck. 'Our' railings were gone for good. We also noticed huge trenches being dug in the park near our block of flats, again for the War effort. But what impinged on me tangibly was the difference in our annual 'holiday' to the hop-fields.

Every September we and hordes of other East End families took to the hop-fields of Kent to earn some extra money, much to the exasperation of our schoolteachers who were faced with depleted classes for three weeks at the beginning of term. But September 1939 was different. We were transported by lorry as usual, but this time in complete darkness. The reason for the unusually late hour for our journey I only learned later. Britain had been put on a war footing, which included among other things, being 'blacked out' at night. I remember being unceremoniously bundled into the dark recesses of the lorry and exhorted to 'Keep Quiet!' although why there should be Germans lurking around the corner I couldn't imagine. The lorry moved stealthily through the seemingly impenetrable darkness of the blacked-out streets, with only the purr of the lorry's engine making any noise. Inside there was an unusual silence of fear and trepidation. This only began to dissipate when we arrived at the hop-farm at Goudhurst in Kent. Unloaded in the early morning into a stygian darkness that was almost palpable, we stumbled blindly around the dark field, again hearing the low curt orders to "Be quiet!" but I was aware only of the sharp, fresh night air and the dark sky studded with bright stars. Doreen and I huddled together, excited and expectant, until our family was allocated the hut that was to be our home for the next three weeks. A hurricane light was rapidly lit in the hut which cast dark, elongated shadows on the walls. Then we were quickly stuffing palliasses full of straw to make up our beds and collapsing giggling onto them. Even the sharp ends of the straw poking into my skin couldn't marr my excitement. Lying in the strange-smelling palliasses and breathing in the other curious odours of grass and manure, I was too excited to sleep at first, but the warmth of the covers and my sister's body pressed close to me made me relax. As I lost consciousness, I thought to myself: "I'm going to see another world out there tomorrow".

That special year, the weather was party to our happiness. Most mornings, a bright warm sun crept through the cracks in the door and we emerged, blinking, yawning and still half asleep to drink a mug of hot, steaming tea and a slice of bread and butter. Then it was time for everyone to start work in the hop-fields. Luckily, our father was not with us, having started work again and my mother was transformed from the grim, forbidding person we knew into a laughing young girl as she enjoyed the companionship of her Irish family, down there in force. Dad could only visit us at weekends and even then he cast a shadow, objecting to my mother going to the local pub at the weekends with her family. But for once he was outnumbered. So we had three weeks of glorious freedom. The long row of huts had fire-irons in front of them where kettles boiled and black pots filled with delicious-smelling stew bubbled away. Some early mornings were wreathed in the white September mists, creating an atmosphere of silent mystery. Strange figures would loom unexpectedly into view around the camp fire, only to be identified as they drew nearer as aunts and uncles. Damp from the autumnal mists, we were soon quite drenched as we pulled down the heavy hop-bines which showered us with dew. Then the sun would emerge, brilliant in the blue sky and we steamed like the pots of stew waiting for us. I was old enough now to have a half-bin with my sister. We picked the bright green hops from the vine, staining our fingers greeny-black, and waited, hearts beating, for the arrival of the tallyman who came with his wicker basket to measure the hops. If any dark-green leaves fell in with the hops, he would walk away in disgust, saying, "Get those leaves out if you want me to weigh those hops!" We would then rummage feverishly through the pungent, feathery flowers to pick out the recalcitrant leaves, and as we beavered away, the sweet-smelling woodsmoke would drift towards us, mingling with the acrid fragrance of the hops. The midday sun gradually released all the mellow odours of the landscape; manure from the horses, the sweet smell of the wild flowers and the sharp smell of the hops. It would shine on our backs bent over the bins, warming them so that I wriggled with contentment. Those scenes in the hop-fields are now set fast in my memory, vibrant and colourful, like the myriad images in a stained-glass window.

I had always had the feeling that we as a family were different from most of our neighbours. Maybe because we were Catholic, or because my father would allow no one in the house except his brothers. We also had to speak properly and were never allowed to swear, although our father was himself partial to the epithet 'poxy' which he applied to whatever was annoying him at any one time. These differences were made manifest when, in August 1940, we were evacuated separately from our school-friends. They went with their school, or with their mothers. For some reason incomprehensible to us, we were sent away on our own. Dad decided that we should be evacuated to Ashford with 'Aunt Mabel', a euphemism for the woman whom we learned later was my father's intermittent mistress. My elder sister and brother knew her well, because they had had the unenviable job of having to follow Dad when my mother suspected that he was meeting another woman secretly. My father would return home from work or wherever he had been, change into another suit and then leave the house, striding purposefully forward, oblivious of others. As soon as he had turned the corner, my mother would grab my sister or brother, whoever happened to be around and shout, "Quick! Irene [or Vic], get after your father! See where he's going, but don't let him see you!" No need for such a remark; paralysed with fear, they would stalk him along the streets, dodging into shop doorways if he turned his head, their hearts thumping with terror. But like beleaguered rats, they had the cunning to avoid detection. If he had caught them, they knew they would be in for a severe thrashing. Usually, all the trepidation they underwent was to no avail, since he would either soon outdistance them or they gave up the unequal chase in fear. When I first saw her, Mabel was regally tall and fearsome of mien. Once the decision was made to evacuate us with her to Ashford, we were whisked away from our home with lightning speed. My father must have had telling powers of persuasion for that odd event to have occurred. I presume, with hindsight, that she thought she would see more of him if she had us living with her. This presumption proved to be false, certainly while we were in Ashford. Of the short time we stayed with her, I can remember only two incidents, both indicative of the woman herself. We always ate in the dining room, the first time I had ever seen one. One Sunday at lunchtime, Doreen fully six years old, raised her plate and enquired plaintively, 'Can I have some mint sauce, please?'

Mabel looked astonished at such temerity and with a malevolent glint in her eye, replied:

'Sauce? You're not getting any sauce! You're saucy enough!' and she was as good as her word. The other memory I retained was the dreadful ritual every Friday evening, when with great ceremony, we were made to swallow a large tablespoonful of brimstone and treacle, to 'keep our bowels regular'. The word 'brimstone' comes from the Old English 'burn-stone', that undergoes combustion to produce a viscous slime and it certainly felt like it. Aunt Mabel would tower above us like the wicked queen in *Snow White*, eyeing us balefully, and force us to swallow the granular sludge thrust at us on the end of a long-handled spoon (we didn't dare regurgitate it). The taste and texture of that glutinous, molten concrete being forced down my throat seemed to me to be one of the major cruelties of my life at that time.

After Ashford, the town of horrors, now transmogrified into the last stop before the Channel Tunnel, my next recollection is being in a hall in Johnstown, a village near Carmarthen in West Wales. I learned later that the Germans had started a heavy bombing campaign, and the South-east of England was the battleground. The 'Battle of Britain' was about to begin; it was feared that any German aeroplanes that did not manage to get to London would release their bombs near the coast. Ashford was considered dangerous, so a second wave of evacuation was ordered, which was why my sister and I managed to escape the clutches of 'Aunt Mabel' and join a cohort of schoolchildren travelling to Wales. Our arrival was mentioned in the local Carmarthen newspaper, with a rider by the councillors exhorting the local populace to take in these poor, unfortunate souls. Apparently, the take-up hadn't been quite as generous as expected, most of the locals eyeing what Arthur Bryant called, the 'shabby, grey-faced, shambling evacuees' with a certain misgiving. We were probably all of that as we stood, with 100 or so other children in a school hall, to be selected by the good people of Carmarthen. The memory of this incident has been engraved on my mind like a Dürer etching. We stood in line as the worthy women eyed us up and down. It was a cattle market, with the sole difference that our teeth were not examined, although we had had a cursory medical examination beforehand, probably to see if we had nits or some other 'dirty' disease. What caused me the greatest shock and shame was that after a seemingly interminable time being stared at by the Welsh women, my sister and I were the only ones left in the hall. Doreen, sniffing, snivelling and occasionally crying, refused absolutely to be parted from me, so we needed accommodation for two. Whether that was the reason we were still there hours after arriving or because we were Catholics, or that we presented a most insalubrious appearance, I never knew, but I felt the shame keenly. Finally, a plump woman by the name of Mrs Whitewood agreed to take us. She already had a child of her own and really could not have had sufficient room to take us in, as was proved by the fact that we had to sleep on an open landing between the two bedrooms. Presumably, the financial benefits outweighed the inconveniences.

Mrs Whitewood's daughter reminded me very much of Violet Elizabeth in Richmal Crompton's 'Just William' stories, which I loved. She was plump and blonde and her mother doted on her, perhaps because the father was away at war. Consequently she was very spoilt and took great pleasure in telling her mother of all our misdemeanours. Doreen and I hated her. I was to remain in Carmarthen for two whole years and moved from childhood to adolescence. My mother, as I remember, came to visit us once in that time and spent most of the time shivering in front of the fire and gossiping with Mrs Whitewood our benefactor. My elder sister, Irene, now resplendent in a WAAF uniform, came to visit us several times and once took us to the nearest seaside, Llanelli, where Doreen and I narrowly avoided drowning in the advancing tide. In spite of being away from Mum for such a long time, I loved the open countryside with its soft green hills. We certainly ate better because we had access to fresh milk and real eggs instead of the powdered eggs eaten in London. Doreen was apparently very unhappy at being away from home or more likely, her constant snivelling got on Mrs Whitewood's nerves and she was whisked back to London after one year. I must have been more acceptable because there was some talk of Mrs Whitehouse adopting me. All these discussions went over my head.

My parents were soon so distant in my memory that to stay in Wales would have made little difference to me. At least I would have been spared my father's rages. Other memories crowd in. One Christmas, I shed bitter tears when I discovered that the parcel from my mother to both of us, which we broke open eagerly and hastily, had a doll in a beautiful, green-sprigged dress in it; unfortunately, the doll was for my sister. I was furious and very upset, and held a grievance against her for some time until I forgot about it. I also enjoyed hanging around the Cow & Gate milk factory with the other children during the holidays, and at the convent school in Carmarthen I discovered a passion for a boy called Lawrence because of his beautiful handwriting. The lessons were taken by nuns in full, flowing robes, which I thought was very romantic. I progressed steadily in my lessons, appreciating for the first time a period of unbroken schooling. When I had been in primary school in London, I had twice been taken away from St Margaret's R.C. school and placed in a non-denominational school for a time, because of my parents' continuous wrangling over religion. In the Convent we were taught Welsh, including how to sing the Welsh national anthem which I still remember. However, during the two years with Mrs Whitewood, fate stepped in and prevented me from becoming a real Welsh girl. The event seemed quite innocuous at first. I developed spots on my face. Mrs Whitewood, in her wisdom, diagnosed these as splashes from caustic soda from cleaning an oven during a Domestic Science lesson. She browbeat me into agreeing that I had, yes, been cleaning an oven, although this was a blatant lie (a venal sin!) She even girded her loins to confront the Mother Superior of the Convent about this dereliction of duty on the part of the teacher involved. She must have soon been disabused of this theory, however, for the upshot was that I was transported with amazing speed to an isolation hospital. It seemed that I had contracted impetigo, a very contagious skin disease, where scabby pustules cover the face. Mrs Whitewood was horrified. She was fearful of what the neighbours would say because impetigo in those days, like scabies, was quite wrongly associated with dirtiness. There were no antibiotics to cure it. The treatment consisted of shutting away the scabby individuals in an isolation hospital, to avoid others being contaminated, and a regime of strict hygiene. To prevent us from touching the sores on our faces and thereby spreading the disease, lint masks smeared with a foul-smelling ointment were put over our faces with holes for eyes, nose and mouth. We wandered around the hospital in our white medical gowns and white lint masks like masked revellers at an eighteenth-century ball. I must have been in the hospital for some months, the time it took for my scabs to clear and for the medical profession to claim success. And by then all talk of adoption had ceased.

While in the hospital, I had received a letter from my mother informing me that I would not be returning to Mrs Whitewood, but to London, to their new address in Prince Regent Lane, Plaistow. The name conjured up the pleasant country lanes I had been used to walking along and I found out in later years that the word 'Plaistow' itself, an old Anglo-Saxon word, meant 'place of play'. The reality proved somewhat different; when I arrived, Prince Regent Lane proved to be a busy highway full of traffic, lined with ugly plane trees with amputated limbs. And no one was playing at this time and in this part of London, which had suffered intense German bombardment in the Autumn of 1940. I was returning after two years away to a family I had almost forgotten and to a bomb-wrecked urban area which contrasted painfully with the countryside of West Wales.

Chapter 3
Images of War

A strange gawky-looking boy with a shock of brown hair was standing at the front door as I arrived at number 22 Prince Regent Lane in July 1942. He eyed me curiously before turning on his heels and going back into the house. This was my brother Vic, now sixteen. He was a total stranger to me. He was already working in a factory and aching to get away both from there and from the endless rows at home. My father seemed to pick on him more than the girls. A middle-aged man's jealousy of his son's youth and vigour? In fact within the year, Jim had lied about his age to join the navy, saying he was eighteen when he was still seventeen, and disappeared once again from my life. He told me later that he hadn't recognised me in my old-fashioned clothes and socks, except to think what a frump I looked. The only incident of note that I remember of him at the short time we knew each other again was when my mother found us both together in his bedroom and erupted with anger. She suspected us of smoking and indeed, such was her anger, of perhaps something much more serious. As usual, in my naïveté, I had no idea of what she was talking about.

The house in Prince Regent's Lane was a solid Victorian end-of-terrace that had seen better days. Outside it was quite dilapidated, with peeling paint and a neglected front patch, but it seemed rather grand to me after the cramped cottage in Wales. As in that cottage, there was still no bathroom or inside lavatory. A fine judgement had to be made regularly as to how long it would take you to get out to the 'lav', as we called it, before any mishaps occurred. At night though, there was the consolation of a chamber pot strategically placed under the bed. The downstairs had a novelty for me, french windows which looked out on what one could euphemistically call a garden, a narrow concrete alleyway which led to the lavatory and beyond that a tangled mass of rubbish and briars interspersed with some green, weedy patches. The french windows remain in my memory as a good example of sibling rivalry or, to put it more bluntly, of how violent my younger sister Doreen could be when confronted with my equally stubborn resistance. We have always had a love-hate relationship. That day, we were sparring fairly amicably until I managed to push her through the french windows and lock the door and run around to the back door to secure that as well. "Let me in! Let me in, I tell you!" A pause: "If you don't let me in, you sodding thing, I'll break the door down". She must have been beside herself to use the expletive, forbidden in our house. I was shocked now but determined to hold my own. I continued with my grinning posturings and mocking grimaces from inside the safety of the locked doors, making her incandescent with rage. There was another pause, while she was obviously thinking how to get back in. Then she disappeared for a moment from my view, returning immediately with an old broom; aiming the handle at the window and grimly determined, she smashed through the window, which shook and almost exploded with the force of her thrust. Fortunately, I had retired to the back of the room and avoided the slivers of glass which showered the room. Even so, I had to leap into the safety of the hall to avoid any stray ones. We were both so astonished at what had happened that there was a moment's silence while the enormity of what had happened sank in. My immediate thought was, "What's Mum going to say when she finds out?" Money still being tight, she would not be too happy to have to replace the glass. Curiously, I have no recollection of the ensuing arguments, but the whole scene was a good illustration of my sister's determination never to be beaten. It was weeks before the window was repaired, its jagged broken appearance a witness to our sibling rivalry. One of my father's favourite sayings was, "Give me the tools, woman, and I'll do the job!" The tools never appeared and consequently the job was hardly ever done.

Although there was no bathroom, my father was fanatical about cleanliness and so we suffered the Friday night ritual of the tin bath in front of the living-room fire. The effort to boil enough water to fill it was a major task for my poor mother and obviously, there was no suggestion of fresh hot water for us all, only the occasional top-up to keep the bath warm. My father, naturally, took pride of place in the bath followed by each of us in order of size as the water became murkier and murkier... When I was older, I would revolt at this routine and in fear and trepidation, would brave the local municipal baths. There was a special procedure to be followed there. Having entered the magnificent portals of the vast Victorian building, you paid your money to the bored attendant who then directed you indifferently to a designated white-tiled bath cubicle, where you undressed and stood shivering with cold to wait. For what? For the attendant to turn on the main tap outside! The bath in the cubicle had no taps, presumably because you might use up too much water while bathing. The water, when it did arrive, gushed out so ferociously from the gaping mouth that the first time I went there I was terrified. Most of the time the water wasn't the right temperature, so you had to open the door, peer round it and call out loudly, 'Too hot!' or 'Too cold!' and your complaint echoed loudly around the cavernous corridors. I was convinced that the attendant took a malevolent pleasure in humiliating me, but even so it was better than the tin bath.

Apart from these exhausting efforts of personal hygiene, there was also the major ceremony of the weekly wash. We had a primitive boiler which took ages to heat up the water, into which the clothes were finally immersed. Depending on whether Mum was around or not, we either poked them around feebly, pretending to wash them or scrubbed them with a scrubbing-board, taking skin off our hands as well as dirt from the clothes. We then lifted them out of the steaming water with a pair of wooden tongs, hoping not to be scalded in the process, and plunged them into cold water in the butler sink. The transportation of the clothes dripping with water was a feat in itself, only to be superseded by the job of putting them through the mangle standing in the garden. This instrument of torture was meant to squeeze out the excess water. To try to coax the clothes through the wooden rollers while at the same time turning the wheel demanded a manual dexterity not easily learned; fingers could also be mangled. The clothes, then somewhat cleaner, were pegged on to the line in the so-called garden and hopefully the weather would smile benignly on them before the rains came. During the War, the government's 'Dig for Victory!' campaign had exhorted householders to turn their gardens over to crops, to supplement the meagre rations. Even the Royal Family helped by turning Windsor Great Park over to wheat. Our house remained immune to these exhortations. My parents laboured under the common impression of working-class people living in rented houses that you didn't have to do anything to the house except keep it reasonably clean. Everything external including the garden was not their responsibility, so my father made no attempts to do anything about it. It must have been a haven for wild flowers. Such areas in the country are now known as 'set-aside' and duly cherished. Cleaning the house was easy because we had the minimum of furniture, mainly cheap 'utility' stuff, a small enamel-topped table and a glass-fronted food cabinet in the kitchen, and a cheap table and chairs and one easy chair in the living room. But we did have a sideboard, which I remember as being of good, solid oak and a beautiful rosewood card table on which my father and his brothers would play cards on the occasional Sunday morning. My sister and I would crowd round to watch this unusual social occasion, but if my father lost the game and therefore his money, his temper would explode, and we would disappear rapidly.

It is difficult to imagine now how arduous housework was in such primitive conditions. We had no refrigerator, no vacuum cleaner (why should we when we had no fitted carpets?), not even a carpet-sweeper. The housework was done with bucket and cloth, dustpan and brush. I remember every Saturday morning when mother had gone out shopping, how I would take up the mats in the hall, bang them on the wall outside, scrub the floor and skirting boards and replace the mats, surveying my resultant handiwork with pride, the satisfaction of a job well done. But then the family would soon return and the hall would revert to its normal shabby state. Since I was always the person designated as the 'charlady', I still prefer housework to cooking, revelling in the resulting short period of neatness and tidiness.

In the weeks that followed my return from Wales, I heard from Mum all about the Blitz of 1940-1941, when the Germans tried to destroy both the fabric of the major cities and the morale of the people. On the way to school, I saw for myself the bomb-damaged houses listing weirdly and dangerously against the skyline. Walls had disappeared and pitiful remains of fireplaces and torn wallpaper were open to the sky. Yet perversely, the buddleia continued to grow in profusion on these bomb-sites, providing some sweetness to counteract the devastation. I learned all about the troubles my family had been through, or more precisely my mother and brother, my father having been drafted into the docks at Swindon. In 1941, the Luftwaffe had launched wave after wave of bomb attacks on London and other major cities, and the docks near us were an obvious target. My mother told the gruesome tale of a school in Silvertown where many of the locals had been sent for protection. Unfortunately during that night, the school was sliced in two by an aerial mine which killed so many people that the limbs scattered around were collected up in baskets. The biggest shock for my mother and my brother was when our street suffered a direct hit. All the houses in the street were flattened. Luckily, they were in the communal air-raid shelter when the raid started, but when the all-clear sounded and they emerged into the eerily silent early morning light, they were faced with a scene of total desolation. No familiar landmarks remained to orientate the bewildered residents, neither did they have time to pick up any personal belongings in the still-smoking ruins. In that one terrible night my mother had lost all her possessions, and the mainstays of my early life, my home, the school and the library had been obliterated, my past wiped out. The residents were then herded on to a bus to be sent to a communal refuge centre, Rackham House in Tooting. Somehow my mother, gossiping as usual, had heard terrible tales of this house, about how it was little more than a workhouse where the inmates were treated very badly. So when the bus arrived there in the still early morning she refused to get off, stating that she would never go into such a place. She recounted this story with great glee and probably some embellishments (after all she was Irish!). Where she and my brother finally did bed down that night was never explained, but soon afterwards they went to Swindon to join my father.

    I had to come to terms myself with such wartime exigencies as carrying a gas-mask around with me everywhere – a rubber and metal contraption in an ugly cardboard box, which, when I put it on for my sister's amusement, almost suffocated me. Fortunately, we never had to use the clumsy things. More affluent people were able to jettison the hideous box for attractive pochettes, like handbags, which sat more comfortably on the hip, but it would be two years more before I could afford one. Torches had to be taken every time we went out in the evening because of the blackout, but the worst restriction of all was the rationing. We each had our own ration book with the coupons in it for bacon, meat, cheese, sugar and tea. Butter soon disappeared altogether, so we had to eat margarine. Each person only had eight ounces a week, reduced at the end of the war to seven. I smile ironically to myself at the modern fad of eating margarine for health reasons. Me, I stick to my butter as if I am still compensating for missing its lovely taste in the wartime. Bananas vanished until the end of the war and, when I did finally get to eat one, I wasn't sure how to open it and when I finally managed to, I was most disappointed at its bland flavour. Worst of all for me, was the four ounce ration of sweets per week. Sweets had been my staple supplement to my mother's monotonous cooking and I missed them tremendously, so I was not averse to stealing some from the local sweet-shop when the occasion arose, even though I dreaded being caught. When in dire need of sweetness, I would raid my mother's pantry, pour out a cupful of coconut, add a spoonful of sugar and wolf the lot down. Other strategies were to use syrup on my bread instead. Interestingly, I seemed not to be so affected by the rest of the rationing, since poverty had rationed food for us all our lives. It was always fish on Friday nights, since my mother tried religiously to conform to the Roman Catholic dogma. There was the occasional rabbit, because it was cheap, but chicken was for Christmas Day only. Frequently, Mum would make a so-called Irish stew, a concoction of grey meat swimming around in pints of water and vegetables. Such embellishments as Oxo cubes or even Bisto were not part of my mother's culinary skills. Once my father and brother had been given the bulk of the lamb, it was quite an interesting exercise to try to find any meat in the thin gruel. The stew would bloat out one's stomach very quickly, only to be followed equally quickly by a voracious hunger. This is why the sweets were so necessary to me. Lord Woolton, the Minister of Food spoke regularly on the wireless, exhorting us to use our rations sensibly and suggesting recipes such as Woolton pie, made with vegetables and some form of gravy made with Bisto. I thought it was execrable! Of course, additional food could be had on the black market from 'spivs' hanging around on designated corners; they peddled perfume as well as the new-fangled 'nylons' and even chocolates. We could never afford any such additions to our plain diet, which consisted mostly of two shredded wheat for breakfast and bread and jam, or condensed milk for tea. I loved that condensed milk! It was meant to replace milk and sugar in tea, but I would steal it from the cupboard and layer it thickly on my bread and hope that no one would come in before my taste buds had fully relished its lingering sweetness. Sundays, being a special day, we would have some sort of lamb or beef, roasted by my mother until it had lost all its tenderness. This was inevitably followed the next day by 'bubble and squeak', the fried-up remains of the vegetables, without the meat of course. Such small amounts of the meat in our diet and the reliance on vegetables is now touted as a much better diet, and the statistics show that people were quite healthy even on such a restricted diet, in the wartime, but my father would not have agreed. At least we did not suffer the indignity of getting fat. Sunday tea consisted of winkles and bread and margarine. I had great fun trying to pick out the winkle from the shell with a pin and then surreptitiously stabbing my sister with it. Her scream of pain was music to my ears. Or we had celery with bread for tea; the celery came in on a plate with water still dripping from it and the game here was to pick up a stick of celery and spray my sister before my parents came in. Sometimes when my father would be absent for a meal, my mother would seize the opportunity to send us down to the market to get 'pie and mash'. We found this meal infinitely preferable.

The most unpleasant shock for me on returning to London was the school I had to attend. I had left a small, caring Roman Catholic convent in Wales and was suddenly pitchforked into a large, impersonal elementary school. I have no recollection of the school, only of truanting from it. Perhaps I found the roughness of the East End children too much to bear after the quieter convent children. I truanted practically every day and wandered aimlessly around until it was time to go home. Most of the time I spent wandering round an urban wasteland called 'The Dump', a bombed-out area at the bottom of our road. Most of the time I was alone but sometimes Doreen would join me. I remember feeling unhappy and terribly lonely. It was as if I were the only human being left on earth as I roamed among the hummocks and hollows of this bomb-site. In parts it was covered with weeds, sparse yellow grass and wild flowers. Ugly as it was, it must have reminded me of the green landscapes I had left; it was my temporary haven from all the unpleasantness at school and the fear of my father at home. No one ever discovered that I was not at school; no one seemed interested.

I could have continued with this way of life for some time, unconcerned about what would happen to me when I was caught, unconcerned about any loss of education or a possible life of criminality. What saved me from the consequences of my truancy was the West Ham Local Education Authority. It suddenly realised that a whole cohort of evacuees had missed out on the 'scholarship' examination, this lifeline to secondary education for bright working-class children. There must have been much discussion about this group of unfortunates. Should they be allowed to sit the examination at twelve/thirteen? Would there be any problems if they were a year older than the rest of the year? This was a risk they couldn't take. So the Authority finally decided to let us sit the examination, but any successful pupil would attend only four years instead of five at the Grammar school. Presumably no one gave us much hope of achieving good results at the end of that time, but lip-service would have been paid to equality. And praise be to God that the councillors took this risk of deciding to let us sit the entrance examination. Looking back, I realised that this was a defining moment for me. A new life was about to open for me, a new world of the intellect and literature and history, which would help to alleviate the misery of my existence. Without this chance I shudder to imagine what I would have become.

Chapter 4
Opening Vistas

The fateful day arrived for the scholarship examination. I walked over to the school from my house feeling sick, wishing I could run away. With other children all looking frightened, I was ushered into the vast hall with its panelled walls, on which the names of successful former pupils were inscribed in gold leaf. I was completely overawed by it, oppressed by the atmosphere heavy with officialdom. Rows of desks were arranged the whole length and breadth of the hall and teachers in long, black academic gowns looking like bats, moved purposefully up and down the rows. I remember wrestling with the Maths paper almost in tears because we had not 'done' decimals in my convent. But the essay subjects eased my dismay and I lost all sense of inadequacy and failure as I wrote copiously about my life in Wales. I walked out of the school thinking I had failed because of the Maths. Months later, my mother received an official letter stating that I had been accepted for secondary-school education with a list of the grammar schools available. The obvious choice for me was the Ursuline convent in Stratford, although it was a long bus ride away. I wanted badly to go there because of their uniform, a dark-brown, pleated box gymslip with a cream blouse and a school hat that was a brown mortarboard with a gold tassel on it which swayed as you moved. Every time I had seen pupils from that school, I had wanted to wear such a hat. The convent would have been a good choice for me, being an all girls' school and given the fact that I was so painfully shy and frightened of boys. It also had a good academic record and was close to East Ham, a subtle distinction, since East Ham was considered to be a cut above West Ham. But in spite of my entreaties and my mother's wish for me to continue to go to a religious school, my father decided that the school opposite our house was easier, although it was lower down in the hierarchy of secondary schools, being quite near the docks. My father was probably secretly pleased at getting one over my mother by wrenching me from the clutches of Roman Catholicism.

Come the day when my mother received a list of all the uniform and the prices, there was a 'volte-face'. I couldn't go. She couldn't afford it. She didn't actually write to the Education Office to decline the offer, writing letters being a very arduous affair for both my parents, but she made me understand that it was out of the question. Weeks went by and I continued to truant from school until one momentous day I returned home to find a parcel on the kitchen table. "Open it, then!" said my mother as I gazed at it. "It's for you."

"For me?" She nodded smiling for once. Tearing open the brown paper, I found inside, a navy-blue pleated gymslip and a white blouse. My mother had somehow found the money to buy the uniform! It was far too big for me, but I would apparently 'grow into it'. I must have kept it until my developing body could no longer fit into it, because I remember pressing and sponging it regularly. Unfortunately, the money found did not stretch to the school blazer and hat. We somehow managed to get a cheaper version of the blazer and Mum sewed the school badge onto it, but the hat proved impossible. Since we never wore hats, my mother assumed I could do without it. Little did she and I know the trouble that the lack of a hat would cause me. On my first day there, I was drawn aside by a teacher as I went through the front door. "Where's your hat?" I was too proud to say I couldn't afford one, so I mumbled, "Please Miss, I've forgotten it."

"Well, just remember to bring it next time, won't you? You must wear a hat to school. You won't be allowed to come into school without one." With this worrying remark she let me go in. I breathed a sigh of relief, saved for the time being.

Plaistow Secondary School was built in the 1930s and was a very attractive two-storey building, built around an open-air quadrangle. Later when I was in the sixth form we were allowed to have lessons out there; it was most pleasant to sit in the summer sun, but it was not really conducive to studying. I paid more attention to the smell of the newly-mown grass than the 1832 Reform Act being explained by Miss Holden, one of my favourite teachers.

The problem of the hat re-surfaced the next morning. That time I was not so lucky and was put in detention. This went on for some time – no hat, so detention. No one thought to enquire why I always forgot my hat. Eventually, with other miscreants who would not wear a hat on principle, it being a badge of academia which they either did not aspire to, or were frightened of being jeered at by the local elementary-school children, a plan was devised whereby some friends would go in to the cloakroom and throw their hats out of the window to the rest of us. Bunched together and watching the entrance door apprehensively, we would grab a hat fast and then nonchalantly pass by the gimlet-eyed member of staff on duty, secretly gloating at 'getting one over her'. I never did buy a hat.

Remember we were a 'special class'. And what a motley bunch we were! It was soon obvious from the sceptical attitude of the staff that we were unpromising material. Missing a whole year of schooling would mean that we would not do so well at the School Certificate exam and it could reflect badly on the school. Some of the boys in the class were quite rough and loud. They all terrified me. One in particular, Wag Bennett, was an absolute tearaway, reducing some of the weaker male and female staff to tears. Later in life, he proved quite a successful entrepreneur, going from barrow-boy, to rag-and-bone man to boxing promoter, proving that a grammar school education might count for something after all. He was particularly nasty to the Geography teacher, a woman who should never have taken up the profession. She was plump, shapeless really with rather nice soft brown hair drawn back severely in a bun, so that her moon face looked even bigger than it was. She was boring in the extreme and could not keep any discipline. I started off feeling quite sorry for her, but when she caught me talking once, she put me at once in detention. I was really annoyed, since I was one of the quietest in the class, but obviously she picked on me because I couldn't stand up to her. I hated her after that episode.

Our first assembly at Plaistow Grammar took place in the hall I had seen before. It was an assembly only for our 'special class' 2D. Several staff were lined up at the sides and on the dais was a slight anxious-looking man who proved to be Dr Priestley, our headmaster. He spoke with a faint Northern accent and the gist of his speech was that we were very lucky to be there, and it was because we had been *chosen.* We were among the top ten per cent of the population for intelligence and he expected us to live up to the standards of the school. This speech was re-iterated *ad nauseum* throughout our school career; it was an effective form of brainwashing which later prompted the thought that such insistence on our superiority would hardly go down well in the area in which we lived. It was so obviously working class, where most of the population had few aspirations to higher education. It certainly caused problems for me much later, when trying to find a boyfriend. After assembly, we were herded into our form room and made to sit in alphabetical order, so I was placed in the back row, my surname being White. This seating arrangement became quite temporary, as the boys usurped our places to sit at the back and do what they liked. Our desks were the old-fashioned sort which combined seat and desk and all our books were kept in there with regular inspections to see that they were tidy. One of my pleasures was to come to school and tidy my desk. Not for us the shoulder-deforming heavy satchels in which today's children carry all their books every day to avoid having them stolen. I was so acutely shy that my head was lowered most of the time while our form master Mr Goldfinch, Head of Science, shadowed the headmaster's speech, but added his own heavyweight interpretation, on the lines of 'God help anyone who tries to misbehave in this class!' That such an important member of staff should be delegated to be our form teacher showed that the school was anticipating trouble. He was known as a disciplinarian. There was an apprehensive silence as he eyed us threateningly. I was rigid with fear and remained so until he left us. Then, suddenly I heard a voice beside me: "What's your name? Mine starts with W, so I'm at the back. I suppose yours does too. I'm Shirley Weinstein". I raised my head and looked in complete astonishment at a really foreign-looking girl with jet-black, frizzy hair, and curiously slanting eyes in a flat face. She looked Chinese, or what I thought a Chinese looked like, never having seen one except in books. She turned out to be Jewish with a Mongolian grandmother and a grandfather from Poland. I opened up to her friendliness and completely forgot my shyness. I was secretly thrilled at her exoticism. We became firm friends from that day on, together through school, college and teaching until she left England for Mauritius, in later years. She was a gifted writer even at that early time, although her indolent nature precluded any commercial success in that field. She would bring in to school every day exciting instalments of the story she was writing, *Letitia's Journal*. It was the diary of a miscreant, similar to 'Just William', but the girls in the class found it funnier. She and I were strikingly different – she, small, plump and rounded, with that marvellous face and I, tall, thin but big-boned and gawky with my head almost permanently bent downwards because of my shyness. We certainly caught the attention of the staff. One day, the Deputy Head stopped us in the corridor to ask us a question.

"I'm sorry, Miss Emsden?" I gazed at her in astonishment not even understanding the question, although I anticipated trouble. Silence ensued for a few moments and I gazed fixedly at the floor.

She repeated, impatient now, "Why is Shirley Weinstein carrying your PE bag all the time?" Comprehension dawned on me. Shirley and I had the same initials. Miss Emsden thought that I was bullying Shirley into carrying my bag! I launched into a long rambling, but I thought quite eloquent explanation, trying to extricate myself from the situation without admitting that I had not even made the wretched PE bag, nor by that time did I have any intention of doing so. Eventually she let me go although I am not sure that she was convinced. When I told Shirley, we both dissolved into laughter. But this event was the first black mark against me. A few years later, we were both in trouble, hauled before the Senior Mistress again, to be told that we were not to spend so much time together. However, her warning was couched in such covert language that we had no idea what she meant. We looked at each other furtively while she made a more explicit order that we must keep away from each other. The suggestion was so risible that I had to be careful not to catch Shirley's eyes or we should have both been convulsed with laughter. Only later did I realise that we were suspected of lesbian tendencies!

Discovering that the daily assemblies were both boring and repetitious, apart from the hymn *Jerusalem*, sung with enthusiasm and gusto, Shirley and I soon discovered a loophole in the school regulations allowing us to claim that our faith did not allow us to take part in Protestant assemblies. The small detail that Shirley was a non-practising Jew and I was fast becoming an agnostic did not deter us. Our supposed devotion to our own religious affiliations impressed the headmaster and we won the day. Five times a week, the rest of the class would file out dutifully to assembly, casting either reproachful, disapproving or envious glances at us, depending on their religious persuasion, and we had a blissful twenty minutes every day to exchange gossip and confidences. It was a heaven-sent gift from whichever God was up above and increased our sense of 'otherness' immeasurably. Unfortunately, we were not allowed exemption from the RE class. This lesson was taken by the youngest male teacher in the school. He was fair-haired and not bad looking, except for his wobbly round bottom. He obviously tried to keep it still by squeezing it into tight, ill-fitting trousers. Shirley and I suspected him of being 'queer', else why wasn't he in the forces? But one day he turned up in a very short jacket which revealed even more of his soft, round bottom than usual. I couldn't take my eyes off it as he wiggled around the classroom and then I suddenly caught Shirley's eye. That was it. We both burst out into peals of laughter. He was surprised, because we were normally like mice in the class. Then he became furious, and approached us wagging his finger. This was even more comical. Our laughter doubled and then I found I couldn't stop, I was becoming hysterical. Sobbing, gasping for breath, with a sharp pain developing in my side and tears streaming down my face, I gazed at Shirley, but that was a worse move to make. She was equally hysterical. By this time, Mr Fairweather had had enough and the class was in uproar. Rushing over to us, he grabbed us in turn, and bundled us out of the room into the corridor. Still hurting with laughter, we slumped against the wall, trying to calm down as we thought of the trouble we were in. But that was the most enjoyable RE lesson we ever had.

One day we were forced to go to a 'special' assembly. Agog with excitement, we listened bemusedly as the headmaster harangued the school about an American pop song sweeping the country called *Johnny Zero*, which was sweeping the country. Not having any means of listening to music at home, since we only had a wireless which was permanently tuned to the Home Service, it meant nothing to me being berated in this way. Apparently *Johnny Zero* was very lazy at school and the lyrics went:

> *The kids all call him Johnny Zero*
> *And when at school they used to say,*
> *'Johnny's got a zero, Johnny's got a zero*
> *Johnny's got a zero today!'*

However this lazy boy subsequently became a fighter pilot and one day, he shot down a German aircraft, and the tune ended triumphantly:

> *Johnny Zero is a hero today!*

Our headmaster was totally incensed at this cavalier attitude to learning and had brought us all together to warn us that our grades were *very, very* important for our future success in life. Of course, the speech had no effect except to make us realise that teachers' lived on a different planet from the rest of us.

Attendance at prize-giving evenings was also compulsory – another boring ritual to suffer. Luckily, neither of our parents came to them; Shirley's parents thought they were a waste of their valuable time and mine were terrified ever to set foot in the school. So we had 'carte blanche' to enjoy ourselves as much as possible, mainly by laughing secretly at the Lady Mayor of West Ham, who came to distribute the prizes. Her name was Daisy Bell and she had the most atrocious cockney accent. Shirley and I had to stuff hankies in our mouths to stop ourselves laughing at her 'poncy' gold-braided uniform with its dangling chain. Apart from Mr Fairweather, the staff in Plaistow Grammar school were unmarried women or older men, the rest having gone to war. In those days, any woman teacher who decided to get married was automatically excluded from teaching. Some managed to circumvent this ridiculous restriction by living in sin or pretending to be single. It was risky in those days to cohabit without being married. The working-class morality was very strong on this point.

One teacher who attracted our attention almost immediately was the French teacher. Not only was the subject thrillingly new and exotic to us, but the teacher was young, dark-haired and quite beautiful. The boys couldn't believe their luck. On first meeting us, she looked us over then said, "I've got a very funny name in French. Do you want to know what it is?" An animated chorus of, "Yes please, Miss!" ensued. She smiled and wrote on the board, 'ARC-EN-CIEL' in big capital letters. Incomprehension on our part. She explained, "It means Rainbow!" From that moment, I was smitten. Learning French, loving French and still teaching French decades later.

Quite the reverse feeling for me was Science. Our form teacher the dreaded Mr Goldfinch, taught us Physics and I vaguely learned something about fulcrums and balances, and fell in love with the photograph of a scientist called Sir Humphrey Davy which was in my science book. He had long curly hair and a romantic look about him, so I tore his portrait out and stuck it in among my collection of film stars. I still remember him for the epigram under the photograph:

Sir Humphrey Davy
Abominated gravy.
He lived in the odium
Of having discovered sodium.

He also discovered the anaesthetic properties of laughing gas, but our Chemistry lessons were no laughing matter to the poor unfortunate Chemistry teacher. He was a veteran of the First World War and suffered from shell shock. He was totally unable to keep discipline. His shakings and trembling as he conducted experiments seemed to me to be quite dangerous, and the boys in the class soon ignored him in order to start fires with a bunson burner. Whether the poor man knew what was going on at the back of the class or not, he resolutely ignored anything that was going on beyond the first two rows in the class.

Maths was also a subject to be endured. Mr Bruce, a fat, bald man who regularly used his black academic gown to wipe the blackboard, had a somewhat military approach to teaching Maths. He would point his chalk at each pupil in turn, fix the victim with his bright beady eyes and bark out a question. Woe betide anyone who could not answer it. Shirley and I would already be trembling in anticipation of the chalk stinging us, but the boys suffered more.

Chapter 5
Adolescence

Apart from school, 'those past, spacious days' beloved of James Joyce, the war still rumbled on, not affecting me in any special way until June 1944 when we were suddenly made aware of Hitler's new, secret weapon. One night Doreen and I were woken up by my mother saying urgently, "Get downstairs quickly! There's an air raid". Still drowsy from sleep, we stumbled down into the hall and were pushed through what I had always thought to be a hall cupboard but which proved to be a cellar. I was thrilled! I felt that I was acting in one of the many adventure stories which had been my staple diet for so long. I was the heroine courageously adventuring into the dark, mysterious cellar, with huge obstacles blocking my way, although the obstacles here were only brick pillars supporting the floor. Now that we were down in the bowels of the house, we could switch on our torches. I played mine over the dirt and cobwebs, trying with the feeble light to penetrate into the darkness, fearful that I would see a spider or even a mouse. Suddenly I glimpsed something white in a corner. It was paper tied in a roll with string. Intrigued, I moved towards it cautiously. It was a map, a map of the world drawn in a spidery hand-writing with the names of all the countries and the big towns. Who was it who had undertaken this labour of love? Then my reveries were interrupted by my mother saying excitedly, "Listen! It's a doodlebug!" I gazed at her in astonishment. How did she know that? My estimation of her went up somewhat. She explained that these 'doodlebugs' didn't have pilots, only bombs inside them. No pilots? How could they fly? I thought. My weakness in Science again. We listened expectantly to the chugging sound of the engine, familiar almost comforting, until it stopped. There was a moment of intense silence and then the sound of an explosion, more of a dull crump really because the aeroplane had hit the ground some way away. We sat frozen for a while, waiting for the next one. But then the 'all clear' sounded and we trooped back to bed, with me clutching my map. We were to live this erratic life for the next three months, as the 'doodlebugs' were sent over London day and night, causing more than 45,000 casualties. They were officially known as V1s, German for *vergeltungswaffen* or 'reprisal weapon' and we all feared them because of the indiscriminate nature of them. We read some time later in the newspaper that Churchill had said with bravado to Stalin, "They have had no appreciative effect on the life of London", which was not strictly true. People were becoming weary now after five years of war. Even going to the cinema you never knew whether you would come back. One of the 'doodlebugs' fell on the congregation attending a church service in the Guards Chapel in Central London, killing sixty people.

I experienced the horror of one bomb some weeks later at close quarters. It was mid-afternoon and I was shopping for my mother at Green Gate, a line of shops not far from us. The area was bustling with the usual traffic and shoppers. Suddenly, the familiar drone of the aeroplane was heard, almost a purring note redolent of bees on a summer's day. No one paid much attention to it, until the engine stopped abruptly, right overhead. There was a palpable silence and looking around me, the shoppers seemed like the motionless stick people in a Lowry painting, then almost simultaneously, they started throwing themselves onto the pavement, going down like ninepins. This was the accepted wisdom, to drop to the ground to minimise personal danger. But they descended in waves, in slow motion. I stood irresolutely in front of the large plate-glass window of the local baker's shop, watching them drop to the ground. Then the aeroplane crashed and exploded. The noise was horrendous. The baker's window shivered convulsively but miraculously, didn't break, otherwise I would have been covered in shards of broken glass. The bomb had gone off round the corner near my home. I was suddenly galvanised at the thought that it might have exploded there. Running furiously around the corner, along Prince Regent Lane, I was stopped in my tracks by the choking, acrid smoke swirling over the street. Peering through it, my eyes smarting, I saw the devastation that the tiny speck in the sky had caused. It was heart-wrenching. Where there had been a tarmacadamed road only minutes before, a smoking crater had appeared; where there had always existed a row of neat, terraced houses, there was now a gaping hole with only vestiges of houses around it. There was twisted metal everywhere, remnants of walls leaning at terrifying angles, showing glimpses of broken furniture, fireplaces open to the sky, sickeningly skewed floors and torn wallpaper. Stumbling through the rubble, covered with dust and with tears coursing in channels down my face, I met Doreen running towards me, her face screwed up with terror. She had had the same fear for me. We clasped each other tightly then ran home sobbing at the desolation all around us. That scene is set in the amber of my memory and the desecration of war was brought home to me with a vengeance. My school was close to the spot where the aeroplane had crashed, but escaped any damage except for all the windows on the east side which shattered. Dr Priestley was not so lucky; his house was totally demolished.

Some time later, we moved from Prince Regent Lane, around the corner to Woodside Road at the end of which was the infamous 'dump' of my former life. Someone must have had a sense of humour to give this road such a name, but perhaps it had been near a wood in the past. Now it was meaner and narrower than Prince Regent Lane, just two rows of terraced council houses. Our house was also smaller, two bedrooms instead of three, and pokier than the other house but with the same lack of mod cons. Why did we move? Couldn't they pay the rent? It was never explained. Life at home was mostly tense silences punctuated only by frightening rows between my mother and father. Now that I was an adolescent, I was much more aware of them and very affected by them. On one occasion, my father in an apopletic rage raised his hand to hit my mother full in the face, when for the first time in my life, I summoned up the courage to intervene. I pushed myself between them, screaming for them to stop. It was useless. My father just shoved me roughly aside, but this movement brought him somewhat to his senses, and he lowered his hand, but continued to abuse my mother verbally. With great sobs of frustration and fear, I rushed out into the garden and stood by the outside toilet, overwhelmed at my uselessness to change anything. What was the point of trying to keep the peace between them? Withdrawal into my own world was the only way I could cope.

A second terrible event shook me in that benighted house, an event that I still recall with shuddering horror. Doreen and I shared the small back bedroom, but at least we had separate beds now. One night, I woke up in terror thinking that something had fallen into my ear. For a nanosecond I thought that I had been dreaming, but almost immediately, I felt something moving, struggling in my ear. I screamed and tried to get it out, whatever it was, but my action of putting my finger in my ear, pushed it even further inside. In a paroxysm of fear and terror, I rushed into my parents' room, screaming, "Mum! Something's fallen into my ear!" Annoyed at being woken up, my father shouted angrily, "For Christ's sake, get back to bed will you? You've just had a dream!" My mother didn't move. Still completely terrorised by this thing burrowing itself into my ear, I rushed back into the bedroom totally distraught. Then the creature suddenly managed to crawl some of the way back, and I could finger it out, a crushed, red-brown bug which left streaks of blood on my hand. Great waves of terror were still flooding over me and I crawled into Doreen's bed, shaking convulsively as she held me tight and tried to calm me. I learned later that bugs were a perennial hazard in poor, neglected houses. They often lived between successive layers of wallpaper, where it was warm and dark, feeding on the wallpaper paste, or in the seams of mattresses. Bugs surfaced again when we went to visit my grandmother Emmeline, the fearsome Emmeline, in Coggeshall, Essex. She lived there with her last daughter who suffered from Down's Syndrome, probably because Emmeline had had her too late in life. We had never been there to visit her and we never went there again. We were supposed to stay the night and were shown the double bed for the three of us to sleep on, with one suspiciously high, lumpy mattresses on top of another. No sooner asleep, we were all suddenly awoken by some sensation. Putting on the light, we saw the flattish, lentil-sized dark-red-brown bugs crawling all over the bed. Leaping out of the bed in a frenzy, the three of us dressed quickly and sat silently on chairs waiting for dawn to appear, so that we could take the first bus back home.

 The bombing continued. No longer with a cellar to shelter in, our house had an Andersen shelter, built courtesy of the local authority, at the bottom of the garden. It was sunk into the soil and covered with grass. It had one major disadvantage. There was a dip in the earth right in front of the entrance, so that when I went in, I had to sit in the dip to swing my legs into the opening. When it rained, as it seemed to often, I had to sit in the puddle and feel the cold water seeping up into my knickers before I could get inside. But once in and bedded down for the night, I was in seventh heaven, in spite of the noise of explosions all around. Lying in my bunk, with the rural accompaniment of the crickets chirping nearby and smelling the wet grass, memories of hop-picking and the Welsh countryside came flooding back to me. At those times, I was blissfully happy in spite of the raids. My sister Irene came home on leave from the WAAF once and experienced a raid for the first time. It was interesting to see her reaction. She was terrified, having seen no enemy action where she was stationed, but we were quite blasé now. Our school routine also continued to be disrupted as the Germans stepped up their attacks on London with the doodlebugs. The air-raid sirens seemed to wail their eerie warning almost continuously, day and night. In school, assemblies were cancelled and many children disappeared from the classes in a second wave of evacuation. Shirley and I loved the break from lessons, although they were supposed to continue in the shelter with the poor teacher trying against all the odds to teach us. But how on earth could we concentrate on lessons when the sound of the 'doodlebug' passed overhead? We gossiped and giggled, oblivious of the teacher. I remember Shirley analysing her reaction to the raids:

"I really like all this excitement, don't you?"

"Yeh, it's a real lark."

"But what are we going to do when the war is over?"

"It'll be really boring, I think."

"Well, let's hope it goes on for a long time yet!"

I agreed, but the headmaster didn't. He became increasingly worried about the disruption to our schooling, especially as our class was a year behind all the others. He even wrote to the Examination Board when the School Certificate exam was imminent, explaining the situation and asking for the Board to take into consideration the loss of teaching time. How successful that ploy was we never knew. When I looked back at the school log years later, however, there were twenty-nine failures out of eighty-seven candidates, and the headmaster's comment: "This was very poor owing to the fact that they were late 1942 entrants." He could have added, "And also because of the disruption to our classes". Perhaps he wanted to make a political point; he never liked the fact that we were allowed into his school so late.

My friendship with Shirley deepened as we became adolescents. Since I lived so near the school, she would come home with me for lunch bringing her neat packet of sandwiches while I foraged around for whatever was in the cupboard. We were alone in the house, my mother having found a part-time job in Trebor's sweet factory. It was soon obvious to all and sundry where she was working, for her figure ballooned out, with the amount of fudge the workers were allowed to eat while working. She even managed to smuggle out some blocks of fudge to us, which we devoured like animals. But lunchtimes were the best times for Shirley and me. Since there was no one at home, we would go to my house, sit by the warm glow of the coal fire in a half-gloom, and talk incessantly about our feelings and our school work. Shirley would also talk about the pain of losing her mother when she was fourteen years old and having to come to terms with a new 'mother' when her father remarried. While talking or listening, I would almost desultorily burn patterns with the red-hot poker in the thick paint on the fire-surround and Shirley would watch, equally unconcerned at the damage I was doing to it, so engrossed were we in our conversations. Fortunately, no one in the family even noticed the peculiar depressions in the paint. We talked a lot about growing up and boys, but never about the changes that were occurring in our bodies. This was the era where children were still seen and not heard and certainly my mother did not prepare me for adolescence. Sex was a taboo subject in our house. My mother would mutter darkly. "That's all men want from you! Keep away from them!" and forbade us to wear lipstick or powder or any form of jewellery. The Roman Catholic antagonism towards sex in all its forms found an apt proponent in her. One day, I discovered that I was bleeding between my legs. Terrified that I had injured myself in some way, and fearful of my mother's reactions, I staunched the flow as best as I could, but at least a day passed before I could gather up the courage to tell her. Quite unconcerned at the fearful news and with no comment, she went to find an old towel and told me to pin it on to my pants. The explanation for the blood I had to find elsewhere. But thereafter the washing of these stained cloths filled me with revulsion, both towards them and towards my body, which now seemed alien to me. Every month the dreaded period pains would come. There was no aspirin or other medication to help, so I took to my bed and groaned out loud in agony.

There was also a half-hearted attempt at school to teach us sex education, a subject considered to be unimportant in an academic institution. When the news got out that the poor Biology teacher, a woman naturally, would talk about the birth of a baby, the boys could not wait to get to the lab. They grabbed the front rows and the girls, overcome with embarrassment, huddled at the back. Needless to say, the teacher did not get very far with her exposition, what with the whistles and catcalls. Class discipline deteriorated into uproar when she started showing diagrams of the sexual organs. When that lesson ended, it was also the end of our sex education. Most of my knowledge henceforth consisted of gleaning mean bits of information in the playground. That was until I went into a bookshop one day and saw a book on sex. I started to read it, and became absolutely mesmerised. Time stood still for me until the heavy hand of the shop assistant fell on my shoulder. I looked up, dragged from this other universe and saw the appalled face of the shop assistant who shouted, 'What *do* you think you are doing? Get out of here immediately!' and I was unceremoniously thrown out of the shop. But I had learnt some new facts. When my breasts started forming, I became ashamed of my changed shape, wore jackets to cover them up and walked around with my arms lapped around them like a hunchback. One day, in the playground we saw a soldier beckoning us to come to the railings. He was in khaki uniform and looked quite nice. Obediently we approached him and he started to talk to us:

'Hello, young ladies! How do you like school?'

'It's OK I s'pose,' I replied giggling. Behind the safety of the railings, I felt quite daring.

'Have you got any favourite subjects?'

'We like French, don't we Shirl?'

Shirley hung back slightly suspicious. Then the soldier laughed and said:

'Do you? I speak French. Do you want to hear? Listen!' He beckoned me nearer and whispered in my ear;

"*Voulez-vous promener avec moi*?" and waited for my reaction with a gleam of interest in his eye. Since oral French was low down on the list of priorities in the French class, it took me some time for the sense of what he said to penetrate, but then I blushed bright red, stepped back quickly and shouted, 'Non!' Shirley saw the look of fear on my face and we both raced back to the security of the middle of the playground. We looked back at him and he seemed quite forlorn, but I shivered at my lucky escape. We also had closer contact now with the boys in our class in the compulsory dancing lessons. What a farce and an embarrassment that was! We were all ushered into the hall, the boys lined up on one side and the girls on the other. After the PE teacher had shown us some steps, we all had to walk towards the centre of the hall until we met the boys in the middle. Then, whoever was in front of you was your partner and the dance began. Since I was tall for my age and the boys were later developing than the girls, I invariably ended up with some short monstrosity, whose head with its slicked-back, heavily greased hair was just under my nose. The smell of Brylcreme was overpowering and I had to keep my face turned aside as much as possible. I died in those lessons, until I decided that I had had enough and truanted from them.

Becoming more aware of others around me, I began to chafe at the unending poverty of our lives at home. All our clothes had to be bought at Granditer's, a sort of draper's in the High Street, because Mum paid weekly for the clothes coupons. I protested vigorously, but the only alternative was to suffer the dresses run up by my mother on her sewing machine. She fancied herself as a dressmaker, but the results were disastrous; ill-fitting and deeply unfashionable to my eyes. The hair fashion at this time was for 'bangs' where the front of the hair was rolled down over the forehead and 'sweeps' where it was rolled up and pinned, none too firmly, on top of the head. In both cases the rest of one's hair hung down thinly at the back, "like rats' tails" my mother said disparagingly. I must have looked an absolute fright because I remember the first time I sported a 'sweep', and staggered into school in my high wedge shoes, Mr Goldfinch stared at me in horror. I thought he was admiring me! Since I could do nothing about our poverty, I buried myself in such escape mechanisms as reading and the cinema. I hated some of the books that we had to read at school, two ghastly examples being Kinglake's *Eothen*, and Hazlitt's *Essays*, but I loved Jane Austen's *Pride and Prejudice* and gained a really good mark in the exam for my answer to a question on Darcy and Elizabeth. As for the cinema, since I never had any pocket money, the only way I could go was when my mother decided to take Doreen and me with her or 'cadge' some money from my father. I would pester him to give me the money to go. I would sit on the settee and say, "Dad, can I have some money to go to the pictures?" He wouldn't even look at me, replying only, "Where do you think I've got the money? All my money goes in keeping you!" Undeterred, I would repeat the question, "Oh, go on Dad! Give us sixpence!" Silence. Then I would start again, "Oh, go on, Dad!" I was quite determined to carry on until he raised his hand to me, but he never did. He would finally concede defeat and hand me sixpence. Then I would rush to the cinema regardless of the programme times and then have to loiter outside, waiting for someone to offer to take me in. The only films I wanted to see carried an A certificate, meaning I had to go in with an adult. This could prove quite a dangerous exercise. Several times I was taken in by soldiers, without any problem, but once there was a different outcome. It was another young soldier who looked at me quizzically as I stood outside the cinema. "You want to go in, do you?" I showed him my sixpence. "OK, Keep close to me." Once inside and beginning to enjoy seeing my favourite film star, Clark Gable, I was suddenly aware of something wrong. I felt that the soldier was moving his hand nearer to my legs. I looked at him but he appeared to be engrossed in the film. Was it my imagination? I was so embarrassed that I turned back to the film, but it happened again. I was mostly annoyed that I couldn't watch the film. But gradually I began to be frightened. I could hardly stand up and shout, "Keep your hands off me, you swine!" could I? I would really cause a stir in the cinema and I would have died if that had happened. So I devised a strategy. "I'm really thirsty," I said with a Cockney whine to my voice. "Can I go and get a drink? And an ice-cream for you?" To my relief, he agreed, felt in his pocket for some money and handed it to me. "Don't be long!"

"Don't be long?" I thought. "You must be joking!" and I disappeared to another part of the auditorium and slunk down in my seat to avoid detection and finally to enjoy the film. Even that episode did not put me off the cinema. At the Granada in East Ham they had a Wurlitzer, a glittering organ which would emerge from the bowels of the auditorium with the organist playing all the popular songs of the period, *The White Cliffs of Dover, Lili Marlene* (which was a German song!) and *We'll Meet Again*, before the film started. I thought it was magic. Then as the film came on, it would slowly descend into the void. The warm, enveloping darkness, the beauty of the film stars, such as Rita Hayworth and Vivien Leigh, the daring exploits of Tyrone Power and Cary Grant transported me into a world of fantasy. These films were pure escapism. They were all about a rich upper-class life even though the bulk of the spectators were working class. We had to wait for 1949 for the Ealing comedies which portrayed more realistic British stories, albeit fantastical in their own way. One film I remember, *Blithe Spirit* with Rex Harrison and Constance Cummings, was so funny that I saw it three times over and staggered out of the cinema after five or so hours completely oblivious to the grim, grey austerity outside. I would try to slip into the house quietly so that I did not have to talk to anyone and so could keep the magic inside me for a little while longer.

There was one last horror before the war ended. The Germans made us a present of their next *Vergeltungswaffe*, in September 1944 just to keep us on our feet. 232 V2 rockets landed in the South of England in one month. It was the last dying throw of the German Reich. It was even more frightening than the V1 since there was no time even for the air-raid siren to warn us and they made no noise until they exploded. They soared silently over London and dropped at the end of their range. They caused havoc. But fortunately the danger did not last long. Preparations were already well advanced for the Allies to invade France; it was the 'Second Front'. As soon as the launch pad stations were discovered, they were bombed heavily and the V2s stopped. Soon to be over as well were my schooldays and some of my innocence. The War had now ended and the country celebrated with street parties. Tables were set up along Woodside Road with flags and bunting and food for the children. There were paper hats to wear, balloons to float, to celebrate our victory. I hated all of it. Since we did not know any other children in the street (my father did not allow any 'fraternising' with the neighbours) Doreen and I were isolated. We also hated the sandwiches and the jelly and custard provided. For me it was a non-event. Much more memorable to me was the showing for the first time on the newsreel at the cinema, of the horrors of the Belsen concentration camp. It was made even more heart-rending because I went to see the film with Shirley, who, of course, was Jewish. The images of the charnel houses, those emaciated skeletons who seemed more dead than alive and the piles of dead bodies in the camp will remain with me forever. We were both in tears and even afterwards, Shirley was sobbing quietly all the way home. A chill settled on our hearts at the realisation of the depravity of some human beings. And yet, being young, more immediate worries pressed on us. Bread and potatoes, the staple diet in my home, were rationed for the first time, because of the world shortage of food. I was also now in the fifth form, in a class which was sadly depleted because many in the class left school at the end of the fourth year because they were fifteen years old. I was now sixteen and a choice had to be made as to whether I could continue my education. Shirley's father insisted she stay on in the sixth form. My mother, on the contrary, decided that I had had enough education to last me for the rest of my life and, anyway, she needed some return for letting me stay on in school. My father who had always been pleased that I never went out in the evenings, but stayed in to study, did not offer any resistance. So a careers interview was arranged for me where I said I wanted to work in a travel agent's, (the call to escape to distant climes, even in my imagination, was strong in me). Unfortunately, travel agents were few and far between at this time and in my area. My mother was not deterred. She needed more money in the house and it was only right that at the age of sixteen I should start work and 'grow up'. In fact very few of our 'special' class stayed on into the sixth form, proof of the lowered expectations of the working class and the more important fact that most could not afford to stay on. Only four out of thirty did so. What was most upsetting for me was that my life would now diverge from Shirley's. We were both very sad about that. I was still very shy, still terrified of my shadow, very immature, and was about to be wrenched from the security and pleasures of school and pitchforked into the outside, adult world.

Chapter 6
The World of Work

The above quotation would have been quoted *ad nauseum* by my mother if she had known anything about Chekhov. But the work ethic had been drummed into us so often, that with very little remonstration, I left school and set about finding a job. Where to start though? The time-honoured way in our family was to look at the adverts in the *Evening Standard*, which at least promised the excitement of a job in Central London instead of the small and probably boring offices locally. So I must have seen an advert for a Comptometer Operator (what on earth was that?) at the Prudential Assurance Co in High Holborn, gone for an interview and been accepted, because within two weeks I was gazing with fear and trepidation at the massive red-brick building in Holborn more reminiscent of a gothic cathedral than a financial centre. I discovered that a comptometer was a kind of high-tech calculating machine. I was shown how to punch mathematical information into the machine with one hand and almost simultaneously, it seemed, it spewed out cards with punch-holes in it at the other end, which were then sorted as if by magic and at breakneck speed into different trays. I quite liked the work, particularly when I was learning the ropes. The other employees in the bright, large-windowed office seemed friendly enough and while I was concentrating on the work, there was little time for social intercourse, for which I was thankful. The problem was the lunch hour. For the first few weeks, I was unsure of myself and far too shy to talk to anyone, so I had to find a place to eat my sandwiches. I was too overwhelmed to go out into the bustle and traffic of High Holborn and there seemed to be no canteen, so I made a beeline for the 'Ladies' where I assumed I could shut myself away in a toilet, eat my sandwiches and read a book. This worked well for some time. Unfortunately, occasionally, there was quite a queue in the toilets and there would be impatient calls to "Hurry up in there!" as I sat on the toilet, in a state of catatonic fear, swallowing my bread silently and holding my breath. Eventually another toilet would become vacant and I could breathe again. This went on for weeks until I was discovered by a couple of girls in our department who had been puzzled as to where I vanished at lunchtime. They were horrified and gently persuaded me to come out and join them for lunch.

The day's work finished at five p.m. and then there was a precipitous rush through the marble hall, down the stairs to try to be first to get in line for the No. 15 bus, which stopped outside the building. Why I joined in I don't know, since I had nothing to go home to, but the panic got to me too. This life went on for about a year, the only break from work being Saturday when I would meet Shirley at Lyons teashop in Stratford East for a chat. Of course, I was now actually earning some money, most of which went to my mother, but I was able to buy some decent clothes for myself. I would buy *Women's Own* every week and learn not only about the latest fashions, but all about the way women had to comport themselves in public. This included making sure that when one was sitting opposite another person, one would have to have one's ankles crossed, because legs spread-out was a *very common* thing to do, and was liable to give men certain ideas. Once again, men were seen as the enemy. There seemed to be so many restrictions on what to wear, what to do, that my ordinary fears were doubled. I remember buying a Prince of Wales check suit, the first I had ever bought and of which I was inordinately proud. When I visited Shirley once wearing it, her grandmother eyed me in astonishment and said to Shirley: "Your friend hàs a lovely figure!" My first compliment! I glowed with pride.

Early on in my new career as comptometer operator, Irene finally emerged from the WAAF after six years in harness, bringing into our life her fiancé Roy. He was definitely different from us; I reckoned him to be one of the aspiring, lower-middle-class types. I'm sure Irene actively sought out someone higher up in the class system to latch on to and she succeeded. The fact that he was a dominating, suffocating personality who eventually broke her spirit was not seen until much later. His parents did not approve of Irene, indeed her mother-in-law once called her 'an aggressive little Cockney' which only goes to show how bigoted some of the members of the lower middle class could be. My sister could never have been described as 'little' since she was five feet eleven inches tall, nor 'a Cockney', with the accent she had cultivated assiduously to cover up her working-class background. I asked her once, quite curious to know: "Rene, how did you manage to acquire this upper-class accent?"

"It's not upper class, it's Received Pronunciation and I 'acquired' it as you call it, by listening to the BBC."

"And does anyone in your camp know where you come from?"

"Well, when they ask, I say London."

"And if they say 'Where in London?'"

"I say *Playstow*." She stared at me challengingly.

"*Playstow*? But you know it's pronounced 'Plahstow [Plaistow]'". My feelings about correct pronunciation were quite strong, as my past experience had testified. She airily waived aside my protestations. I was torn between outrage at her cavalier dismissal of the locally accepted rule of pronunciation and envy at her ruthless attempts to eliminate her background. I don't suppose anyone discovered her secret except Roy. I had met him several times when she was home on leave and was usually highly embarrassed when he came. This was because we had so few chairs in our kitchen, that it gave her a good excuse to sit on his knee, gazing at him adoringly while he carried on some sort of conversation with me. I would wriggle in acute embarrassment as we discussed so politely the latest news.

Irene decided that her wedding should take place in St Martin-in-the-Fields' in Trafalgar Square, a very beautiful neoclassical church and a fashionable place for a wedding. It had an impressive nave and the occasion should have been wonderful. Irene looked very smart in a tight-fitting dark-brown suit with a matching pillbox hat and a beautiful spray of freesias. Mother was resplendent in a long fur coat that she had managed to acquire from a second-hand shop. I, however, felt quite miserable because I was convinced that the green suit that I had bought specially for the wedding did not go with the only jumper I had, a navy-blue one. What with that *contretemps,* my long unruly hair and thick lisle stockings (no nylons in those days), I suffered agonies of self-consciousness. Roy's parents and his two sisters and a brother were barely polite to the motley East End group who had come to share in my sister's happiness. That group included my maternal grandmother in a long shapeless coat and black hat with flowers on it and several Irish aunts and uncles.

At the end of the service, we trooped out for the obligatory photographs and then the Groves family disappeared as if by magic, taking Irene and Roy with them. We stood around disconsolately for a while, then the Irish contingent having taken one look at my father's grim face and obviously judging there would be no Irish fun to be had there, also vanished. But then my father then rose to the occasion and stated that he would take us to Lyons Corner House for lunch. A meal in a restaurant – my first! Lyons Corner House seemed very 'posh' to me with its waitresses called 'Nippies' who were dressed in black dresses, with white cuffs and caps, and frilly white aprons. Unfortunately I did not choose my meal wisely. Seeing 'braised duck' on the menu, I decided that duck would be something special, a superior type of chicken, which we only saw at Xmas anyway. So I expected something white and tender to appear on my plate. What arrived was a brown gluey-looking sauce swimming with lumps of brown meat. I was close to tears but had to pretend to enjoy it to avoid the wrath of my father.

When I went for my regular meetings with Shirley on Saturday mornings, Shirley would regale me with all the work she was doing in the sixth form, Shakespeare and Milton, the causes of the American War of Independence and the naughty things she was learning about mistresses in French novels they were reading, Then she would ask me what I had been doing. What *had* I been doing? The realisation then dawned on me that I had nothing to tell. Having learned the comptometer, I did the same thing every day and there was no gossip to recount. While a whole new world was opening up to her, my greatest excitement was to be one of the first to get on the No 15 bus. Having realised that, I became more and more disenchanted with my work and decided to leave. Marks and Spencer was advertising for trainee managers. I liked the idea of the training, wasn't too sure of the management side, but decided to give it a go. I had three months training, learning all about sales, conversion of fraction to decimals, percentages and general book-keeping. It was like being back at school. At the end of the three months, we had an exam and I passed with 100% marks. I, who had only just scraped through Maths at School Certificate! The supervisor was duly impressed and called me into her office: "Miss White, we are very pleased with your results and would like to suggest that we by-pass the next stage in our training programme and move you onto something else." She looked at me inquiringly, obviously waiting to see a pleasant reaction. I stared at her with misgivings. What was she suggesting?

"We have in the main store in Central London a small office which is currently without a manager. We'd like to offer the post to you. Of course, it will mean quite a big increase in your salary, commensurate with the extra responsibilities you would be undertaking. If you agree, you can start next Monday." Through the euphoria of the accolades I was receiving, a sudden chill wind blew around my heart. Me run an office? The mere thought of it filled me with horror. Supposing I did something wrong? Supposing I couldn't deal with the problems brought to me by the others in the office? I would be a focus of ridicule and humiliation. I mumbled some non-committal response and asked for time to consider the proposal. She agreed and I left, but I already knew the answer I would give. By the time Monday came, I had already written a letter of resignation and that was the end of my career in Marks and Spencer. I've often wondered since what my life would have been like if I had taken that job. I might have earned quite a lot of money...

What to do next? I was desperate to get away from home now and toyed with the idea of joining the Land Army, mainly because I loved the uniform – those khaki breeches, green sweater and very fetching hat. My father refused to let me – he thought that working on the land was common, but wasn't averse to my joining the WAAF where Irene had been for the last five years. Whenever she was home on leave, she had waxed enthusiastic about the camaraderie of the forces, the social life and the men. She had met her husband there, and whereas I had no such thoughts, I did like the idea of becoming a car mechanic and learning to drive. So I duly presented myself to the recruiting office and was told that we would have an initial training period during which we would take vocational tests to discover whether we were suitable material for the WAAF It seemed that now that the war was over, the WAAF was being a little more selective. Thus in a state of high excitement I joined a group of other girls in a lorry and was transported to the training centre in Kent. On arrival we were shown our sleeping quarters, which didn't impress me much. A long low building with a corrugated iron roof and whitewashed walls. Inside, the walls were lined with what looked like hospital beds and seemed just as inhospitable. To me it smacked of clinical desolation, with the grey blankets and the coarse sheets. The other girls didn't impress me either with their raucous voices and terrible cockney accents. Worse was to come the next morning when we were dragged from sleep at 6 a.m. for ablutions and square-bashing. What was I doing there marching up and down in the freezing cold? As usual my imagination had run away with me. Then we were taken into another building and had our medical examination. This lasted some time, but apparently I was in good health and there was no bar to my joining the WAAF. There was only one slight problem. Nits had been found in my hair and I would have to undergo some treatment for this. Regardless of the fact that nits were a perennial problem among poor children, the shame of this discovery overwhelmed me. I had always prided myself on my cleanliness. I suddenly remembered that the only time mother would clasp me to her bosom was when she was regularly searching my head for nits. She would use a special steel comb which scraped painfully across my head and the discomfort was only assuaged by the softness and warmth of her breasts, the only physical contact I remember with her. But I was now eighteen years old and had just had a perm. How could this be? I felt dirty and unclean and was terrified that the news would get out and that I would be a butt for other girls' jokes. I wanted to run away and was even contemplating it, but was saved by the Intelligence Officer, of all people, from God knows what punishment I would have incurred. We had completed the series of vocational tests, and apparently my results showed good verbal reasoning and auditory skills, which were the skills needed to become a wireless operator. This job involved sending and receiving messages in Morse code to the wireless operator on the aeroplanes. Curiously enough, this was the same job that Irene had done in the WAAF.

"Unfortunately," said the officer, "there are no vacancies in this field at present. Do you have any idea about other jobs that would interest you?"

"Well sir, I really joined the WAAF because I want to become a car mechanic." I didn't mention that the inner mechanisms of the car had no attractions for me, I merely wanted to drive one. I can only imagine what his thoughts were on this suggestion.

"I'm afraid that there are no vacancies in this field either," he replied. "In fact the only vacancy we have at the moment is as a dental assistant."

I looked at him in disbelief. Was this the exciting life I had joined up for? Preparing fillings for a dentist? Looking at the gaping mouths of patients for the next few years? Then a faint ray of hope flitted through my mind. This might be an escape route for me from the anguish of finding out about the nits. Carefully and in a neutral voice, I said, "I don't really see myself as a dental assistant, sir. If you don't have any other vacancies, I suppose that means that I leave the Service?" He nodded and added helpfully, "I'm sorry we can't offer you anything else at the moment, but you can, of course, apply again at another time." Halleluya! God was in his heaven and helping me at that moment. I thanked him and made my escape, back to Plaistow, back to the bosom of my family and back as F.R. Leavis put it, "to the vigour of a prolonged adolescence", because I had decided that, come what may, I was going to try to get back to school.

Obviously on my return home, my first job was to get rid of the nits, which I did successfully. I had my hair cut short and smacked some evil-smelling stuff on it every night so that no self-respecting nit would ever consider taking up residence in my hair again. Then there was pressure on me from my mother to get another job. But I prevaricated. I wanted to go and see Dr Priestley to ask if he would take me back in the sixth form. I was becoming ever more jealous of Shirley and her studies, and wanted to be part of that life again. He was quite hesitant at first. "You realise that you have missed a great deal of work, Sylvia?" I concurred. "You will only have just over a year to in which to prepare for the Higher School Certificate?"

"Yes, I realise that, headmaster, but I am a good worker and I really want to continue my education," I pleaded. Finally he agreed. I left his room, hugging myself with glee, imagining with some amusement the talk in the staff room when the staff heard the news:

"That tall girl, Sylvia White who left more than a year ago, wants to come back."

What! One of those in the special class? Wants to join her little Jewish friend again?"

"Well, she won't be in the same year, but it will be interesting to see how she copes after all this time."

"As long as there is no 'hanky-panky' between them!"

Actually I was probably maligning them. Miss Holden, the History teacher, would have been quite glad since she only had one student in her sixth form, but the others would have been quite disinterested. Then, of course, I had to face my mother with the news.

"Mum, I've decided to go back to school in the sixth form."

She stared at me in disbelief. "What are you talking about? They won't have you back after you've been left for so long!"

"Dr Priestley said I can go back."

"You've been over to see him without telling me? Well, I'll tell you something, my girl. You don't decide. I say you've got to go out and get a job and help out with the money I need in this house!"

"But, Mum, I want to go back! It's important for me! I'm sick of all these rotten jobs I've been doing. I want to get a better job!"

"I'm not having anything of this," said my mother really angry now. "You'll get up on Monday morning and you'll go looking for a new job. You've had enough learning to keep you going for a lifetime!" She refused to talk any more about it and left me brooding on the unfairness of life. True to her word, the following Monday morning, she came early into our bedroom, saying, "Come on, get up – you've got to look for a job!" I shouted out, "Mum, I'm not going, I told you!" secretly quite frightened and pulled the bed-covers over my head. Eventually, realising that she could not forcibly drag me out of bed, my mother had to accept the situation, although with a bad grace.

Back at school, I realised how much work I had missed when I was confronted with sixth form French and even worse, Chaucer's Middle English. My first test results were abysmal – two out of ten for Chaucer, four out of ten for French. I needed to work really hard. It was made more difficult because our French teacher was a Dr Arnold, a tall, willowy figure, straight out of a Pre-Raphaelite painting. She *drifted* in to the class dressed nearly always in black with her black academic gown floating gently behind her. She was highly academic but a useless teacher. She had prolonged absences, but when she did deign to teach us, she spent most of her time quoting French poetry to the uncomprehending sixth form with a look of supreme beatitude on her face. I didn't understand a word of any of it. What I needed was a crash course in my forgotten French grammar, but I didn't get it. Once she turned up with what looked like a gnome in tow, half her height with what I thought of as grotesque features and a broken English accent. He proved to be her new husband, a very learned professor, but for the class he was the focus of ribald merriment. Luckily there were no more than five or six in any of my classes, so that we did have a great deal of attention. English was not so bad. We had a superb teacher, a Miss Crow who funnily enough looked rather like her namesake, with her black academic gown and her short, shining, black hair. She would invite her small band of devotees to her house where we read and discussed Browning and Tennyson and listened to her expounding on Milton's *Samson Agonistes*. I had to read bits of the Bible before I could even begin to understand it, having only learned the Catechism at my Catholic school. Another of our set books was Thomas Hardy's *The Return of the Native*. I remember visiting my sister Irene who now lived in Bristol and had a large three-bedroomed house which I thought very grand. It bordered a large stretch of common land which really attracted me. I would go there day after day, in the high summer, to read Hardy's book. I would sit, surrounded by the tall grasses and the wild flowers, whose perfume intensified in the warmth of the sun, and listen to the murmuring of the summer insects, while reading the description of Egdon Heath. It was as though I was there on that heath in the company of the wild, capricious Eustacia Vye. Wonderful days! Not so pleasant was the afternoon that Irene decided she would unload onto me all her experiences in childbirth, having recently given birth to a son, John. I sat on the settee for what seemed hours while she recounted all the gruesome details of the birth and the pain she had suffered. Not only was I annoyed at having to sit and listen to it all but she made the whole experience sound so awful that I vowed then and there never to get married or have a child.

I made another friend in the sixth form, Irene Hallybone, so totally different from Shirley. She was a very keen Ranger, the adult section of the Girl Guides, and excellent at games, but not as academic as Shirley. She helped me with my struggles with Chaucer. In its wisdom, the English Department used an expurgated text of *The Pardoner's Tale* and every so often there would be lines of asterisks instead of text. We were all really intrigued to find out what we were missing, expecting some salacious descriptions. Irene and I couldn't get to the library quick enough to find a complete version of the tale. One of the expurgated lines, Chaucer's description of the Pardoner turned out to be: "I trow he were a gelding or a mare". I had to look up 'trow' and 'gelding', since they weren't in my vocabulary and then when faced with the explanation 'castrated', had to resort once more to the dictionary. "What one learns in the sixth form," I thought.

Apart from academic lessons, the sixth form was encouraged to take part in games lessons but were excused PE One day, a new PE teacher arrived at the school, a Miss Goodeve. She was young, enthusiastic and as small as Shirley but with a fearsome energy. In her wisdom, she decided that the sixth form should not be exempt from PE So perforce, we had to present ourselves in the Gym for our first lesson. To Shirley and I, this was a torture chamber, with its wall-racks on which we were supposed to climb and hang on to like performing apes. This was not to my liking, but worse was to come. We had to vault over the horse. I managed it with great difficulty, hating this presumptuous little woman, not much older than I was, for inflicting such ignominy on me. Shirley fared even worse. Her short plump body was not designed for such acrobatics. Twice she ran up to the horse and twice baulked at it. When ordered to try again, she stood stock-still, crimson with the effort and her embarrassment and then quite simply refused. Silence in the hall as we all waited curiously to see what our new teacher would do. Foolishly she tried to make Shirley run at the horse again, whereupon Shirley burst into tears and rushed out of the room. And that was the end of PE lessons for Shirley and me. We decided to truant every time it took place. We would saunter casually out of the school and make a beeline for the sweet shop at Greengate. The heavens didn't open, we weren't punished. I can only assume that Miss Goodeve was as glad to see the back of us as we were of her.

Higher School Certificate time arrived. I remember sitting at the kitchen table trying to revise, surrounded by the rest of the family listening to the wireless and sitting there until two a.m. in the morning trying to stuff dates into my head. But I did well in the exams and the question of continuing my education was broached. Obviously I could not go to university having no Latin and neither could Shirley. She had spent the last year teaching infants in a local school and already had a place at Avery Hill Training College for the next year. I decided, along with Irene Hallybone, to try for the same college. I was accepted for an interview and had to take a tram through the Blackwall Tunnel, which proved to be a bone-shaking experience. The tram careered at what seemed breakneck speed through the dark, narrow tunnel, round the vertiginous bends, throwing all the passengers against each other with malicious glee. But when I finally arrived in Eltham I really believed that I was back in the countryside, surrounded as I was by leafy trees, just turning russet-gold. I walked along the road skirting the high walls of the college and was pierced with a sudden, sharp sensation of pure happiness. The interview was a mere formality given my results, but when asked by the Principal why I wanted to teach, I was well prepared, having thought long and hard about my response. Prissily and pedantically, I mouthed the words: "I would like to impart my knowledge to children." There was a silence, then a "Hurrmph!" from the Principal as she probably tried to smother a laugh, but I was accepted.

I intended to study French at Avery Hill College. There was only one snag, I had never been to France, this being impossible during the War, so my spoken French was pretty poor. I had also had a gap of eighteen months from study and the poor quality of Dr Arnold's teaching did nothing to remedy this problem. So I asked Irene Hallybone if she would like to go to France with me for two weeks' holiday. Money was the stumbling block both for Irene and me, but by working in a hospital during the Xmas holidays we managed to save enough to get across to France and then we hoped to hitch-hike down to the south in search of the sun. It was Easter 1949 when we went; and there were still travel restrictions in place, not least the fact that one was only allowed to take £25 out of the country. This did not worry us because we had very little anyway. The ferry was not as exciting as I had imagined; I had to stay on deck most of the time because the motion of the ship made me feel queasy and indeed for several nights after we arrived, as soon as I lay my head on the pillow, I experienced the rocking sensation of the boat. A most unpleasant beginning to the trip. We decided to stay in Paris only the night; we wanted the sun. So the next morning found us on the outskirts of Paris vigorously thrusting our thumbs forward in pure hitch-hiking mode. And so we spent two of the most exciting and potentially dangerous weeks of our lives hitch-hiking through France. We looked pretty peculiar, both of us still wearing socks and blazers and with rucksacks on our backs. Every pick-up by car or lorry was either hilarious or frightening, depending on one's outlook. We hitched a lift to Dijon, but had to sit in the darkness of the driver's cab for over an hour at about midnight waiting for the driver to have a sleep. But arriving in Dijon as the morning broke and feeling the warm sun on one was pure heaven. The next lift was from two men in a small Citroen van, a *quatre-chevaux*, which had space only for the driver and one passenger. When it stopped for us we hesitated noting the lack of space for extraneous passengers but the two men beckoned to us laughingly, so spurred on by the fact that it was at least a lift, we squeezed in between them. I had to sit with the gear-stick between my legs, which the driver, with what I thought was unnecessary force would pull back between my two open thighs. Of course, women didn't wear trousers in those days so he managed to get the gear-stick quite far up my thighs. Luckily, it was a short journey and both men were very good-natured. I was beginning to improve my spoken French rapidly. I certainly needed it when another lorry driver gave us a lift. He seemed quite a taciturn type, not smiling or open to conversation. Then suddenly he said to me: "*On fait l'amour sur la route?*" Not understanding his rapid delivery, I replied: "Comment? *Je ne comprends pas.*" He repeated the phrase in such a tone and looked at me so meaningly that the sense of his remark hit me fully. He wanted to stop somewhere to make love to me (the modern, more appropriate word being 'shag', I suppose). Since it was deemed to be a question, I answered firmly, "*Non*! *Non*!" while Irene, ignorant of what was going on, stared at me. Whereupon, he pulled the lorry up sharply and told us in no uncertain terms to get out. We were pushed out at breakneck speed, Irene following me bemusedly, and then the lorry had disappeared into the night. We were on a dark country road with not a car or lorry in sight.

We stayed there forlorn and somewhat apprehensive for more than an hour and then, out of the gloom, an expensive-looking car drew up. A head poked out, a man with a dark beard. He asked us politely what we were doing there. I explained and he said that if we did not mind going with him, he was on the way to his château which he wanted to open up for the summer. We could stay the night there. Did we mind! When we finally arrived at the chateau, in a very isolated spot, it loomed up at us forbiddingly, a huge bulk of classical architecture. Stepping out of the car, waiting for the driver to unload his belongings, we could hear the faint murmur of a river at the bottom of the garden. It was the river Rhône. The owner of this awe-inspiring chateau took us in to a large imposing hall and then a grand room on one side of it. I remember the clouds of dust billowing up as he took off the furniture drapes and the piles of dead flies scattered over the windowsill as he opened the internal shutters. The Frenchman was very courteous – he asked us if we had eaten and when we shook our heads, suggested we walk to the village nearby for a meal. We stuffed ourselves voraciously, having eaten only croissants for breakfast and a piece of baguette for lunch. He also plied us with wine, the first alcohol I had ever tasted. We walked back across the dark fields lit only by the stars shining in the velvet depths of the sky. I remember we giggled uncontrollably as we stumbled in the rough grass and he laughed with us, holding on to us as we staggered and wove our way back to the château. He then showed us our room, a vast high-ceilinged bedroom with a grand double bed and said: "*Bonne Nuit. Dormez bien, mes jeunes filles.*" He closed the door quietly behind him and I was suddenly aware that there was no lock on it. I shook Irene. "Irene! Supposing he comes in during the night? We can't lock the door!" She looked at me foggily but was also conscious of the inherent danger of our situation. So together we clambered out of the huge bed and manoeuvred a large commode to the door to barricade ourselves in. Then we collapsed on to the bed still with our shoes on and fell asleep immediately. I woke up dazed in the middle of the night to hear a noise. I listened acutely; it was the Frenchman, softly turning the doorknob. Finding an obstruction, he started to push at the door, but the heavy oak commode resisted his onslaught and suddenly it was quiet again. He had given up. But the next morning, as soon as we woke up, we were off and hitting the road as fast as we could. A similar episode occurred in Toulon. Running out of money now, we booked into the cheapest hotel we could find, in the dock area. Without realising it, we were in a hotel which was a meeting place for prostitutes and sailors. We were eyed lasciviously by a raucous gang of sailors in the bar as we made our way up to the bedroom. Once again, we barricaded ourselves in, although even more effort was made to get to us than in the château. We were kept awake most of the night by the various unsuccessful attempts to enter our bedroom. But suddenly we realised we had a more pressing problem than the oversexed French men. We had very little money left. By the time the rooftops of Calais reappeared, we had virtually run out of it. We needed a drink; we couldn't drink the water, the coffee was too expensive, so all we could afford was the really rough red wine available in the bars. We drank a couple of glasses of that and then, reeling up the gangway, carefree and very much wiser in the ways of the world, we made for home.

It was back to Plaistow and the perennial problem of finances, this time for college. Tuition was free but we had to find our own living expenses. I was expecting to get a bursary from the local authority to cover my living expenses, since Shirley had already been given one, even though her family were much more affluent that mine, her father being a self-employed hairdresser. Unfortunately when all the forms were sent in, I was refused a bursary. Apparently my father had earned over the limit on the previous year. This was a bombshell both for my mother and me. She demanded to know from my father what it meant. The painful and unpleasant facts emerged; he had had a good year in the docks with full employment, but chose not to let the rest of the family enjoy this bounty. He had instead indulged his passion for 'the dogs' at Walthamstow dog track. He was also deaf to any pleas to help me out with my college expenses, saying that he wasn't earning so much this year. Since he had never, ever divulged what he earned to my mother, she could do nothing. The college course was in the balance. But my mother, to my eternal gratitude, decided that I should go and that she would take on an extra cleaning job to help me out. Such a sacrifice on her part overwhelmed me and for the first time in my life I hugged her. Yet she obviously could not afford to give me much. I had five shillings a week pocket money from her for the next two years, which was nowhere near what I needed, but like Scarlett O'Hara in *Gone with The Wind*, tomorrow was another day. It was October 1949 and I was on my way.

Chapter 7
College Life

Avery Hill Training College was set in magnificent parkland in Eltham, south-east London. Eltham had many claims to fame, not least the surviving Great Hall of the medieval palace much frequented by Edward IV and Henry VII. It also had a country house called Well Hall which had been lived in by the novelist Edith Nesbitt. I was thrilled to discover that she wrote *The Railway Children* there – one of my favourite books when I was younger. It was so wonderful to have my own room! I remember reading Virginia Woolf's *A Room of One's Own* when I was in the sixth form and longing for my own space and now I had it. It was obviously small, room enough only for a bed, a wardrobe and desk and chair for studying, but it was my own to shut myself away whenever I chose. What was not so quickly dispersed was my feeling of intense homesickness, especially on Saturdays. Saturday night was my father's 'dog' night, and it meant that we, my mother, Doreen and I could enjoy ourselves without his brooding presence. We went out every Saturday to the cinema and would talk about the film on the way home, only to fall into a tense, expectant silence as we went through the front door. Was he in a good mood or a bad one? If he had won some money, we could relax, but if he had lost, Doreen and I would disappear fast leaving my mother to bear the brunt of his mood. So to arrive at the college and find that no other student had this routine, but were quite happy to do other things on Saturdays was quite a shock for me. I was so homesick that my friend Irene took it upon herself to inform my mother of my state of mind. What she expected my mother to do, I had no idea. But when I found out that she had written to Mum, I was really annoyed. I wanted to deal with my emotions in my own way and not let my mother be privy to them.

The college was a single-sex establishment and in the early 1950s it was run like a girls' boarding school. We had to be in by 10 p.m. not that most of us found this onerous since there was very little nightlife in Eltham. But we had to obtain written permission to leave the college at weekends. I chafed at these restrictions. My parents were not that enamoured of writing letters. Return to college after the weekend was quite hazardous. The main doors were locked and the only entry to one's room was through the kitchens. Unfortunately, these kitchens were also the favourite abode of many cockroaches, and the decision had to be made; should one put the lights on and watch the shiny hard-backed creatures scuttle back into the dark recesses of the room or should one grope one's way in the darkness, to the door at the other end and hope that one did not feel the sickening crunch of a cockroach squashed under foot? Many times I stood outside the kitchen door in the darkness of the evening, trying to gather up the courage to undergo this ordeal. I'm amazed, in retrospect, that no complaint was ever made to the authorities, but we were a passive lot, much in awe of the teaching staff. Although still unnaturally inhibited and reserved, I was bolstered by the presence of Shirley and Irene and Thora Richmond, the daughter of a rabid Welsh Baptist. Although she had been born in Plaistow, she retained a strong Welsh accent (deliberately?) and was very pretty and very intelligent. She should have gone to university, but her father would not countenance any association with the opposite sex, and so forbade it. She was also quite 'fey' and otherworldly, probably because she had been incarcerated for so long with such a parent. To this day, she has never married, although pursued quite relentlessly by men at different times because of her beauty.

As far as the teaching at college went I was quite disappointed, finding it much more superficial than the work we did in the sixth form. It appeared that to teach in a Secondary Modern school, one needed very little learning. At Avery Hill College, French was taken by a Doctor Cowie who had an overwhelming personality and a stature to reflect it. Tall, stocky, she resembled a rugby half-back rather than an academic. She terrified me. I had only scraped through French at HSC because I had missed so much and I was totally out of my depth. She would reel off dictations with breathtaking rapidity and would eye me maliciously as I faltered and waited for the inevitable blast of withering scorn. So I abandoned the struggle and took up English instead. The main English lecturer was a Miss Nesbitt, who must have been quite pretty when younger, with her dark, curly hair, but years of teaching at the college had obviously dried up any emotions she might have had. She was now a desiccated spinster. Her pursed mouth and peevish expression gave her the look of a dried prune. After the disaster of French, I had high hopes of the English lectures, expecting to experience the widening horizons and deepening understanding that the study of English literature had given me in the sixth form. But with one eye to our future, teaching in Secondary Modern schools, Miss Nesbitt decided that she would fill in the gaps left by the very narrow study undertaken at sixth form level. So we galloped frenziedly and chronologically through the whole of English Literature, starting with the Greek tragedies, through to the medieval mystery plays, Shakespeare, the Jacobean tragedies, the Restoration comedies, the growth of the novel with Laurence Stern and Henry Fielding, the Victorian novelists Dickens and Thackeray and ran out of steam with Oscar Wilde and the early 1920s. It was all quite superficial and unmemorable. I remember being congratulated for having written a good essay on Wilde, whose comedies I found delicious, and castigated for a criticism of *Hamlet* on at a London theatre at that time. Given that I could not afford to go to see the play myself and had to rely on newspaper articles to help me concoct some attempt at a critique, I wasn't surprised at my poor grade, but I was far too proud to let on.

As we were being so-called *trained* to teach adolescents, we had to become familiar with other subjects on the secondary curriculum, such as History, Geography, Maths but most hilariously and unbelievably Art, Book-binding, Weaving and Needlework! The Art lesson was taken by a plump woman with hair pulled back in a grey bun who fancied herself as some sort of psychiatrist. Perhaps she had read some Freud. We would all stand in front of our easels, brushes poised expectantly and listen to the music being played on the gramophone. Our job was to transpose this music into some form of art, which she would then examine and give a judgement on. I remember having a penchant for drawing boxes, being useless at any other kind of drawing. So since no other picture was suggested to me by the music, I proceeded to cover the paper with interlinking boxes, feeling quite pleased at my geometrical patterns. However, Miss Webster was not happy with my endeavours. When her eyes fell on the work, she cried out spontaneously: "Oh! My dear! You poor dear! What will become of you?" and launched into some spurious psychobabble about how introverted I was, how I was trying to shut myself away from the world in my little boxes and there was no way out. I was totally amazed at her outburst and privately thought, "You silly cow!" She put me off art for many a year. Needlework was even more of a disaster. I had managed to escape this drudgery at school by claiming that my eyesight was a lot worse than it was. So I had never learned anything about needlework, couldn't even pick up a needle without pricking myself. Shirley was not much better, being so academic. Our first lesson proved also to be the last. We were told to sew a sampler. I had to inquire of a more assiduous student sitting next to me what that was. She went into explanations about cross-stitching and chain stitches while I looked at her in increasing fear. I could foresee trouble. We had two hours in which to produce a finished sampler. Galvanised into researching in a book how to do these stitches, I think Shirley and I managed about five stitches each before the lecturer descended on us. She obviously thought we were being insolent, would brook no arguments about our ignorance of the finer points of embroidery and hauled us before the Principal. I remember reiterating my overworked excuse about my eyesight to this tall, awesome figure, to which she replied, "Don't be silly, ducky!" which completely floored me. But somehow we did not have to do needlework any more.

After the initial excitements of all these different experiences, it was soon impressed on us that we were there to train as teachers, so our education lectures were considered to be the most important. It was a pity then that these lectures were so superficial. We had a very 'jolly hockey sticks' type of lecturer for Education Studies. She would be very important to us because she would be our Inspector on School Practice. It behoved everyone to keep on the good side of her. She gave us potted sociology lectures, of which the class struggle as adumbrated by Durkheim was the only part that interested me, given that I had come from the bottom of the pile, so to speak. I remember reading about the 'Theory of Delayed Gratification'. Apparently this excellent principle was found in the members of the middle class, but not in the working class. The middle-class had the necessary discipline to withhold themselves from eating sweets or spending money, for example, and could save such pleasures for a later, more appropriate date, while the working class lacking such discipline, wolfed down sweets as soon as they bought them and went on regular spending sprees which they could ill afford. I found this principle hilarious and even more surprising that it contained a grain of truth. There were also lectures in the History of Education and School Health. The textbook for this subject had horrendous pictures of poor children with rickets, small-pox and TB which really put me off meeting any of them. We were also taught something about adolescence, although there was no practical help as to how one would deal with any recalcitrant children of this age. In fact, we were quite unprepared for the real problems we would face in front of a class, such as class control and discipline. It was as if these mundane aspects of school life were of no interest to our lecturers. Consequently, my first school practice, two weeks in a local secondary school in Mottingham, a poor area near the college, was not only a shock in itself but nearly the end of my career as a prospective teacher.

The workload for School Practice was very heavy. We had to prepare proper lesson notes beforehand, stating our aims and objectives, not that I knew the difference between those, but also write our conclusions when we had taken the lesson, and state whether we had actually achieved our aims. I would have settled for just keeping the class quiet. Hanging over us during this time was the knowledge that one day during those two weeks our lecturer would appear in the class to inspect us. I remember little of my experiences at Mottingham Secondary school, except for the history lessons. I think I must have blocked the rest out from my memory. I only had three lessons of history, the rest of my timetable being English, so on that first history lesson, I decided that attack was the best form of defence and put the fear of God into the class by saying that they were going to be inspected to see if they were working properly. In lurid terms I described what would happen to them if they failed that inspection. I also hit on the novel idea of teaching the same lesson three times over if necessary, banking on the fact that the lecturer would appear at one of them. Which proved to be the case. The class was preternaturally quiet when she appeared during the second week and answered all my questions beautifully. I was later complimented on my class control and teaching methods... Luckily, we only had six weeks School Practice during the whole of the two years at college, and no one failed. I imagine that they were so short of teachers that unless the student committed some grievous sin, there would be no question of failure.

Worse was to come when we were expected to find a school near our homes during the summer vacation to observe some experienced teachers and take the odd lesson under the supervision of the form teacher. I looked forward to this, and found a headmistress in a school in Stratford, a very poor area, who was willing to take me on. The school was housed in one of those huge red-brick buildings in neo-Gothic style built at the turn of the century. They were all about six-storeys high with all the classrooms grouped around a central hall on each floor. It was like teaching in a goldfish bowl. I shuddered at the possibility of having to teach a lesson there. I was taken on arrival to meet the headmistress, a fat, ungainly woman with a loud booming voice. She immediately thrust a timetable into my hand and said: "Your class will be 1D. You'll be teaching them all the general subjects, including PE." I gazed at her in astonishment. "But, Miss Watson, I'm only here for observation." "Observation?" she boomed at me. "We haven't got time for observations here. I'm too short-staffed for such luxuries" and ushered me out of her room rapidly. So I had this class for a whole week, poor 1D, eleven- and twelve-year-olds who were thin and small, with dull skins and an undernourished look. Discipline was no problem; they were lethargic and apathetic. I was supposed to teach every subject. Needless to say, I didn't, realising early on that no one was going to come near me for the whole week. I taught English, History and Games. But there were few problems since the class was very depleted with only about twelve pupils each day on average. I was startled to see some of them coming in the classroom in high-heeled shoes, staggering and clacking across the wooden floor. When I inquired as to the reason for this, I was told by one pupil, "Please, Miss, I ain't got no shoes now and me Mum said I had to go to school in these." The others chorused agreement. I also learned soon enough that the reason why there were so few in the class was because either they had no shoes to go to school in or were kept at home to look after the younger ones in the home, the mothers believing that school was an irrelevance for girls. I checked with the headmistress that this was the case and she agreed. I was really shocked. I had now discovered girls who were even poorer and more disadvantaged than I had been.

College vacations were the only time I had to earn some money to keep me going for the next term. The first one proved to be quite an ordeal. I was employed as a ward orderly in Plaistow Hospital. This euphemistic title encapsulated a multitude of really nasty jobs, including washing the walls and giving patients bed baths. Early on I was designated to give a bed-bath to a fat woman who seemed so old to me that I was amazed she was still alive. She sat in her bed, naked to the waist waiting for me to wash her. I eyed her huge pendulous breast with apprehension, but summoning up my courage made tentative attempts to apply a wet flannel to the more respectable parts of her anatomy, namely the neck area, keeping well away from the wrinkled, brown nipples. My half-hearted movements finally irritated her and she grabbed my hand, flannel in tow and thrust it forcibly on one nipple. I closed my eyes and winced as I felt her protuberance under the flannel. I felt in the whole fibre of my being that I was being abused, and completed the bed-bath in probably the fastest time ever. Another dreadful experience was with the Matron, those fearsome controllers of the ward who have long since disappeared, although I understand there are now attempts to bring them back to maintain order and discipline. This one came up to me as I was on my knees scrubbing the skirting board and bellowed, "Nurse!" I shot up like Jack-in-the-box. "Fetch me the callipers. I'll be at the other end of the ward."

"Callipers?" I had never even heard the word, let alone knew what it meant. I, who prided myself on my vocabulary. I backed away from her and retreated to the far end of the ward as if I were really going to fetch them. I searched feverishly for someone to ask what these things were, but the ward was empty except for the moribund patients lying in their beds. I debated whether to ask any of them what callipers were, but decided that if I did, I would either be letting the nursing profession down or cause one of them to have a heart attack. So I wandered aimlessly around, too terrified to return to the Matron. Then suddenly I saw and heard her descending on me, white, starched apron crackling, skirts billowing, bust thrust out and eyes narrowed. I wanted to die. But she just brushed me aside contemptuously and picked up something from the corner, which looked like an instrument of torture but which proved to be a steel splint with straps attached. She departed without saying a word, callipers in tow and I breathed again. The only other experience I remember in that hospital was being on night duty all by myself in an ENT ward, because of the shortage of staff. Most of the patients had recently come back from the operating theatre, having had their tonsils taken out (still very fashionable at this time.) I spent hours in the darkened ward listening to gurgling, choking noises, terrified that someone would soon choke to death...

Something much more exciting happened on my next vacation job. Thora Richmond and I applied to teach English to foreigners in a Brighton School of Languages. We were accepted and had two glorious weeks in a very elegant eighteenth-century mansion house near the coast, teaching English to foreign adult students. Most were German or Scandinavian and all were unfailingly courteous and grateful for our help. The social life was very pleasant; we sat in the lounge after dinner, setting the world to rights or went for walks along the beach. I felt very much at ease with these foreigners, who were unaware of my class background. And for the first time in my life I fell in love. With a Norwegian named Odd. He was tall, blonde and charming, and when he smiled, his eyes wrinkled up in the most attractive way. I was smitten and he seemed to like me, congratulating me, of all things, on my perfect enunciation. He was quite puzzled as to why I sounded the ends of every word so clearly, almost like a foreigner, he joked. I didn't know what he was talking about but it was obviously a compliment. Of course, given the time and the place, there was no way that this relationship would develop, but it was an extra dimension to a holiday that was so pleasurable in every way.

Stirrings of what I suppose could be called sexual feelings had already affected me at college. A group of young men came from the nearby Men's Training College for an inter-sports tournament and I was immediately attracted to one of them. He was not particularly tall, quite stocky in fact with dark hair and a square face, but he had a very pleasant smile which attracted my attention. Alas, it was love from a distance. He treated me exactly as he did the other women students, with friendly courtesy, but that did not prevent me from feeling quite weak at the knees about him. Such episodes did not often happen. The opportunity for mixing with the opposite sex was very limited at Avery Hill College. There were always end of term dances to which other men's colleges were invited, but one had to wear evening dress, and that was way beyond my means. I secretly agreed with Scott Fitzgerald the American author that "The rich are different from you and me". I would look at the young ladies going into the ballroom at the college, dressed in stunningly beautiful dresses, but was on the outside just looking in. I was obviously coming out of my shell, however, and feeling more at ease with the opposite sex. Then my third vacation job helped me even more along the path to normal relations with men. Thora came with me again to a farm in Tiptree, Essex where we had a week picking soft fruit, mostly in the rain. We stayed in quite basic farm accommodation with many other foreign students, including the Italians and the French whom we all hated, but secretly envied for their ability to shirk on the work. While the English, the Dutch and the Germans slaved away picking raspberries, the Italians would take early siestas in the fields sleeping off their excesses of the night before. In the evenings, there were 'hops', local dances in most of the villages around, to which we went. Since we were all working together, there were plenty of opportunities for Thora and me to dance with the other students, but one evening a local boy came up to me to ask me to dance. His name was Steve and he was gorgeous, with a lovely, country burr which was even more of an attraction for me. Accents meant a great deal to me. I could not begin to imagine falling in love with a man with a cockney accent. He was tall, blond, stocky, rather shy and slow in his manner but for me it was the *coup de foudre*, love at first sight. The next day it continued to rain and we were all sent to work in the local canning factory. Our job was to examine all the cans of jam on the conveyor belt. Any which did not have the protective glaze painted all around the can had to be removed, the missing strip painted in and then replaced on the belt. This went on from 9 a.m. to 5 p.m! There were rumblings of discontent among the students at the end of the day. We had not come to work on a farm to spend all day long looking at a conveyer belt. However it rained again the next day and most of the group seemed to vanish. So when Steve asked me to go with him for a spin on his motorbike, that was it. I downed tools and went off with him. We spent the next four days touring Sussex, his home county. The sun came out, the corn was high and golden, the quiet lanes were shaded by the heavy, summer foliage. It was heaven. We would sit by the riverbanks clasped in each other's arms, in a daze of unfulfilled sexual passion. We kissed and cuddled and hugged each other, our bodies straining together. But it was the 1950s and that was as far as we went, being respectable working-class people. The excitement and fatigue soon got the better of me and I came down with a heavy cold. I felt terrible, but couldn't stop seeing him. He was solicitude itself, commiserating with me and even taking me to spend the evenings in his parents' house.

Then the week was up and since I had already arranged to meet Thora in the Isle of Wight for the second week of our holiday, we had to part. The wrench was terrible and the Isle of Wight was a very poor substitute. But we agreed to meet up in London the following week. And sure enough he appeared in Plaistow, on his motorbike, a bronzed, blond giant of a man radiating health and sunshine in that grey, poverty-stricken place. The euphoria lasted a few weeks longer. Then one weekend he came to my home, my parents for once had gone out somewhere and we were alone in the house, on the couch kissing each other passionately, real 'French kisses'. Then he grew bolder and snapped my bra, fondling my breasts lovingly. How I would have loved to respond and to go up to bed with him, but my parents would soon return and I had to push him off gently, saying, "We can't do this. Mum and Dad will be back in a minute. Let's wait, shall we?" Reluctantly, he let me go and when my parents returned, we went separately to bed. Sunday he went home, more kisses, more promises to meet next week, but he never appeared again. No explanation. I sat in the house waiting for him until the realisation came to me that he would not arrive. I was beside myself with grief, could not wait to get out of the house to avoid explanations, took my bicycle and rode furiously towards Wanstead Flats, the nearest open area to us. There, riding on my bicycle, I cried heart-rending sobs which shook me and the bike. I was almost blinded by tears. I rode and rode, oblivious to everything except my grief. Finally, in desolation, I returned home, making up excuses to give my mother. This was my first real love, intense and poignant, and never would I experience such a deep feeling of loss again. I have often wondered why he did not turn up. Was it our poverty-stricken home and the environment in which I lived? Was it the realisation that we were from such different backgrounds? Was it that he could not persuade me to have intercourse with him? I shall never know.

Luckily, college life was coming to an end and we had to start looking for a permanent teaching post. I applied to Bristol where my sister was living, but was not accepted, the explanation being that the first jobs went to those students studying or living in the Bristol area. I muse sometimes as to how my life would have been so different if I had been accepted there and had managed to get away from the East End of London. But it was not to be. With the rest of the 'Plaistow set'

I was offered a job by East Ham Education Authority. Of course I accepted, but was surprised that I had to sign an agreement to join the National Union of Teachers before I could be accepted. It was the 'closed shop' syndrome, the first intimations of the power of the teaching unions. We had to wait a few more weeks to see where we would be placed and then Irene and I were offered posts as Assistant Teachers at Essex Road Secondary Modern School for Girls. I remember receiving the letter from the headmistress, telling me to report on 10 September 1951 to the 'Eyrie', her office on the top floor of another Victorian, red-brick building to start my teaching career. It seemed strange to me that she should call her office 'The Eyrie' and I wondered at her personality. I soon found out.

Chapter 8
Initiations

1951 was a momentous year for me, starting out on my first real job, dreading it in some way, but longing to start earning some proper money. To fortify myself before facing the rigours of teaching, I went with my family to see the Festival of Britain. That my father had decided to take us there was astounding in itself, but he must have also been caught up in the euphoria and the media hype. There was still an air of grim austerity around at this time, not helped by the many bombsites still lying open to the sky. We were enduring Attlee's 'Austerity Programme'; higher taxes, which gave my father more cause for bad temper, and the endless continuation of rationing, especially sweets. In fact rationing did not finally end until 1953-54 when, with great glee, Doreen and I tore up our ration books into tiny pieces and scattered them to the winds. There *were* some changes; some improvements in living standards, such as washing-machines now in the shops at prices suitable for poorer people and even television sets to be had for the fortunate few, but we were not among them. I still looked like an over-grown schoolgirl in my socks and flat shoes, cardigan and skirt, teenagers not having yet been invented. But the Festival of Britain was meant to cheer us all up, 'pleasure officially licensed for a time'. We had won the war (with the help of the Americans, of course!) and although we had lost the Empire in the process, it was time to draw a line under all that gloom and enjoy ourselves. So we marvelled at the Skylon, that elegant forty-foot pencil soaring up into the sky seemingly without any visible mean of support, found the Dome of Discovery very interesting and were amazed at the really futuristic-looking Festival Hall.

Then it was back to reality and my first day at Essex Road Secondary Modern School for Girls. Once again I was in the same type of massive, red-brick four-storey Edwardian building, once again I tramped up the endless stairs lined with the glazed white tiles on the walls, reminiscent of a prison, up to the 'Eyrie' on the top floor, where the headmistress held court. As I walked into this forbidding establishment on my first day, it was the smell which struck me most forcibly, a combination of mustiness, stale sweat, chalk and repression. The plan of the building was a replica of the Stratford school. Three central halls with classrooms encircling them, so that the poor unfortunate teachers and pupils were exposed to all eyes. The headmistress was a Miss Harris, one of the many unmarried, career women who became headteachers of Secondary Modern schools after the 1944 Education Act, rising to this exalted position after long service in the profession. Most of those whom I met were fairly limited educationally, having been trained in the teachers' training colleges. But they made up for this deficiency by becoming power-mad eccentrics. I decided after a few weeks that Miss Harris was quite batty, but fearsome in her battiness. She ruled the school with a rod of iron and her diminutive figure was to be seen everywhere, careering down the stairs at breakneck speed, barging into classrooms without any apology if she did not like what she saw going on in them. She would then castigate the teacher in full view of the children, which of course did wonders for the poor teacher's discipline. She was also very erratic and would alter the timetable whenever it suited her. I particularly remember one assembly when she announced that normal lessons were being disbanded for the day. Amid the buzz of excitement at such news, she raised her voice and with arms flailing in various directions announced in a shrill voice, 'One half of the children will go into the Lower Hall, one half into the Middle Hall and the rest are to remain here." Of course pandemonium ensued. Obviously Maths was not one of her strong points. Most of the staff agreed with me that she was deluded, but were very careful not to cross her.

    I was shown to my form room, a high-ceilinged, tall-windowed barn of a place where the desks seemed to huddle together for protection, quite lost in the vastness of it. It had been built for a much larger number of pupils taught under the monitor system at the turn of the century. Facing the children on the far wall was a large fireplace with a fireguard around it. In winter, there was a coal scuttle filled with coal by the side of the fire and it was my duty to appoint a coal monitor to keep the fire alight. As ever with open coal fires, those nearest benefited from the warmth, but the other poor souls had to suffer the cold. We also needed a milk monitor to hand out the small bottles of milk which were brought to the classroom at the Break. This practice was only discontinued in the 1970s under Margaret Thatcher and, for this decision, she had all manner of epithets thrown at her including 'milk-snatcher', both by the Opposition MPs and angry mothers. There was also a dais in front of the class, on which was a high, heavy oak desk which I had to climb up to in order to sit on the seat. From there I had an excellent view of all the children, and could note their misdemeanours, but not get down very easily to curtail them. I was often in danger of getting caught up in my own skirt and falling ignominiously on to the floor. Fortunately, it never happened.

As was usual in schools at that time, any new teacher was given the worst class in the school, the existing staff having felt that they had earned promotion to better classes year by year. The class allocated to me, 2D, would be described today as 'intellectually challenged'. They were the bottom stream of Year 2. I have a class photograph of all of us, I in socks, sensible shoes, skirt, blouse and cardigan, they, dressed in flimsy dresses, some with cardigans and some with no warm woollens on at all. They really did look a poor, wretched lot, but smiled eagerly at the camera. Being so shy and diffident myself and conscious that we were in full view of the hall, most of my energies were spent in keeping order in the class, to the detriment of my teaching. During these first few months, I made no attempt to get to know the girls better or to structure my lessons around their experiences. I was more concerned to regurgitate the notes I had spent writing up the evening before. There were meant to be twenty-five in the class but often we were down to fifteen, because of the usual absences "to help me Mum". Many could barely read. One girl I remember particularly. She was a Cypriot, with dark, frizzy hair and a swarthy face, which stood out dramatically from the wan, pallid ones around her. She had forgotten all her Greek and had learned very little English, so it was almost impossible to communicate with her. I would often catch a movement out of the corner of my eye as I was in full flow and would raise my head to see her shinning up the window pole to hang on the topmost window frame like a large, brown bat. The class took this as a signal to have their own fun and it was all I could do to get them back in order. I could never get her to come down and there was no way I would go to the headmistress for help. That would have been marked down as a sign of weakness. In the end I would decide to ignore her and she would eventually decide to come down. She needed remedial help but there was none available. That first day was the worst day of my teaching career, as I suppose it must have been for many other fledgling teachers. I walked home in a daze of exhaustion, collapsing onto our settee, closing my eyes, trying to forget my ordeal, plotting how soon I could give my notice in; I was determined to leave Essex Road by Christmas.

Fortunately, I had some other classes for English and History apart from 2D and they were slightly more receptive. There were still problems; reading around the class was an ordeal both for the poor wretch picked out and for me. The class would become restive, shuffling and shifting their feet in boredom as they listened to the stumbling, hesitating delivery of the reader. Even when, in exasperation, I took over the reading, their powers of concentration were limited, and I had the difficult task of trying to motivate them by injecting some drama into the story, while at the same time fixing the class with a gimlet eye, daring them to misbehave. Poetry lessons as can be imagined were even more of a nightmare. Many times, their blank, uncomprehending faces made me question inwardly: "What am I doing here? What is the use of this to them?" But they did manage to learn chunks of poetry by heart and I would hope that some of the verses have stayed with them after all these years. I can still recite John Masefield's *Cargoes* by heart... What saved me from complete misery during that first year were the extra-curricular clubs I was allowed to organise. When not on dinner duty, (another ordeal to be suffered, where one had to try to keep about two hundred children quiet in the large dining room), I ran a country dance club and a drama club after school. There I enjoyed teaching those children who were really interested in learning something and we had some successes in the local festivals of dance and drama, and Inter-School competitions.

I started to become more confident, and relaxed somewhat. Having learned that none of my class had ever been to Epping Forest, a mere five miles away, I arranged day excursions at the weekends for them. We went about twice a term, and it was a sheer delight to see them running about in the forest, crunching the dead leaves underfoot, shrieking and throwing leaves over each other. We took our own picnics, played Rounders and Hide and Seek, and they blossomed. I was even invited to accompany the deputy headmistress, a Miss

Browning, on a school excursion to Clevedon. She was a most sensible, good-natured woman, trying most of the time to repair the ravages wrought by the headmistress. I survived the first year, and even managed a glowing report from Miss Harris on my classroom control. Unfortunately, this proved to be a two-edged sword. Since she was now convinced that I was an effective disciplinarian, she called me into her office one day and said, "Miss White, I have been very impressed with your command of classes this year, and think you now have enough experience to take on a more challenging task. So I have decided to allocate 4D to you next year as your form." 4D? Not only were they the least intelligent of the fourth year, but that year was always the most difficult. Those pupils could see light at the end of the tunnel – they could leave school at Easter if they wished and so school was almost an irrelevance for them. I gazed at her in horrified silence, seeing unfurled before me the dreadful scenes of confrontations with 4D. I was so overwhelmed by the prospect that I blurted out loudly, "4D? There is no way, Miss Harris, that I will take 4D. I have taken 1D for a whole year, and I don't think it is fair of you to give me a lower class again."

She was most affronted. "Don't you shout at me, Miss White! 'Fairness' as you put it does not come into it. As the headmistress of this school –" she drew herself up to the limit of her diminutive stature "– I decide on the timetable and you will take the class that you are given". I was seething with anger by now, both at her duplicity as I saw it and her use of her power over me. I was ready to throw my whole career away, so frightened was I of having to take responsibility for a group of large, loud-mouthed fourteen-year-olds. I decided to take a chance. "Very well, Miss Harris. If you insist that I take 4D, I'm afraid that I shall have to hand in my resignation."

There was a silence in the room, both of us sizing up the other. She took a quick look at my face, which was white with anger, indignation, but most of all fear and then changed her tack somewhat. "Well, I'm sorry you feel so strongly about this, Miss White. I thought you would enjoy the challenge," eyeing me somewhat maliciously. The liar! She knew full well that other members of staff must have already staked their claim to the better classes. "However, since you don't feel able to accept that offer, I shall have to find another class for you." It was a climbdown on her part, but such a blessed relief for me. I was finally allocated a new first form, 1A with whom I was able to do so much more.

Weekends were the highlight of my life at that time. Shirley was abroad, having decided to take a third year course in France to stave off the fateful moment when she would have to teach. So I spent most of my time with Thora Richmond, who had taken a teaching job in a nearby primary school. We would go most Saturday evenings to the Palais de Danse at Ilford Town Hall in the hope of picking up a boyfriend. Only one of our group at college had a steady boyfriend. That was Irene Hallybone, but she had met her future husband at the Rangers, the senior group of the Girl Guides organisation. The rest of us suffered from the fact that we were that much more educated than our peers, and most of the young men eyed us with suspicion if not downright fear. Yet in that working-class area, if you were not at least engaged by the time you were twenty, you were considered to be on the shelf. Thus the imperative to get a man. So Ilford Palais was the obvious choice, at least to try. The dances took place in the impressive, neo-gothic town hall. The main hall, all burnished panelling, rich carvings and busts of Victorian worthies, became the setting for most of my humiliations. A shining chandelier, hanging from the ceiling, would revolve slowly around casting coloured shapes on the walls, and the band would play the popular Glenn Miller tunes. The young girls, dressed up 'to the nines' in the fashion of the day would stand decorously on one side of the room, with their bodies tense with excitement and the men would lounge against the opposite wall. Segregation of the sexes was very much in evidence. Most of the men were quite happy to size up the young girls from a distance, but were not so courageous when it came to asking someone to dance. A few intrepid and obviously good dancers moved on to the floor with a partner to show their prowess, much in the manner of Victor Sylvester's style of ballroom dancing, but the majority would eye the girls, sizing up the possibilities before they ventured to ask them to dance. Desperation would come in the second half of the proceedings; after they had fortified themselves with the weak beer on offer, they had to get their money's worth before the end, so they ventured forth. That was usually when I was picked, after having suffered the agonising boredom of watching others dancing for the best part of the evening. Of course, Thora with her curvaceous figure and pretty face was always chosen before me.

The other problem after having been 'picked' was the

conversation one had to endure while dancing. The opening gambit of, "Do you come here often?" having quickly been dealt with, there remained the puzzle of what to talk about. My mind would race to think of things to say, while at the same time being very conscious of this foreign body so close to mine. These East End men were hardly loquacious, more concerned with squeezing their partners as closely as propriety would allow, than keeping up a conversation. Woe betide Thora and me if we said we were teachers. We were dropped like the proverbial hot coals. So we devised other strategies, choosing nursing as a more favourable alternative. This also had its dangers. We would have to endure all the medical insinuations and remarks such as, "Cor! I wouldn't mind you giving me a bed bath!" but at least it was preferable to being a 'wallflower'. Then the last dance would start and the romantic song, *Who's Taking You Home Tonight?* played and I would be in a fog of uncertainty as to what I should say if a man *did* ask to escort me home, with all that that entailed... If no one did, as was often the case, there was then the shame of not being asked. Fortunately Thora, even though the men flocked around her, would never allow anyone to take *her* home for fear of her father. So we would run out together to catch the last bus back home.

Shirley sent me chatty letters describing her life at the British Institute in Paris and the interesting lectures, but the even more interesting meetings with her French friends in a café called 'La Shope' in the Latin Quarter, where they spent the evenings discussing philosophy and politics, among other subjects. It sounded incredibly romantic to me. She invited me to visit her during the holidays and since now I was earning a respectable salary, I was off like a shot. It was the first time I had really seen Paris and I fell in love with all its eccentricities and idiosyncrasies and its sheer 'foreignness'. Her lodgings were in a typical Parisian *immeuble*. On the ground floor the dreaded concierge had her flat, so that she could keep a beady eye on the comings and goings of the residents. The ground and first floors were always inhabited by the wealthier residents where the stairs had carpets on them, but as you climbed up, the carpets disappeared, to be replaced by coconut matting and then finally on the top floor there was nothing but bare boards. Shirley lived in one of the garrets on the top floor. I cursed the *minuterie*, the lighting system in her block of flats. It was a most ingenious method to save electricity. One had to press a button near the huge entrance door and light would flood the hallway for one minute only. Consequently one had to race up the stairs to find the next *minuterie* before the light went off. Being unused to such a contraption, I was too slow and was left feeling my way along the wall in pitch darkness – quite an unnerving experience.

Shirley had changed immeasurably; more vibrant, colourful, warm and giggly, showing none of the Jewish melancholy to which she had often been prone. She took me to 'La Shope' to meet all her friends. She was very flirtatious with all the men but sat very close to one young bearded, swarthy character. I was not impressed with the café; it seemed seedy and run-down to my eyes and was filled with cigarette smoke and rough-looking men. The rapid French issuing from the mouths of all those sitting around the table was quite beyond me. One evening in her tiny flat, Shirley confided in me that the young man who had sat next to her was her lover. He was not one of the French students but an Italian who was looking for a job in Paris. I was appalled – what about the risk she was taking? She brushed this aside as a mere bagatelle, going into minute details of his prowess in bed. Still riddled with my mother's views on sex, I thought she was mad playing such a dangerous game, but found her descriptions of their sexual antics very exciting. Fortunately, nothing untoward happened to her and by the end of the academic year, she was back to reality, back that is in East Ham teaching French in East Ham Grammar School for Girls.

On her return, now fully experienced sexually while I was still a virgin and still terrified of men, she said I must find somewhere better than Ilford Palais de Danse to meet some men. We started frequenting some of the teachers' dances put on by the teachers' social clubs. There we had some more luck than in the Ilford Palais. We met two very eligible men who did not think we were something out of a horror film just because we were teachers. They took us out on various jaunts, including such cultural experiences as classical musical concerts. John, my boyfriend, was very passionate about classical music, which was a closed book to me. As soon as the music started, he would close his eyes and I might not have been with him for all the attention he gave me. I was quite peeved at this, but tried to emulate him. But for me there was no transportation to some wonderful world. My thoughts would sheer away from the music to much more mundane things such as "Do I really like him? Would he ask me to marry him? What would I say?" This after only a few months of his acquaintance! The most hilarious episode of that time was when we had a picnic in Epping Forest with Shirley and her boyfriend. We found a bright sunny clearing in the middle of the forest where we laid out our spread. It was very quiet and peaceful, with only the damp, pungent odour of the undergrowth and the somnolent murmur of the insects as an accompaniment to our feast. The shafts of sunlight penetrating the deeper part of the forest heightened the illusion of a magic wood. After the meal and lots of giggling and jokes, we settled down for a pleasant session of kissing and cuddles. I was really happy, what with the sun, the forest, the company, I stretched out voluptuously on the grass. Then a noise wrenched us from this blissful interlude; it was a distant rumbling sound as of hooves. It became louder, more insistent and eventually changed into a thunderous drumming which frightened us all rigid. We sat up ready to flee from any danger, when from the forest into the clearing, a herd of red deer came surging towards us, squashing bread, cakes and scattering other detritus in all directions. We leaped up and ran from the spot just in time. There must have been at least twenty of them, beautiful beasts with enormous antlers, their flanks heaving, nostrils snorting as they leaped over the makeshift tablecloth and remnants of food and disappeared into another part of the forest. The drumming of the hooves receded into the distance and silence ensued as we tried to digest what had happened. Then we started laughing weakly with relief and excitement, all thoughts of amorous grapplings now far from our minds.

1953 was the year when my family could finally leave that bug-infested house in Woodside Road. Along with other local authorities, West Ham had started a programme of bomb-clearance after the Second World War. Because of the extensive damage in the area caused by the bombing of the docks nearby, it had taken some while and was still going apace in 1953, the year that we were offered a new council house in Abbey Arms. It had three bedrooms, a garden and a real bathroom with hot and cold running water. It was heaven! I was so proud of it, particularly the bathroom, that I invited Shirley and our two boyfriends home to see it. Having ascertained that my parents were going to the 'Dogs' one Saturday evening, my friends duly turned up. I had bought a new record for the occasion to put on our second-hand record player. It was Ravel's *Bolero*. And we danced and danced most of the evening to it. That sensual music with its passionate crescendo sent us all crazy with frustrated sexual excitement and, but for the fact that my parents would be home before long, who knows what would have happened that night? It was not to be and, soon after that time, both men seemed to tire of us and disappeared from our lives. I was obviously now slowly emerging from my frigid fear of men and sex and was ready for an affair, but only three more encounters with men were vouchsafed me before I moved on again. One was rather serious. Shirley, Thora and I had dared to travel as far as the West End to go to a dance in Tottenham Court Road. We caught the last bus back and our ways parted at Aldgate. I finally arrived at the Abbey Arms at about midnight. I was just walking up the side street to my home, when a man barred my way. He was obviously drunk and quite aggressive.

"Where y'going, gel?"

"I'm just on my way home."

"Home, eh? Where's home, then?"

"Just up the road there."

"Well, if it's just up the road, I'll come with you. It's a bit darker there, innit?" with a lascivious leer.

"Oh thanks, but there's no need."

But he still wouldn't let me pass and I was becoming frightened. I looked around but there wasn't a soul to be seen. I tried another tack: "Look, my Dad'll give me hell if I don't go in soon. Would you like to meet me somewhere tomorrow? For a drink?" Although sozzled with drink, he moved back somewhat, seemingly surprised at my capitulation. He hesitated, mumbling incoherently to himself. Then he said, "Yeh, all right. It's gotta be tomorrer. 'M workin' Monday."

"OK, I'm going home now."

But he still insisted on accompanying me to my house, so chatting aimlessly to him, we arrived at my front gate. Fortunately the hall light was on. With my key in my hand, I rushed up to the front door, opened it, slammed it behind me before he realised what was happening. Once behind the front door, I stood panting and shivering and tearful at my lucky escape.

Another, seemingly similar incident occurred a few weeks later. As I got off the bus at Greengate, a man stepped forward and started talking to me. But he proved to be a teacher who had seen me doing the same journey every day and had now plucked up courage to speak to me. He invited me out to 'the pictures', which was still one of my passions. I agreed, calculating that not much could go wrong there. I can't say I liked the look of him very much; he was heavily-set, heavy in personality and shambling in his movements. I found out later that he had a deformed arm. I don't remember the film because during it, he started to stroke my upper arm. No one had ever done that before and the sensation was quite pleasurable. It was some time later that I read that the upper arm is one of the erogenous zones. But he blew it all afterwards. We took the bus home from the cinema, and walked towards Woodside Road. As we approached my turning, his breath suddenly began to quicken until he was almost panting. I was both revolted and fearful and could not wait to get into my house. He continued to follow me for some days after that until I was forced to find another route home to avoid him.

The third encounter with the opposite sex was when I joined the local drama club. The director must have seen some latent dramatic talent in me because I was chosen straightaway to play the heroine in a play. We even had Bryan Forbes, a well-known actor at that time to give us some tips. The story was a Cinderella one about a poor young girl who makes good and falls in love. I was obviously typecast. I was very good as the poor, downtrodden heroine, but less successful as the assured beauty who falls in love with the handsome hero. My lack of confidence was compounded by the fact that we had to provide our own costumes. I had plenty of cheap clothing but my wardrobe did not run to a sumptuous ball-gown, which was needed when I became transformed into a beauty. Nor did I have the money to buy one. My mother added her opinion: "You're not squandering your money on something you're never going to wear again!" So I compromised with a long cotton skirt, but I realised by the less than enthusiastic applause when I appeared in the second half of the play, supposedly transformed into a beauty, that my costume fell far short of what was expected. But the bonus of the play for me was that the man playing the role of the hero actually took a fancy to me and we became friends. We spent months together, going to films, walks, outings. He was very handsome, with fair curly hair and a lovely smile. He was also very easy to talk to. Social conversation had always been one of my weak points since no one spoke much at home, except my father of course when he was in a rage. My mother was extremely chatty with all the neighbours, but once at home in the brooding presence of my father, even her chattiness disappeared. Consequently I had no 'small talk'. Before going out on any date, I would make a list of topics that I could talk about. This usually meant that the man could hardly get a word in edgeways, as I ran the gamut of the topics of the day. I still suffer from this fear of silences in conversation, but have managed to disguise it by plunging wildly into any subject that comes into my head. My family now think I am very talkative... Ron however had a pleasant flow of conversation and I could relax much more. One memorable occasion, Ron invited me to go to Wimbledon with him to see the tennis. The snag was that it was during school time and I would have to telephone school and pretend I was ill. For days, I wrestled with my conscience but the lure of Wimbledon proved stronger than my fear of Miss Harris. So I went, but to my horror found that we were positioned near a television camera. I imagined all sorts of consequences, the worst being that Miss Harris *herself* would see me on television, when I was supposedly laid up in bed. In fact, I read soon after in the newspaper that someone had been discovered missing school and had lost his job. Luckily God was smiling on me on that occasion.

Ron also took me to see the Queen's Coronation. That was a momentous occasion, a double one in fact. Four days before the Coronation, on June the second, Everest, the highest mountain in the world, had been conquered by a British team of climbers. The two who had the honour to get to the top were Edmund Hillary and his sherpa, Tenzing. The first ever team to reach the top of Everest was a British team. The news was held back until the day of the Coronation, but when the news broke the country went wild. It was total euphoria. Even the government was affected and decided to relax rationing for a short time which meant that we could have an extra pound of sugar and four ounces more of margarine. We went to Trafalgar Square to see the Queen's procession wend its way to St Paul's Cathedral. The crowds were so dense that Ron put me up on his shoulders – quite a feat since I was no lightweight – and I was able to see better the rich spectacle unfolding before us. The Queen was radiant and so beautiful. Fifty-six per cent of the population saw the Coronation on television. Although we did not possess one yet, my mother, along with many other working-class families was able to join in the excitement by seeing the show on a neighbour's television. The newspapers spoke of the occasion as the dawn of a new Elizabethan age. It proved, unfortunately, to be a false claim.

I broke with Ron soon after, the first time I initiated the break-up. He was a good friend but not passionate enough for me. I think he was probably as inhibited sexually as I was, so we were not much use to each other. I wrote him a long, polite letter explaining my reasons and did not feel the separation very much because soon afterwards, Shirley, Thora, Irene Hallybone and I went on a week's holiday to Scotland. It was a laugh from one day to the next, but the funniest time was when we had managed to get as far north as Oban on the west coast. We spent about three days there and each evening went to the local 'hop'. We felt quite superior to these locals, since we came from London. They in turn were very pleased to see a bevy of young girls, new faces, appearing in their small town. These men had none of the inhibitions of the callow youths on the dance floor in Ilford. We had partners all the time. After the first, very successful evening, when the four of us were back in the hotel bedroom, conducting the usual inquests on our successes, we found that we each had had a similar experience. Each one of us while dancing had felt something hard knock against our thighs! Could all these men be having an erection at the same time? It was very puzzling. The second evening, the same experience occurred. We had to find out what was going on, or revise our estimate of Scotsmen. So, I gathered up courage to ask one chap what it was all about, almost dreading the reply. The young man, with a sly grin on his face suddenly produced a small flask of whisky from his hip pocket. Apparently they kept up their courage with surreptitious nips of the amber liquid. This explained their amorous attention at the end of the dance. One young man, by the name of Roderick, had taken quite a shine to Shirley and she, as usual, was like putty in his hands. Not that they had any real opportunity to do anything serious. We teased her about her infatuation for him, but had a shock, when, after a few days in Oban, Shirley announced that she was getting engaged to Roderick. We could not believe our ears. I don't know how serious Shirley was, but there was no doubting the sincerity and the intensity of the Scotsman. They had it all planned. Since he was a telephone operator, he would be able to telephone her every evening on her return to London, courtesy of the Telephone Co. and as soon as he had some holidays he would come to her home and meet her family and they would take it from there. We couldn't wait to get her away from Oban. But their relationship went on for weeks. As agreed, he telephoned her every night, long conversations of an hour or more. Distance eventually took its toll; she began to tire of him and her family left her in no doubt about their opposition to such a mismatch. They were planning their own arranged marriage for her.

School was beginning to pall and there were no serious boyfriends on the horizon. I now wanted desperately to get away from home, away from the strictures of my mother and the now blessedly intermittent rages of my father. I could never invite someone to stay and I chafed at the restrictions. I started looking in the *Times Educational Supplement* and one day an advertisement caught my eye for a post as a teacher with the British Army residential school in Wilhelmshaven. On an impulse, I applied for the post but heard nothing for some time, so quite relieved, I dismissed it from my mind. After all, Germany was a long way away and I did not feel very kindly disposed to the country, since we had suffered five years of war and deprivation as a result of their *lebensraum* policies. I imagined it would be a grim place, still recovering from a terrible defeat. Also, it wasn't France, of which I had fond memories. Then, some weeks later, I came home to find a very official-looking letter for me. It was from the War Office inviting me to attend for interview. So I decided to go, more out of curiosity than interest, rationalising to myself that it would be a good experience for me. I did not think that I would get the job; after all I had only ever been a teacher in the working-class area of London and now I would have to face education officers of the British Army. But, having made the decision, I really wanted to impress them, so borrowed a long black winter coat from my sister, which may sound quite dowdy, but it had a vivid emerald green lining, which flashed out as one moved. Shades of my history teacher's skirt which had always fascinated me. The interview went well even though I had to face a whole line of people. I even made the panel laugh about something and, within a short time, I had been offered the post of teacher of English and History at the British Army Residential school in Wilhelmshaven, on the North Sea coast of Germany. Trepidation immediately kicked in, and I nearly did not accept the post. But the alternative, to remain at Essex Road School and continue living with my parents, was even less attractive. So I accepted. My parents were so shocked that they had nothing to say. My mother, realising the importance of the occasion came with me to see me off at Liverpool Street Station. She shed a few tears as we clung together, but ever a model of resilience she soon recovered. After these affecting goodbyes, I sat in the compartment on my way to Harwich and thought: "This is a momentous time in my life. Will I be able to cope with it?" Once more I was on the move, but this time a long way from my family and more importantly, with no friends to keep me company. I was off alone to foreign climes.

Chapter 9
Foreign Climes

The loud noise at our front door and the huge pile of papers that had fallen onto the mat had been my travel documents to Germany – Hamburg via Harwich. After embarrassingly tearful farewells from my mother and sister in London, I reached Harwich in the deepening dusk of the evening. Exciting sounds of clanging iron and shouting voices resounded around the port and the great white outline of the ferry ship, ghostly in the darkness, loomed out at me. I went down what seemed like endless stairs into the very bowels of the ship, and finally found my cabin. I opened the door. Inside, nothing but darkness greeted me, although peering around I gradually discerned a figure on the top bunk, obviously a woman, since I doubt I would be sharing with a man. She seemed to be asleep for she made no movement as I barged in. I was afraid that if I switched the light on, she would wake and I would be subject to a spate of polite conversation which, in my state of tension and exhaustion, I wanted to avoid. So I stumbled around in the gloom, feverishly searching for my pyjamas. I lay down on the bunk and immediately fell into a fitful sleep, lulled by the muffled throb of the engines. A noise awoke me with a start. I listened and heard what seemed to be a hoarse, strangulated sound and the hairs on my neck rose in fear. Gradually as I strained my ears, I realised that the noise was coming from the toilet, where a thin thread of light was visible under the door. I suddenly identified the sound as of terrible wretching, of someone being violently sick. Immediately I was aware of my own stomach, which began to respond to the lurching movement of the ship like waves on a shore. At each heave of the ship, nausea flooded through my body but I could not be sick, probably because I had eaten so little all day. Sleep was now out of the question as I fought to control my stomach, willing myself not to be sick. The night seemed endless. My poor companion spent most of the night in the toilet, while I lay wide awake in the darkness, my face stuffed into the pillow trying to avoid the smell pervading the cabin. It was a bad beginning; I felt lonely and unhappy and desperately ill. I prayed for the morning to come. I must have slept somehow because I woke to the engines throbbing to a different rhythm, a long slow beat as the ship slowed down. Hearing voices outside and anxious to escape from the noxious atmosphere of the cabin, I went up on deck in the hope that the fresh, early morning air would revive me. I drank in both the cold morning air and the sight before my eyes. The ship was gliding majestically along the River Elbe towards Hamburg. Laid out before me was Germany, its quaint villages with the rounded domes of the baroque churches, its fields open to the sky. It looked so *foreign*. I stood entranced, thrilling to the strangeness of it. As we neared the port of Hamburg, the charming pastoral aspect was replaced by one of industry. Huge warehouses, factories and container ships were anchored along the coast. But I had no time to reflect on the scene before I was bustled off the ship and climbing into the waiting train, thankfully without any problems of luggage, which had been sent on separately. Destination Bremen and then Wilhelmshaven, named after King William I of Prussia, later the Kaiser of all Germany. Once settled in the compartment, still feeling delicate, I looked around at my fellow passengers. They were mostly burly men dressed in queer green buttoned-up jackets with corduroy collars, some even in knee-breeches. The women had plump, red faces and stared at me silently, seemingly in a hostile fashion. I was conscious that I did not speak any German and I was obviously a foreigner from a country that had been at war with them only nine years before. I withdrew into myself, watching the green fields speeding by, feeling dreadfully homesick. A mood of depression settled on me. I longed to get to Wilhelmshaven to speak to some English people, yet dreaded meeting complete strangers. For some time, I wallowed in feelings of self-pity, unaware of the passing countryside. Then a thought flashed into my brain, lightening my depression. OK, so, at that moment I was alone but that did not mean I had to feel lonely. In fact I could not be lonely because I had *myself* as a companion. I had that inner core of *selfhood* which had succoured me all my life. I would meet all these new people and would try to integrate with them, but there would always be my own inner life to which I could escape when necessary. I began to feel better and enjoyed the rest of the journey until Wilhelmshaven appeared on the horizon. There, I was met by a British soldier and driven in a military vehicle to my new home.

Prince Rupert School was set up by the British Forces Educational Service in 1947, two years after the end of the Second World War, when the partitioning of Germany into four sectors had been agreed by the Allied powers. This arbitrary division of Germany had not been without a deal of wrangling between the United States and Russia, Berlin being an obvious problem. This was the early start of the Cold War between the two countries, causing great anxiety and some shocks, such as the Cuban missile crisis. This part of North Germany which included the major towns of Hamburg, Bremen and Hanover, famous for sending one of its royal family to England to become George I, was placed under the jurisdiction of Britain. The rumour among the British was that the United States had commandeered the warmest and most attractive part of Germany, Bavaria, for itself. This story was repeated *ad nauseum* in the officers' mess as they shivered from the intense cold of a Wilhelmshaven winter. The town was endowed with Germany's deepest harbour, had been an important naval base and so had been heavily fortified during the War. A string of solid bunkers had been built along the coast to protect the shipyards. Most were still there, but there was one, near the town itself, which the British occupying force had tried to demolish when they took over, but so thick were the concrete walls and so heavily had it been reinforced that they succeeded only in tilting it slightly, so that it seemed to teeter in mid-air threatening to collapse at any moment, a surrealist sculpture among the grim, grey buildings. My first glimpse of the school was of the high wire fences surrounding it, so that to my tired imagination it resembled a prison more than a school. The campus with its ten two-storey buildings had been built by the Germans to house navy personnel during the War and sprawled out towards the North Sea. The red-brick facades were still warm and glowing in the late summer, but my gaze was suddenly arrested by the sight of two concrete military bunkers rearing their heads menacingly, shocking in their raw, brute size, a permanent reminder of the war. We drove in silence through the long central road and pulled up in front of one of the buildings, where I was introduced to a member of staff and shown to my flat, a pleasant, airy room at the top of what was known as Collingwood House. The pupils in the school were divided into four houses, and this was the home of about fifty girls, with the next building housing the boys of Collingwood. I learned quickly that as well as teaching English and History, I had boarding duties. These consisted of getting up with the girls to take breakfast with them and checking that they were all in their beds in the evening, before I put out the lights and retired exhausted. I was technically 'on duty' during the whole of the night, but mercifully, I was seldom woken up. I found it particularly wearisome to have to keep up pleasant conversation with the girls at breakfast and was not very happy at my loss of freedom. The teaching itself did not satisfy me, either. There was a constant changeover of pupils as their parents were posted to different parts of Germany to take up new duties. Hardly a week went by without some pupils leaving or arriving, so it was impossible to get to know them very well. They seemed very self-contained, presumably because of their constant change of environment. Even worse, we had school on Saturday mornings until twelve o'clock. All in all, one worked very hard for the admittedly generous salaries paid. Most of the staff who boarded at the school, became exhausted towards the end of the term because of the constant exposure to children. One young teacher admitted that he slept for two whole days at the end of each term to recover from the rigours of the job.

The high spot of the week for all staff was the gathering at the Officers' Mess at twelve-thirty p.m. on Saturdays, a custom to which I was introduced very early on. The main attraction of the Mess was that the prices of the alcohol were subsidised, presumably by the War Office. Gin and tonic, a favourite tipple, was only thirty pence, in today's money and other drinks were similarly ridiculously priced. Consequently a merry time was had by all. After a while the married types would weave their way home, but a hard core of teachers would remain for the best part of the afternoon. Most of these were the newly appointed men who had no devoted wife waiting at home for them. They had a singular pleasure to celebrate, that of not being able to bring their family with them for the first term. It seemed that the Administration, in its wisdom, felt that new staff needed time to concentrate on settling in to their new posts for three months, unencumbered by marital duties. Unfortunately, this concern for the welfare of the staff was rather misplaced, for it did not have the desired effect. Most of the men took advantage of this felicitous situation and concentrated all their attentions on the single women in the school, with dire consequences for me personally. Being so naïve and immature, knowing little really of men, never having drunk any alcohol except for the couple of glasses of cheap wine in Calais, I was probably considered fair game to some of these men. I had never spent so much time with the opposite sex in my life. Every Saturday afternoon I would be tipsy after the first glass of gin and tonic, giggling at anything and anyone, to the great amusement of the company. Usually, I had enough sense to restrict my intake of alcohol and would weave my way unevenly through the blocks of buildings to my flat, and there fall into a deep sleep. I have a photograph of my new life, surrounded by three men, all of us drinking and smoking and laughing, a far cry from my previous existence. But the first Mess party was my undoing. Drinks in quick succession, music, dancing, the conviviality made me quite drunk. I remember only flinging myself onto a sofa, laughing so much that I had a pain in my stomach. I then proceeded to kick my legs up in the air and in the process flung one of my shoes off which was quickly grabbed by someone and hung on the ceiling light. Around me was a blur of faces, swirling in and out of my view and suddenly disappearing as I lost consciousness. Several hours later I woke up in my own bed groaning with the most horrendous of headaches and being violently sick. My first hangover. I felt so ill that I wanted to die. Soon after, the school doctor came to see me and I remained in bed for about three days. Apparently I had had alcoholic poisoning. Once recovered, I vowed never to drink so much again and have kept that promise, more or less.

I began to get to know the staff. Two women became particular friends, one tall, dark and elegant and one short with light-brown curly hair who had a piercing intelligence. Both were from the north and were career women, seemingly with no interest in the opposite sex. To me they seemed already staid and almost middle-aged, although they were only in their early thirties. One day, a man emerged from the crowd and made a beeline for me, a man who looked like a caricature of a flying officer, replete with handlebar moustache. His name was Gordon Craig, he was very amiable and he was the new head of Art. I have no idea what he saw in me but I was flattered by his attentions. He courted me assiduously, overwhelming me with his boisterous charm, his quick wit and ready smile. Most importantly to me, he had a lovely voice with an educated accent. My two friends disapproved of him, probably because he was married. I remember one occasion when he excelled himself in the courting stakes. One of the 'perks' of our job was that we were entitled to first class travel on the railways and my friends and I used it to good effect at half-term by travelling to the Harz mountains to learn to ski. When I was shown to my room in the hotel, my eye caught a splash of bright red on the pillow of the bed. There were six red roses laid out and on top of them a poem, written in Gordon's handwriting, a copy of Andrew Marvell's *To a Coy Mistress*. What a romantic gesture! As I read the poem, the perfume from the roses wafted over me and lingered sweetly in the room for hours afterwards. Another time we travelled to Copenhagen on the night train; it was real luxury. But Copenhagen was a disappointment. It still seemed guilty at its sudden capture almost overnight by the Nazi tanks rolling into the town; the Tivoli was closed and a grim, gloomy atmosphere reigned everywhere.

Back at school, Gordon persisted in his wooing of me. I don't ever remember feeling any strong sexual feeling for him apart from the pleasure of his company. There was no *coup de foudre* and there was, of course, the insuperable barrier of his wife. As a good Roman Catholic, although beginning to lapse somewhat, I could not even begin to imagine a serious relationship with a married man. He was often at pains to tell me that they had married young and the marriage was not a success, an explanation that was past its sell-by date, I think. But she would be coming out to Wilhelmshaven in January and I could not see any possibility of continuing our friendship then. In fact, I was secretly quite contemptuous of him for behaving as if he were a single man. Yet we talked easily and amicably together and took interesting walks along *das deich* looking out at the vast North Sea which would regularly freeze in winter, the steely expanse of water metamorphosing into a patchwork of huge white slabs of ice and glinting, grey waves which broke through the surface. Not that we were ever really cold. Like most northern Continental towns, central heating was a fact of life long before Great Britain succumbed to its pleasures. When I was on duty in Collingwood House in the evenings, Gordon would come to my flat to keep me company. Once I had 'done the rounds', checking that all the girls were safely tucked up in their beds, we had the rest of the evening to ourselves. It was strictly forbidden to entertain a male colleague in one's flat in the evening, but the rule was regularly broken by staff, who tried to ensure that they were not caught *in flagrante*. Gradually, Gordon became more assiduous and more amorous. He was quite besotted with me. Whether this was because of my coolness physically to him, (my usual inhibitions) I don't really know. But one evening he became very passionate, kissing and stroking me as we lay together on my bed. His hands became more bold as he stroked my whole body, and then he started undressing me. First he undid my blouse and removed my bra, caressing and stroking my breasts which sent me into a swoon. Then he lifted up my skirt, took off my stockings and finally my knickers. I lay on the bed almost fainting with the strength of my desire, and my body, as if reluctantly, began to respond to his caresses. Murmuring loving words, moving his hands up and down my thighs, his hands gradually moved to the Mound of Venus and then he was massaging my clitoris. I was like someone disembodied, my brain now aware of how my body was responding eagerly to his touch but also coldly conscious of the dangers. Suddenly, my body arched up in a frenzy, my brain reeled and I groaned deeply uttering a piercing cry. Without even knowing it, I had had my first clitoral orgasm. Yet, somehow, that was as far as it went. I stopped him in his tracks and pushed him off me. I was terrified of becoming pregnant. Scenes flashed through my mind of my mother's face if I appeared at home, a 'fallen woman'. She would probably have turned me away immediately.

Yet it seemed as if by stopping him, Gordon was made more determined. He was so enamoured of me by this time that he wanted to meet my parents during the Christmas holidays. He actually proposed marriage to me one evening as we walked along the *deich*. I listened to his protestations of love and then looked at him in amazement and annoyance:

"How can you talk about marriage to me? You're already married and soon to bring your wife back here!"

"Listen to me! My marriage is a sham, it's only a convenience now. My wife doesn't love me and I don't love her. If you promise to marry me, I'll start divorce proceedings at once." Warning bells rang in my head. Was he sincere? How could I believe him? What would his wife say? I didn't want to get involved in such a messy affair. I rounded on him:

"You have no right to ask me that. If you're serious about me, you must first divorce your wife and *then* ask me."

"But I can't take the risk of losing you! Just say you'll marry me."

"I can't *do* that, because you aren't free. Ask me again when you are divorced!" And with that parting shot, I stomped away on my own.

When Christmas came most of the staff went home to their families. Gordon returned to his wife in West London while I went back to Plaistow, clutching a bottle of *Liebfraumilch* and a dinky little carousel of tin angels who twirled around gracefully on their golden stand as the heat of a candle below reached them. Very *gemütlich*. Wine was always available on our communal table in the Staff Dining Room and I had developed quite a taste for this sweet white wine and hoped to impress my family with it. My parents had never tasted wine; my mother had taken the pledge in the 1930s when it was fashionable to do so, and had remained a teetotaller ever since. She couldn't even be persuaded to try the occasional glass of Guinness with her Irish family. It was not until my father died that she enjoyed the occasional glass of whisky. I had only once ever seen my father under the influence of drink, when one Christmas Eve, he must have been persuaded by his workmates to go into a pub for 'a couple', before returning home. When he *did* arrive back, he was really the worse for wear. The predictable result of that 'sortie' had been that he was in an absolutely foul mood the next day and our Christmas was ruined. But on the occasion of my homecoming, my bottle was standing resplendent on the table, although eyed suspiciously by all. In my mother's eyes it was 'the temptation of the devil' and a foreign one at that. They did condescend to try it, but none of them liked it, sweet as it was, so the rest was poured down the sink.

While at home during the holidays I told my family about Gordon and they listened passively. Presumably they thought that I was old enough to do what I liked. I then mentioned that he wanted to meet them and they were again non-committal. But shortly before he was due to arrive, I felt I had to tell my mother that he was a married man. They had already dressed in their best clothes to meet him, but on hearing that momentous piece of information, she gave me a venomous look, turned away and called out, "George! Come on, we're going out!" There were no recriminations, just a complete refusal to meet him. And within minutes they had disappeared through the front door. I was mortified. By this action, my mother had expressed her complete disapproval of the situation and it was more powerful than any words. When Gordon did finally arrive, dressed in his best suit, I made the pretext that they had to go somewhere urgently. I don't know whether he believed me.

The spring term brought with it the usual combination of pleasure and stress. The Mess was quite a bit depleted now that the wives had been installed in their lodgings. Gordon returned with wife in tow. She was a small, artificially-blonde woman with very little personality. I had decided to try to socialise more with others, having come to the conclusion that a *ménage à trois* was not to my liking. One day, my friends and I accepted an invitation to an all-night ball at the RAF officers' mess in a neighbouring town. Transport was laid on for us, but we were more concerned with the problem of how to keep awake during the night. We still had to teach the next morning. For the first and last time in my life I took an amphetamine pill to help me keep awake. It did the trick and I went from the ballroom to the classroom without any trouble. But did I feel ill once the school day was over! The ball was a great success, the men very attentive. I met a Scotsman, six foot four inches tall who took a great interest in me. We agreed to meet again sometime. In the meantime, he wrote me long, romantic letters *daily*, perhaps to fulfil his literary inclinations. After having read the first few, they palled on me, far too romantic for my liking. Gordon became intensely jealous and began drinking heavily. He waylaid me whenever he could, to the point where I decided that I would not see him any more. That was not easy, since we worked on the same campus. One evening, there was a dance put on particularly for the wives newly arrived. By this time in the school year, most staff had paired off. Of course, I had been most of the time with Gordon, but he had to be very careful now his wife was around. With my two friends, I went reluctantly to the dance, but it was boring to sit there, waiting for someone to invite us onto the floor. I was graphically reminded of the Ilford Palais de Danse. I did manage a dance with the headmaster but eventually decided to leave. I returned to my flat, angry at myself for going and at Gordon for putting me in this position. Suddenly the telephone rang, it was Gordon pleading with me to return to the dance. I refused. He then rang me several more times until I eventually took the telephone off the hook to avoid his maudlin protestations of love. Several minutes later, there was a banging at the door and it was he, pleading and calling out, "Sylvia! Come back in the dance! What's the matter? Don't you feel well? Open the door so I can at least talk to you!"

I remained silent, leaning against the door but was inwardly quite scared. The scene was all too reminiscent of my father's rages. Gordon was making such a noise, he was even crying. He had obviously drunk too much and had lost control. I started to cry myself, frightened of what he would do and the possible repercussions. The top floor of Collingwood House could surely hear the rumpus but nonetheless, Gordon stayed outside my door for some time. I heard him slump against it and then there was silence for a while. He must have fallen asleep there and I fell into an exhausted sleep myself. By morning he was nowhere to be seen. I trembled at the thought of what the authorities would say to me.

Sure enough, next day we were both called in, but separately, to see the headmaster. I remember going into a toilet while I was waiting to be seen, and staring at myself in the mirror. I was deathly pale, but what was even more disconcerting, I suddenly noticed two deep frown lines between my eyes, which wouldn't go away. I was twenty-six years old and already the first lines were appearing on my face! I became more and more dejected. When I went into the headmaster's study, there was the whole Board of Governors sitting around the table. The language used to warn me to stop associating with Gordon Craig was so hedged with obfuscations, that if it hadn't been for the events of the night before, I might have had no conception of what they were trying to say to me. I listened to the stern tones of the headmaster and felt deeply aggrieved. I wanted to say that it was not my fault that I had tried to disassociate myself from him, but after that last night, I knew they would not believe me and I was too proud to attempt any explanation. I was warned that if I continued to associate with him, I would be dismissed from the school. I left the room quite devastated and once outside, my eyes filled with tears of self-pity and rage at Gordon. I resolved to cut him whenever I saw him and to spend as much of my free time as I could with my new-found Scottish friend.

It was useless of course. Gordon had also been warned by the Board of Governors, but the warning had no effect on him. He was like a man facing the abyss and actually wanting to fall into it. He was obsessed with me and I didn't know why. I really couldn't understand how he, a married man, could try to continue this relationship which was so dangerous for both of us. I tried to analyse his conduct. Was it because men enjoy the thrill of the chase and become even more interested in the object of their desire once they are baulked? Or the fact that we had not had sexual intercourse, and he would not give up until he had? Or that he was so weak that he was willing to endanger both our jobs for his selfish ends? These thoughts whirled around in my mind constantly. Writing about it now, however, I realise that many men behaved in the same way to me. It may be that I wanted to be liked (because of the years I had spent, deferring in fear to my parents?) so played up to their male egos. Consequently, they would almost begin to idolise me, believing that I was a really charming girl. Unfortunately, I could not sustain this mistaken impression. In fact, I was being dishonest with them, playing a game in effect. Whatever the reason, to get away from Gordon, I turned to Ian, the Scotsman, who continued to send me his interminable letters. He was not such a good companion as Gordon, being as inhibited as I was and with rather a cold personality. But we had some good times together. We went on a day trip to Friesland and the island of Sylt in the North Sea just by the Danish border. We had to get up very early to take the train and the boat to get there, but it was worth it. Sylt is really a giant sandbar forty kilometres long, Germany's northernmost island. During the war it had been packed with seaplanes and guns trained on Great Britain, but they had long gone. It is now considered to be the 'St Tropez of the North'. For me, it was a paradise of fine white sand dunes and coarse waving grass. On this pleasant, summer day it was a revelation, after months of staring at the iron-grey North Sea and the constant relics of war in Wilhelmshaven. We spent the day swimming, sunbathing and lying close to each other feeling the warmth of the sun coursing through our bodies. It was a wonderful occasion. Another time I remember, we spent the evening in my room, drinking a whole bottle of Glayva, a Scottish liqueur unknown to me, while he went into minute details of the history of the Scottish borderland, which was where he came from. He was actually rather boring, a dour, very respectful man, given only to discreet kisses to show his affection for me. Eventually, he asked me to marry him and I agreed. Why, when I didn't love him? Flattered, I suppose, and intrigued at the thought of being married. It seemed to me it could never really happen. Being so romantic, he suggested that we spend our honeymoon on the Isle of Arran on the west coast of Scotland. His enthusiasm was infectious and it all sounded so exciting and exotic to me. I was not so sure, however, of another of his suggestions; that when we *did* get married, we should buy a boat instead of a house, at least for the first year or so. Secretly, this was romanticism one step too far for me.

The spring term was coming to an end, and my friends and I decided to spend the Easter holidays touring southern Germany. I invited Shirley to come with us for the fortnight. We had a hilarious time, stopping in picturesque villages, admiring the houses with the bright frescoes painted on the walls and the white, neoclassical churches with their lovely domes and glittering baroque interiors. Wherever we stayed, we sought out the 'local colour', frequenting the village dances to flirt with the local men. Once, I remember, we had underestimated the time it took to get to a village on foot and with darkness descending, we looked around for somewhere to stay. But we were *en pleine campagne*, not a house in sight. Trudging further along, becoming weary and rather apprehensive, we spied a house in the process of being built. It was open to the sky and not all the walls were yet built, but it was somewhere we could stay. We climbed into our sleeping bags, because it was damp and cold in this shell of a house, but gazing up at the night sky and the myriad of stars glittering above, I slept happily. We toured through the Schwarzwald, suffering the interminable rain, and visited Hitler's Berghof in Berchtesgarten, perched high in the mountains like an eagle's nest above the small town below. It had been his command centre and holiday home. Looking at the Berghof, I thought of Eva Braun, his constant companion and wondered what she was like, how she could have associated with such a monster. He would not marry her until many years later, when they were both in the Berlin bunker sheltering from the invading Russians. It was a short marriage ceremony and then a double suicide. So much for a woman who had devoted her life to this man. Today, the Berghof is being turned into a 140-room, luxury hotel. The wheels of history grind on slowly but inexorably.

We had only a few more days holiday before it was back to school and one of the last places we decided to visit was Königssee on the lake itself. Another local dance to round off the evening, but this one proved to be extremely interesting. Shirley and I happened to meet two men travelling together. They were on their way to Vienna and suddenly asked us if we would like to go with them. Would we! With no more ado, we said goodbye to our dumbfounded girl friends and were speeding across the border to Austria (exciting in itself) and across the Oberösterreich plain to Vienna. We arrived very late at night and there the city lay below us with all its myriad lights twinkling merrily – it was magical. The two men, quite pleasant types, seemed to know of a hotel where we could sleep for the night. They booked two double rooms and with hindsight, I assume they thought they were onto a really good thing. I was quite tired, since once again the burden of trying to converse with them on the journey fell upon me, and I couldn't wait to get to bed. To my surprise, Shirley started to move to one of the rooms where the men had deposited their luggage. I stopped her. "What on earth are you doing?" She looked at me with similar astonishment and somewhat challengingly said:

"I'm sleeping with Otto" (or whatever his name was).

"What? Don't be such a fool. You don't know him from Adam."

"I like him! It'll be a laugh."

I was so outraged, thinking of all the possible consequences of her behaviour, and suddenly made up my mind.

"No, you're not to. I can't let you do this. We shan't see them after tomorrow!"

"So what?" and she moved nearer the bedroom door. She can be very stubborn at times. Meanwhile the two men were wondering what on earth was happening, their English being very limited. I turned on them both and in my best teacher's manner and my pidgin German, harangued them. What sort of girls did they think we were, we were respectable people, we had trusted them as decent men, they were taking advantage of us, they should be ashamed of themselves, etc. Of course, I realised my argument was rather flawed in that Shirley was now half in the men's bedroom, but my indignation and eloquence silenced all of them and within minutes Shirley and I were safe in our own room. Fair play to the two men: the next morning they bore no grudge, even looked at me with great respect and proceeded to show us Vienna. I saved Shirley from a fate worse than death, but I don't suppose she was grateful...

Once the summer term dawned, I was beginning to chafe at the lack of any intellectual stimulus in my teaching, and becoming rather tired of the incessant socialising which was *de rigueur* in the school. I decided to try to learn some German and started having lessons with a middle-aged German living in one of the grim, solid three-storey blocks of flats so prevalent in Germany. He was exactly my idea of a character in Grimm's fairy tales; short, corpulent, with grey hair and a grey beard, he was typically German, very *ernst* and erudite. All I remember of the lessons was the enormous blue and white tiled stove in the corner of the room belching out warm air. But I must have had some grounding in the language, albeit very cursory because when I was speaking French the next year, the lecturer said that I spoke it with a German accent. More of that later.

I continued to see Ian regularly, and in the summer term, we became engaged, despite my reservations as to a boat instead of a house. As far as school was concerned, things went from bad to worse. Not only had Gordon been in my room in the evenings, but Ian also. I wanted to shout it to the rooftops that NOTHING EVER HAPPENED ON THOSE EVENINGS, but what was the use? My stupidity consisted in being so open about it all. Gordon continued to pursue me in spite of the warning we had had, and at the beginning of the summer term, we were once again hauled up before the headmaster and his posse of governors. No prevarication on the headmaster's part this time. He was quite blunt: "Miss White, it pains us to have to call you once again before the Board. The last time, you were warned about continuing your relationship with Mr Craig, a married man, but you have chosen to disregard this warning. We have no complaints about you professionally. In fact, you have carried out your duties with commitment and integrity, but you have allowed your personal life to intrude too much upon your professional life and this cannot continue. You may have your own reasons for not wishing to end the relationship with Mr Craig, but my responsibility is to the school and the pupils. To be blunt, you have violated the rules of the school and you do not set a good example to the pupils." My face flamed with shame at this criticism and anger at the whole situation. He continued, his voice resounding in the tense silence of the room:

"The governors have thought long and hard about this but have come to the conclusion that your contract must be terminated at the end of the year." So that was that. Gordon had been seen staying in my room in the evenings (as had Ian) and the powers-that-be had judged that we had been *in flagrante delicto*. Would that we had! My life might have been entirely different. I was offered a sop, however. "Miss White, we recognise that this will come as a shock to you and we are concerned that your career does not suffer. If there is anything that we can do to help you, please let us know." Quite out of the blue, in my distress and shame, I suddenly realised that I was quite relieved. There was the possibility of escape. I could leave Prince Rupert School, leave the unsatisfying teaching commitments, get away from

Gordon and the interminable social life that was getting on my nerves, in fact leave the whole sorry mess behind. I was also hesitant, aware that to be sacked from a job could affect my career. Yet I wanted to run away, from relationships and from teaching for a while. I thought for a moment. I wanted to study again, to experience once again the pure pleasures of scholarship. Could I be helped to do this? I blurted out, "I should like to continue my studies. I should like to go on a course in France, if that could be arranged." And so it was arranged. At the end of the academic year, I left Prince Rupert School under a cloud, but glad, glad that I was being released from an environment that did not suit me, did not satisfy me, glad to be shot of Gordon. He fared somewhat better than I, being a man, although most of my problems stemmed from his behaviour. He was offered a teaching post in Singapore, a down-graded position, but he had not been sacked as I had.

Chapter 10
Paris

The problems of my love-life, for want of a better word, did not disappear when I waved goodbye to Prince Rupert School. I had ten weeks to kill before I could present myself at the British Institute in Paris, and with no money to spend on frivolities, I had perforce to remain at home. Ian, my fiancé, insisted on taking leave to spend a week with me at home, a fact that I viewed with great misgiving. However, for whatever reason, whether because he was an officer, or Scottish or probably that he was such a kind, gentle soul, my parents took to him and offered him Doreen's room. She was now married and had left home, all in my absence. Ian was such an idealist. He tried to get tickets for us to see the Proms but was unsuccessful. In no way deterred, he went out and bought a radio so that we could listen to the concerts in my bedroom and to make an occasion of it, suggested we should dress up to listen. So for several evenings in my tiny little room, he donned his formal RAF uniform and I made some attempt at a long skirt and we sat on the bed, listening in dignified silence to the great composers. What an incongruous setting for Beethoven and Mozart! It was quite farcical, but humour was not one of Ian's strong points. My parents must have thought us mad.

Gordon had also written wanting to visit me, but obviously I had to dissuade him from coming to my parents' home. I could just imagine the scene if he ever met Ian, and it was not a very pleasant one. So I prevaricated, using my parents' dislike of him as an excuse and suggesting we meet the following week in central London. He agreed, so I was saved. Ian had suggested that since it was a sunny day, we should take a picnic to Hyde Park, so we walked up to the corner shop to buy the goodies. Suddenly I saw the familiar figure of Gordon turning the corner. I stopped dead in my tracks, my heart beating, my mind racing as to how I was going to extricate myself from this mess. Casting around wildly for some solution, I said to Ian,

"Oh God! I've forgotten Mum's shopping list. Can you go back and get it, Ian? I'll walk along slowly and meet you outside the Abbey Arms pub." Before he could open his mouth to say anything, I twirled him round, pushed him back towards the house and marched purposefully to the corner. My heart thumping like it would break I was in no mood for niceties. I accosted Gordon at the top of the road, my voice raised hysterically in my fear. "What are you *doing* here? Can't you leave me alone? You are so pathetic! I *told* you my parents don't want you round here." The poor man stepped physically backwards from my onslaught, bereft of words. I had never been so rude to him before. I calmed down somewhat after that and we had a brief conversation. Then I sent him packing just in time. I could see this six foot four inches tall figure coming towards me in the distance.

The rest of the holidays dragged along slowly. I spent hours talking to Shirley on the public telephone in Barking Road telling her of all my escapades and glaring at anyone outside who was waiting to use the telephone. I was worried about money. All I would have was a small grant from West Ham Education Authority which I suspected would not go far in Paris. But the die was cast, the day arrived to depart, this time without any emotional farewells from my mother. In the fifties, it took practically the whole day to get to Paris – tube, train to Dover, ferry and then a five hour train journey from Calais to Paris. Arriving at the Gare St Lazare, I did not feel confident about making my way across Paris with my suitcase, so opted rashly for a taxi. I had enough sense to ask how much it would cost to get to the Cité Universitaire where the university students' accommodation was. Unfortunately the taxi-driver's rapid French reply floored me completely. Not wishing to look stupid, I accepted and got in the taxi. It was quite a long way. I was trying to peer at his clock which seemed to be racing along, but it made no sense to me. Only when I arrived at the Cité Universitaire and had time to work out how much I had given the driver did I realise that I must have been fleeced. Bad luck continued to dog me. It was now about eight o'clock and dusk was descending. I went into this ugly building, purpose-built to house all the French and foreign students who did not have private accommodation and in the gloom saw a man with an evil expression sitting behind a desk. The rest of the area was as silent as the grave. I tried English and he just looked at me and shrugged his shoulders, so in my almost forgotten Higher School Certificate French I explained that my name was White and I had been allocated a room here. A pained look came over his face as I massacred the lovely French language, then he turned to a huge ledger-book and looked down the columns. Another shrug of the shoulders, a splaying of the hands and a most unsympathetic stare. "*Il n'y a pas de nom White ici.*" My name wasn't on the list. I was completely bewildered. What was going on? I launched forth again, embellishing the previous bald statements with what I hoped would elicit some sympathy for me. He erupted and shouted: "*IL N'Y A PAS DE NOM WHITE ICI!*" I promptly burst into tears of fatigue and frustration. For a few moments there was silence except for my attempts to control my emotion. Fortunately, a door suddenly opened and a woman emerged who spoke some English. There was obviously a problem. There were no rooms available, except a small attic room which I could have until the morning when they would see what had happened. So I followed the woman into the massive cage which was the lift, up to the top floor and into a tiny, almost bare room and I was left alone. I was distraught, exhausted, hungry, hated the French and cried myself to sleep.

The next morning, I seriously considered jacking it all in, but the thought of all the hassle I would invoke deterred me. I found my way to the canteen, a vast high-ceilinged room which resounded deafeningly with the sound of vociferous French voices. I joined the queue of students, managed to acquire a piece of bread and a cup of coffee and sat morosely dunking and eating. Somehow soon after, the room situation was resolved. I was given a better room, with a bookcase, desk and chair as well as a bed. I spent some time unpacking my suitcase and then decided to take a shower before going to the British Institute. While attempting to manipulate the shower, I discovered that the French love of economy, not only applied to electricity (i.e. the minuterie system of switches), but also extended to water. It gushed out from the shower when the button was pressed, but the moment you removed your finger, the water stopped. One does not need to be overly intelligent to deduce from this fact that it was extremely difficult to soap one's body with one hand while pressing on the button with the other. How ingenious of the French. Somewhat cleaner and more refreshed after this battle with the shower, I successfully navigated the Métro and arrived at the British Institute to meet my fellow British students and began to feel better. They were a very friendly group, many older than me and most of them married.

They were all serving teachers and were very serious about their studies. After the initial welcome, we all had to face French bureaucracy to get our *permis de séjour* and other official passes. We queued up for hours at the Hotel de Ville, arriving at the front of the queue just as twelve thirty struck. Immediately the shutters went down, the doors closed. It was the famous French lunchtime. The office would not open again until two thirty. We could not leave our place in the queue, so we took it in turns to forage for some food to keep us going. We were to encounter this type of French officialdom constantly. The French civil service was a mammoth institution.

I became friendly with a large girl from Bradford by the name of Brenda. She was much older than me, had long blonde hair but was in no way sexy-looking. She fitted the stereotype of the Northerner completely; down-to-earth and stolid, but very serious and conscientious. She did not have student accommodation, but lived in a small garret in the centre of Paris. I admired her knowledge of French and her supreme confidence. She also had a fiancé back in England and we spent much time discussing our respective *beaux*. The lectures at the British Institute and the Sorbonne were a delight and I plunged into studying with enthusiasm. The teachers were excellent, determined that we should learn as much as possible about French civilisation. We studied French Literature, History, Art and Architecture and Phonetics, a subject that was all the rage in academic circles. My mind expanded as my French improved. One lecturer, a Mademoiselle Priny taught French Art and Architecture and gave impassioned lectures which imbued me with a love of art. I got off on the wrong foot with another lecturer, a Mademoiselle Dupont who taught language. I was talking about being full up after our meal and said quite innocently: *Je suis plein*. One look at the expression on her face which had changed from interest, (probably simulated) to horror and I was peremptorily sent out of the room and later called back in for an explanation. Apparently, I had said that I was pregnant. And she wasn't sure whether I meant it or was being insolent. Such are the pitfalls of learning another language. Every morning we took the Métro from the Cité Universitaire to Cluny-La Sorbonne, walked along the Boulevard Saint Michel to the Institute, surrounded by a throng of students and swiftly moving traffic to the Institute. It was always rush hour. We were packed tightly and sweatily in the carriage, which reeked of Gaulois cigarettes and garlic. I was always in fear of two things on the Métro. One was of not being able to push my way out at my stop, so great was the crush, until I learned to say as forcefully as I could: *"Vous descendez?"* and so managed to part the commuters somewhat. The other fear was of another type of pushing; when a ghastly type with a 'hard on' would press his body purposefully between my legs while staring impassively into my eyes. That was quite an ordeal and happened frequently.

Paris was a revelation to me. After the mean streets of London where I had lived for so long, the grand, wide, tree-lined boulevards and avenues of Paris with always a vista of a magnificent building at each end filled me with awe. I used to enjoy walking along the *quais* of the River Seine to the *bouquinistes* who had their large packing cases of second-hand books on display. One could buy all sorts of books there even those that were banned in Britain. One such book was Henry Miller's *Under Capricorn*. Banned because of its sexual explicitness. I couldn't wait to read it, but I was revolted by it, especially the scene where the man had intercourse with a woman in a toilet, standing up. I also bought *Lolita* by Nabokov, banned in Britain because the protagonist had sex with an under-age girl. The cinema was included in our pleasures. It was a time when French cinema was breaking new ground. I remember having to sit on the floor of the cinema to see Cocteau's *Orphée*. It contrasted strongly with an American film featuring the latest musical craze, Rock and Roll. I preferred the French hit *Pigalle*, with clever lyrics describing that sleazy *quartier* of Paris. The sheer classical order of nineteenth-century Paris amazed me. One could stand under the Petit Arc de Triomphe with its Quadriga of Victory and see in a perfect straight line, through the Tuileries and the Louvre all the way down past the exclamation mark of the Obelisk at the Place de la Concorde, along the Avenue des Champs Elysées to the Grand Arc de Triomphe at L'Etoile. We walked all the way once and having arrived at the Arc de Triomphe with its simple, sombre grave of the Unknown Warrior and tried to read all the names of Napoleon's victories carved in the stone, we climbed to the top of the great arch and saw the twelve great avenues radiating out like wheel-spokes and connecting with the other boulevards of the capital. The older parts of Paris, the Ile de la Cité and the Ile St Louis were the domain of Mademoiselle Priny who swelled with pride as she described the rose window of the twelfth-century cathedral of Notre Dame and the jewelled stained-glass windows on the gothic Sainte Chapelle.

Christmas seemed to come around very quickly. Both Brenda and I, having experienced so much in this short space of time, had misgivings about facing our respective fiancés. It would not be easy to resume the same old relationship, albeit for three weeks only. I was still receiving loving letters from Ian and the occasional ones from Gordon extolling the pleasures of Singapore. I really wanted to extricate myself from the engagement, but did not know how to do it elegantly without hurting Ian. In the event, it happened quite suddenly and brutally. I had arranged to do a temporary job during the Christmas break, delivering mail for the Post Office, even though Ian was coming for Christmas. I needed to supplement the subsistence level of the grant I received from West Ham. I had some vague idealistic notion that Ian would get up at six a.m. with me every morning and help me. Not at all. It was his break from the air force and he wanted to lie in. He offered to give me money so that I did not have to work, but I was too proud to accept it. But as I left early on every one of those cold, dark, winter mornings, I nursed a sense of resentment and grievance. He was my fiancé, should he not have been sharing the burden with me? Consequently I was not in the mood and anyway was too tired to socialise in the evenings. The situation came to a head on Christmas Eve. We went with my parents to a local pub for a pre-Christmas drink, but I was by now in a foul mood. I started to pick a quarrel with him and eventually and dramatically, threw my lovely sapphire and diamond engagement ring straight at him; the ring that we had chosen together. He was very upset and astounded at this virago shouting at him. He refused to accept the ring. He wanted me to have it even if I did break the engagement. I was adamant that I would not accept it. I wanted nothing to remind me of him. All this in front of the appalled gaze of my parents. Suddenly, my father, with an oath, sprang up and said, "For Christ's sake, Ag, let's get out of here! and turning to me: "You're enough to make anyone bleeding sick!" and made for the door. The next morning, Christmas day, I packed Ian off and was left to face the wrath of my parents. My mother now railed against me, "What do you think you are doing? Giving up such a nice man as that? You don't even deserve him. Mark my words, you'll regret it. You won't get another like him. You and your stuck-up ways! You'll come a cropper, you'll see!" Prophetic words which proved later to be true. But I didn't love him and that was that. I was only sorry afterwards that I hadn't kept the ring.

I was very glad to get back to Paris, only to find that Brenda had also broken off her engagement. We felt so free and started 'eyeing up' the local French men. I had bought some contact lenses with some of my Christmas earnings and felt quite attractive, able to counteract the old saying: 'Men never make passes at girls who wear glasses' which was a very cruel adage but I believed it. So, sporting my new lenses, I met a tall, rangy Italian who was good fun to be with and who also didn't want any encumbrances. He took me to meet some French friends with him and mentioned to them that I had very attractive almond-shaped eyes. One of them, a trainee doctor, looked closely at me and said, "*Ils brillent trop.*" I thought that was very clever of him to spot that the lenses made my eyes brighter, but he didn't know why. I also went dancing with the Italian. We danced the *Paso Doble*, the latest passionate, rhythmic dance from South America. I was so excited dancing it that I felt I could have sex then and there. But there was no opportunity for sex, although I did learn what a 'French' kiss was. I can't say I enjoyed it; I felt as if I was choking. And then soon afterwards, I fell in love again. Brenda had remained good friends with her 'ex' and received a letter from him saying that he and a friend wanted to spend a week in Paris. Would she show them around and bring a friend along? Would she? We both 'cut' lectures for the whole week so that we could be tourists for once. When I saw this friend, Tom, I was smitten. It was the *coup de foudre* a second time around. He had brown, curly hair, a crinkly smile, and a marvellous sense of humour. He lived in Harrogate, worked as an electrician and played the trumpet in pubs and other venues in the evenings. The four of us hardly stopped laughing the whole week. Paris is compact enough to walk around. This was something one did only as a tourist and we felt just like tourists that week. We went up the Eiffel Tower and saw the silver ribbon of the Seine curving around the islands, saw the *Mona Lisa* with her mysterious smile in the Louvre and visited the Gendarmerie, the old prison of Paris where so many hapless royalists had been kept during the revolution before facing the ultimate scourge of the guillotine. It was wonderful to walk around Paris in the spring, with the trees coming into delicate, pale-green leaf and the sun shining the whole time. One evening, we went to a nightclub, which offered reduced rates to students if they came in early to create an 'ambience'. Inside it was dim and the plush furnishings glowed in the light of the table lamps. It was almost like a *maison de plaisance*. We were also offered a free glass of champagne. Some time during the evening, a cabaret was put on, the central part of it being an enactment of a 'wedding'. The compère looked over at our table, where we sat giggling and drinking, and chose Tom and me to be the bride and groom, amid loud applause. Incredible as it was, we went through the motions of a real wedding, with vows and exchanges of rings (courtesy of the establishment). There was I, in a nightclub, one of the few I had ever gone to, madly in love and taking part in a marriage ceremony. It was really bizarre. It was as if our fate had been decided for us. The next evening, Tom and I walked along the quais of the Seine, on the Ile St Louis, gazing at the moonlight reflected in the Seine. The trees moved delicately in the light breeze and the leaves of the weeping willow trailed in the water, sending out ripples which gleamed in the moonlight. The week was up and the two men had to return to work. We talked seriously of seeing each other again and continuing the relationship. I promised to come to Harrogate and stay with his family as soon as I could. We kissed each other, solemnly and chastely, promising eternal love. Reality kicked in a few months later, however, when I went to Harrogate. The romance had gone. There were not even a few warm embers to remind us of that intoxicating time.

    Life continued to be full of interest. We were studying medieval architecture and had to write an essay on St Marie-Madeleine in Vézelay, the twelfth-thirteenth church and basilica in Burgundy. It was famous because it was on the pilgrim route to St Jacques de Compostelle in Spain and the setting-off point for the Third Crusade, led by Philip of France and Richard Lionheart in 1190. A small group of us decided to go to Vézelay for the weekend to see the cathedral for ourselves. It would be a pleasure to see the rolling green fields of Burgundy after our hectic life in Paris. We stayed in a small hotel in Vézelay itself, a village of narrow, twisting, cobbled streets high up on a hill and leading higher to the church itself. It was like going back in time to the Middle Ages. Nothing prepared us for the sheer size of the church with its vast nave, where the pilgrims would bed down for the night before continuing on their gruelling way. The round romanesque arches were emphasised by alternate bands of dark and light stone. On the capitals were magnificent sculptures of devils, goblins and peasant figures grimacing horribly. Outside was the colossal romanesque arch of the main portal and on the tympanum above, rich sculptures of Christ stretching out his hands, from which rays of light descend onto the apostles to tell them to go out into the world to preach the gospel. We spent two whole days looking at the church, writing about it and some of the more artistic in the group spent time sketching the façade. None of us had cameras to record the magnificence of the building, yet we had to have some sort of pictorial record. I was useless at drawing, but one of the men on the course kindly helped me out by drawing a marvellous architectural sketch of the church. It became a World Heritage site in 1981.

Shirley decided to come to Paris for a weekend. Having no boyfriend, she was in a mood for adventure. She insisted we walk along the Champs Elysées and then sit outside at one of the expensive cafés lining the Avenue. It was early evening, the lights along the Avenue were just coming on, vying with the strident lights of the restaurants. We looked around us. So much movement and colour and excitement! We were in a happy, expectant mood, two bright, vulnerable foreigners looking for a thrill. We ogled all the passing men to see if we could 'pick up' anyone handsome. Soon, two very well-dressed, attractive men sat down at a nearby table and proceeded to engage us in conversation. One was dark and swarthy-looking, with melting eyes and the other blond, heavier, slower with a huge wide grin. I liked him the best. They asked us if we had ever been to the Bois de Boulogne, the large open space, the 'lung' of Paris similar to Hyde Park in London. We hadn't, so before long we were in a car going to the Bois de Boulogne with them. The wide tree-shaded paths were all covered with shingle, the spring flowers in full bloom and the limpid lakes gleamed in the setting sun. Before long Shirley had acted in her usual fashion and vanished with her escort. I was in a quieter mood now, slightly wary but still game. We continued walking and talking in the deepening dusk. His name was Pierre and he spoke very cultured French. Then we stopped and sat down under a tree. Soon, darkness descended and he began kissing me passionately, murmuring romantic phrases in my ear. The sharp smell of the grass, the rich odour of the earth both mingled with the warmth of Pierre's body. I stretched out voluptuously and began to respond to his caresses. Then, shockingly, our amorous interlude was interrupted by a dazzling flashlight shining into our eyes and lighting up the darkness and behind it, the burly shape of an *agent de police*. He saw these two bodies entwined in each other's arms and was not happy. A rapid conversation ensued with the Frenchman, and among the spate of words I heard, "*Pas permis!*" and then, swiftly and unceremoniously, we were arrested. We were bundled into the Paris equivalent of a Black Maria with its small, high windows with bars across them and taken to the nearest police station. There we were separated and questioned. I learned that there is a law against 'courting' in the Bois de Boulogne and we had infringed it. My passport was taken from me and I was told that I should be taken to court the next day to be sentenced. Meanwhile, Pierre was pushed roughly into another room and I was taken to the women's quarters where there was mayhem going on. There was a large cage in the middle of the room and in it were a whole group of prostitutes, flashily dressed, screaming and shouting. The door of the cage was opened and I was made to join this screeching band. The contrast between the calm of the Bois de Boulogne and this cacophony of the women can only be imagined. I was totally devastated. It seemed as though I was in the cage all night, but it must have been only a few hours before the cage door was opened and I was told roughly that I could have my passport back and that I was free to go. The authorities had obviously wanted only to frighten me. I enquired solicitously of Pierre only to learn that he had already been freed. Apparently, he came from a well-known wealthy family who had procured his release almost immediately and he had taken my earrings with him. My socialist tendencies came to the fore. I was livid with rage and resentment at the unfairness of it all, but more prosaically, I had to find my way back through the dark streets of Paris in the very early morning on foot. Shirley had somehow not been arrested by the police and was safely tucked up in bed.

To supplement my meagre income, I decided to take a part-time job looking after two young French children while their mother was at work. The family lived in a very elegant flat behind the Champs Elysées, replete with Louis XV furniture, yellow damask curtains and drapery and two very obnoxious children. On the first day, I was ordered to take them to the Tuileries to give them some exercise and fresh air. They took their model boats with them to sail on the small circular pond in the gardens. Once in the park, however, they raced ahead of me and I was forced to run after them. The big problem was that I could not understand their toddler's French and they appeared not to understand me. I managed to get to the pond just in time to prevent one of them falling into it and dying of pneumonia, and I proceeded to berate them in my halting French. They took not the slightest notice of me. The sailing boats were not a good idea. One of them screamed in a tantrum because his boat had floated to the middle of the pond and had capsized. The other joined in when his boat collided dramatically with a much superior yacht, causing it to list dangerously. It needed all the efforts of a patient stranger to fish both boats out of the pond and by that time I was exhausted, and couldn't wait to get them back home in one piece, regardless of the curtailed exercise and fresh air. This incident so unnerved me that I decided I would rather remain hungry than undergo such an ordeal again. Money continued to be a problem. Once a month, I trekked to the Place Vendôme to my bank to receive my monthly cheque from West Ham Authority. It was totally insufficient for Paris. To make matters worse, I hated the food in the canteen at the Cité Universitaire. It consisted mostly of spaghetti and macaroni and meatballs in a glutinous sauce. I was able to eat only the copious amounts of bread available and supplemented my diet with sweets and chocolates. Even so, I lost a stone and a half in weight in Paris. My ankles were like those of Minnie Mouse and my figure the slimmest it had ever been. That may be why my future husband was attracted to me, but more of that later.

Summer was approaching and examinations loomed. The French system of examinations included orals as well as written exams in every subject, which was quite an ordeal. I remember having a very interesting discussion with Mademoiselle Prinet during my oral exam in Art and Architecture, about Watteau and Corot and gained a distinction in that subject and in Phonetics. I garnered Merits in Literature and Essay-writing and emerged from the year's study with a Certificate of Merit, with a good accent (thanks to the phonetics) and a reasonable command of the language, I was now able to apply for teaching posts back in England and start earning some money again. I did not particularly want to go back to East or West Ham, so applied for posts in other areas. Fate stepped in, however. I received a letter from a Miss Fletcher, MA, AKC at Brampton Manor Secondary School for Girls, offering me the post of Head of French. She was friendly with the headmistress of East Ham Grammar School for Girls where Shirley taught and must have heard that I was returning to England and looking for a job. She had studied my application and although another teacher, who was a French graduate, had applied for the post of head of French, Miss Fletcher felt that my year in Paris gave me the edge, even though I did not have a degree. To be offered a post with responsibility for French and for the two other staff in the French department could not be refused. I accepted. So once again I would be back living in Plaistow and teaching in East Ham, but the wanderlust had seized me. Long discussions with Shirley made us both decide we would only teach for one more year and then we would emigrate to Canada. But fate stepped in once again.

Chapter 11
Love and Marriage

One of the few pleasures when coming back to Plaistow, apart from the sense of relief that one was back in England and that if anything went wrong, the good old British bobby would be there to sort it out, was seeing my mother and Shirley again. Shirley was still teaching in East Ham Grammar School for Girls and still 'unattached'. Her father and step-mother were still pressurising her to meet a 'nice Jewish boy', but she steadfastly resisted all blandishments on their part. We continued to meet in Joe Lyons café in Stratford every Saturday morning, exchanging gossip and making plans. We both decided we were quite fed up with this boring suburban life after our experiences abroad and that at the end of the year we would find that new life in Canada. This may seem strange when I was about to start a new job, but all I needed was to earn some money before we set off again abroad. Fortunately, Brampton Manor was not one of those ghastly Victorian buildings that had been my lot for so long. It was a modern two-storey building, full of glass and light – much more attractive. The headmistress, a Miss Fletcher, was another of those formidable spinsters who had dedicated their lives to education. She was built on a grand scale, solid and most of the time immovable, but very jolly. It was at Brampton Manor that I finally began to enjoy teaching. This was partly because I was now teaching French. Languages are a 'linear' subject like Maths and demands a much more teacher-orientated approach. Unlike English or History, the pupils can't do much at home except revise what they have already been taught or supplement their learning with their own reading. I was the sole person who could help them. Nor, thankfully, could they indulge in their own opinions in class, which was always fraught with problems and I could also avoid having to divulge my own feelings and emotions. I could shelter behind the language, so to speak and still remain in control. The other reason I enjoyed myself so much was because I was teaching the 'A' classes, the most intelligent girls in the school because Miss Fletcher, in her wisdom, did not think that the B to D streams were capable of learning a language. Of course, if she had ever studied Comparative Education, she would have realised that this was a total fallacy. In most of Europe, all children were introduced to a second language in the primary schools. So three quarters of the Brampton girls were considered less intelligent and suffered from a restricted timetable and this was from the age of eleven onwards. Then at fifteen, they could leave school, most of them quite ill-equipped to face society. The eleven-plus examination was in full swing at this time and even the very bright girls that I taught must have been emotionally and academically affected by the fact that they had failed the examination. They were definitely grammar school material, but because there was only one girls' grammar school in East Ham, numbers were obviously limited. They were just below the dubious IQ 'cut-off' point and were branded as being insufficiently intelligent for a grammar school education. I knew that the whole system was grossly unfair, that success in the exam was influenced by the number of grammar school places available in an education area. Thus, in Wales, many more children went into the grammar schools and then became teachers, because there were so many more grammar school places available. There is no doubt that pupils suffered from this inequitable system. Of course, in the 1970s the Labour Party's remedy for such inequities was even more disastrous, to turn most schools into comprehensive schools and in the process abolish whole swathes of grammar schools, to the detriment of the many bright working-class children for whom a grammar school education was a passport to university. Most of the 'A' classes in Brampton Manor tended to stay on for an extra year to sit for the same O-level examination as the grammar school pupils. At the end of my first year at the school, my fifth year class did spectacularly well in French. There were fifteen girls in the class and all passed in French; twelve received an A grade and three a B grade. Miss Fletcher was in seventh heaven and I became one of her favourites, able to indulge myself with any ambitious schemes to promote the learning of French, such as a French club and French films. But I felt so sorry for those girls; most wanted to take A-level French but it was impossible, unless they managed to get into the sixth form in East Ham grammar school and most did not have the self-confidence to attempt this. Some continued at evening classes and kept in touch with me for some time. Of course, the news spread of the excellent results and I had teachers from other schools asking if they could sit in my class to watch my methods. I couldn't see what all the fuss was about.

It was also a pleasure to work with the two other French teachers in our department. One of them, Thelma O'Callaghan, was a very attractive blonde with curly hair and laughing eyes and a 'penchant' for the men. We became firm friends and together we organised French plays, French Assemblies and at Christmas taught the girls French carols. We also took groups of children to France for holidays. These journeys had their ups and downs. One girl on her first night away was so homesick and got into such a state of hysteria that I had to give her some of the medicine I brought with me for the pupils in the event of just such a problem. It was called Dr Collis-Browne's mixture and it certainly solved her problem. She quietened down almost immediately and went to sleep quite happily. It was only when I looked closely at the bottle of mixture that I noticed one of the ingredients was morphine... Fortunately she was bright and cheerful the next day. Another trip was fraught with danger; one of our girls was caught shoplifting in the 'Galeries Lafayette' by the police Fortunately, it was only a small souvenir, but it took all my powers of persuasion to get the police to drop the charges and take her back home as soon as possible. There was also the occasion in Annecy, when the bus to take us back to the station did not arrive and we all had to hare along the streets, as if the Furies were after us, our cases banging painfully against our legs. As I ran, I envisaged the chaos that would occur if we missed the train and all its connections, but we caught it with minutes to spare.

Since Shirley would not go to any dances, I turned to Thora Richmond, my erstwhile Welsh friend. I was surprised that she was still in Plaistow and even more surprised that she was teaching in a primary school. As far as I know she stayed in that same primary school during the whole of her teaching career. But she was happy to go to dances with me. We decided we were now quite superior to the locals, so went up to town to dances where we could meet foreign men. We met Cypriots who danced on tables, Frenchmen who kissed divinely, Spaniards who wanted us to dance the tango. It was really exhilarating. I was taken by an Asian to a concert where Ravi Shankar, a famous Indian musician played the zither; I was proposed to by a Colonial who wanted to take me to Zanzibar to live, a proposal that I gracefully declined; and I had to exert a great deal of energy rebutting the advances of an Irishman. Thora and I enjoyed teasing them, but resisted very firmly their constant attempts to court us. Of course, there were dangers. We were standing at a bus-stop in Tottenham Road at midnight one evening, and realised the last bus had gone. Minutes later, we accepted a lift from two men in a car, who said they were going our way, and did, indeed, for much of the way, only to veer off from Plaistow and turn the car towards Wanstead Flats, that green belt around London which was a regular meeting-place for courting couples. At this time of night the 'Flats' were quite deserted and only the ghostly shapes of the trees dotted around lightened the darkness. Memories of the Bois de Boulogne! But since there were two of us, we did not feel afraid. The driver stopped the car and both of them settled down for what they imagined would be a pleasurable interlude. The silence, when the engine cut off, seemed to scream out at us and then suddenly a real scream rent the air. It was Thora, screaming like one possessed, frightening them and me too. She made such a fuss and they were so taken aback by her fury, that thoroughly shaken, they turned the car round and drove us home.

I was not so fortunate another time and it was in Cheltenham, of all places. I had kept in touch with one of our college friends, Elizabeth Robson, who invited me to come to a special dance being held in the Town Hall. Since it was quite an occasion, we both dressed up in long skirts and pretty blouses and sallied forth. The evening was a dream. I danced most of the evening with a chap with a very attractive West Country 'burr'. When the dance concluded, Elizabeth disappeared with her beau and since my companion had a car, he offered to drive me home. All was well for most of the journey, although I was slightly uneasy since I did not know the area. Then we turned into a road which I recognised as being near Elizabeth's house and I relaxed somewhat. Suddenly, some few houses from where Elizabeth lived, the chap stopped the car, locked the door and proceeded to kiss me. This was 'par for the course' and I acquiesced in the game. Then he started to become more passionate and began to pull up my long skirt. This was not part of the bargain and I pushed him off, which only made him more passionate. Before long, his hands were on my thighs moving upwards. I gave him an almighty shove, so that he fell against the door. This made him become quite violent. With an oath, he began to pull at my open-necked blouse, ripping a button off in the process. Suddenly I was fighting in earnest, seized with fear. I could not believe this was happening to me. Thora and I had run the gamut of all the advances of the foreigners in central London and yet here, in this respectable, genteel town I was being attacked. Fury made me stronger and for a few minutes we were locked in a desperate struggle. I scratched his face whereupon he shouted, "You bitch!" and wrenched my head back. I started screaming; my skirt was up to my thighs, my blouse undone and my head hurting where he had pulled it. Then suddenly it was over. He opened the door, kicked me out into the gutter and the car sped off. I remained there, sobbing and trembling and then finally gathered myself up, straightened my clothes composed my face and knocked on Elizabeth's door as if nothing had happened. I was too distraught, too ashamed to tell her what had in fact transpired. But it had been a near thing.

Perhaps this event triggered off my feelings of dissatisfaction with my social life. Shirley and I were still committed to going to Canada, but the end of the school year was still a long way off. In this mood, I went with Thora to a NUT dance organised for the local teachers. The dance hall was above a pub and quite shabby. The dance itself seemed very tame after the excitements of Paris and the men behaved as predictably as ever, unable to summon up the courage to ask the women to dance until they had sunk a good few beers. I was bored and looked for an opportunity to go home, but did not want to let Thora down too early. At one point, I was standing alone when a man came up to me and said, "I don't dance very well, but would you like to have a go round the floor? I'll try not to tread on your toes." I looked at this rather stocky man (I seem to prefer the heavy-set type of man) and noticed that he had the most amazing hazel-coloured eyes. He spoke in a light, sibilant voice with a pronounced Welsh accent. I decided that it would be less boring to shuffle round the floor with him than to stand decorating the wall. Surprisingly, he had little to say, none of the usual patter that one had come to expect, and appeared to be as bored as I was. I learned only that his name was Stan and that he taught Maths in a boys' secondary school in West Ham. I prattled on while he listened to me carefully and when the dance ended I took him back to meet Thora. I calculated that they might have something in common being Welsh and I could slip away surreptitiously. He had the next dance with her and then disappeared among the throng of men propping up the bar. It was only towards the end of the evening that he appeared again and stood before us. Turning to me, he said he would like to see me again. Would I mind going out with him next Saturday? I was quite astonished because he had shown no real interest in me and anyway Thora was Welsh and much prettier than me. I stammered, blushing, "Oh! You can't mean me. Thora's the one you should be taking out. She's the Welsh one." Thora looked suitably embarrassed and I wanted the floor to open up. I didn't really fancy him and hoped to divert him to her. He shook his head seriously and said, "I'm sure Thora is a very nice girl, but I'm asking you." He raised his eyebrows enquiringly and suddenly smiled. His whole face changed when he smiled. His eyes creased up and his mouth widened, showing small, regular white teeth. Well, a 'date' was a 'date' and he intrigued me somewhat. So we set a time and place and then he disappeared again. None of the usual, "Can I see you home?" routine. Thora talked about him on the way home. I wasn't too sure now about going out with him. I said, "He's got a very small mouth, quite mean-looking." Thora countered with, "Yes, but he's got lovely, soft eyes," which I could not dispute.

We met for the second time at Plaistow station. I insisted on buying my own rail ticket and he did not argue. We were going to the London Welsh Club in Holborn. I'd never heard of it, but it was a home from home for expatriate Welshmen and the drinks were cheap. I was amazed again on the tube when he made no attempt to talk to me, burying his head in a newspaper instead. Decidedly, he was different from all the other men I had been out with. I alternated from being intrigued and being annoyed at his apparent indifference. The London Welsh Club was pretty basic. Most of the men were short and dark, not very prepossessing. Stan made no attempt to talk to any of them. He bought us drinks and we sat in silence sipping them. Was he shy? Or just plain boring? I couldn't decide. In the event, it was not until we had both had three drinks and I had started giggling that he began to talk. His full name was Thomas Stanley Jones and he came from a small village in North Wales called Llanberis. Its only claim to fame even today is that it lies at the foot of the Snowdonia range of mountains and has a small train on a narrow-gauge railway that takes tourists to the summit. In the fifties it was quite undiscovered and the train was used mostly by railwaymen working on the track. Like Ian, my former fiancé (both Celts, of course!) he loved to talk about his home, the mountains, the lakes and the tiny villages clinging precariously to the mountainsides. He explained that he did not learn to speak English until he was eleven years old when he went to the grammar school. At home the family always spoke Welsh. His weakness in English was to cause him some difficulties later. His headmaster decided to keep him in the fifth year until he passed his School Certificate in English and it took so long that he was called up for National Service soon afterwards. From there, he went to Teacher Training College in Bangor to study Art and Maths. His father was a slate quarryman and his mother the daughter of a Baptist Minister. It was an unlikely coupling. The father was a pleasant, easy-going man who liked a pint, especially on Fridays when he had his wage packet in his pocket; the mother a teetotaller, a tiny virago of a woman, who apparently had only two aims in life, firstly, to prevent her husband from going to the pub and spending most of his wages and secondly, to prevent her two sons becoming quarrymen like their father. She succeeded in the latter, but alienated her children in the process. Stan told me how she would lock him in his bedroom to do his homework and he would then climb straight out of the window to join his mates.

The pattern of that evening was to be repeated for most of our whirlwind courtship; sporadic conversation until our tongues had been lubricated with a certain amount of alcohol and then I would collapse into giggles and he would talk about his plans for the future. He wanted to own his own house and wanted to get married and 'settle down'. I could identify with such aspirations, they reflected my own feelings at that time. I wanted to get married and most particularly, I wanted to have children. So it was not long before we became engaged. Buying the engagement ring proved to be something of a nightmare. When I was not satisfied with the first few I saw, Stan became bored, gave me the money and told me to choose one for myself. Yet somehow, his boorishness did not worry me. For some unfathomable reason, Stanley seemed 'right' for me. I had this atavistic feeling that he was the one I should marry. I reasoned that he was from a working-class background and was a teacher, so had a similar level of education, but it was this feeling of 'rightness' that persuaded me. When I told my parents, they were not pleased. Because he was quite inarticulate, they mistook his silences for churlishness and didn't like him. But his quietness after the years of hearing my father's loud, aggressive voice was quite a relief. I would meet him after school and go back to his rooms with him, just to get away from my father. He rented two upstairs rooms in a small terraced house in Plaistow, a small bedsit and a tiny kitchen. It was in a double bed rammed up against the window in that cramped living room that I finally succumbed to sex. I rationalised that I no longer had any need to worry about any consequences, since I would soon be a married woman. He was an expert lover, having none of the sexual timidity (sensitivity?) of my other boyfriends. He played on my body like a musician plays a violin. The thought did cross my mind that he must have had a lot of practice, but I was the one benefiting from it. We would spend hours in bed in the evening, caressing each other. It seemed he knew all the erogenous zones of my body and waited until I was afire with desire before penetrating me. I learned of the other orgasm a woman could have, the vaginal orgasm after the clitoral one. The two feelings were so different. Stan's gentle caressing of my breasts and then my clitoris sent shudders through my body, shudders which became more and more intense until I convulsed, and cried out, almost sobbing with the exquisite pain of the orgasm. My body seemed to explode, unable to contain the powerful feelings coursing through it. Then, almost immediately after the crisis, my body was urging him to penetrate me. Hastily, desperately, I drew him downwards and his body moved in rhythm to my urgings. We were both caught up in the ecstasy of our feelings, totally absorbed in assuaging our needs. I was now transported into a different kind of euphoria, deep, intense and satisfying, until with a deep groan he would let loose his sperm on my stomach and collapse exhausted on me. In spite of our passion for each other, we both wanted to avoid an unwanted pregnancy. My body still felt the need to hold him inside me, until the emotion subsided and I lay languorous, replete and contented, smiling at the wonder of the moment. I was amazed at myself how easily I opened up to him and gradually became as daring in my love-making as he was. Usually, he would then get up and start to prepare a meal for us while I lay on the bed feeling the cool, night air coming in from the open window, fanning my face. We were like a long-married couple as we washed up together and talked about our future life. I discerned in him sensitivities which I had never suspected. When I had flu at one time, he cosseted me and was assiduous in his attempts to make me feel better. He had a very 'feminine' side to him which he would have stoutly denied, but it appeared in our relationship.

Practising 'coitus interruptus' after a time was not very satisfactory and I still did not trust Stan to control himself at times, especially after we had been out for a drink. So I decided, like the educated young woman that I was, to go to the local family planning clinic to be fitted for a 'dutch cap'. The only other contraceptive available at that time was the coil which was fitted in to one's body and left there for six months. I certainly didn't fancy that. I had visions of it going septic inside me. So, perforce, it was the dutch cap. The family planning clinic was a bare, unwelcoming establishment, with a main reception area and small cubicles leading from it. In my state of extreme tension, it seemed imbued with a permanent air of disapproval, to which the demeanour of the nurses seemed to contribute. I suddenly thought of my mother who would have looked askance at me for attending such an establishment, believing a good Catholic would either abstain from sex or accept fatalistically what God had ordained. Residues of her strictures that sex was dirty buzzed around in my mind and a fleeting image of the angry bookseller throwing me out of the bookshop for reading a book about sex flitted across my vision. An officious nurse in a white starched uniform sat behind a rickety desk and proceeded to question me as to my reasons for wanting to practise birth control. Was I really intending to get married soon? I had to show my engagement ring to prove the point. Then I was put quite summarily into a small cubicle and waited. Thinking about what would transpire, I realised how little I knew of the inside of my own body. Panic began to set in until a nurse arrived and thrust this rubber thing into my hand, saying, "This is the 'dutch cap' which is guaranteed over ninety percent success if used properly. You insert it like this." She twirled it around expertly. "I shall come back in a few moments to see that you have put it in the correct position." I turned the cap around, very inexpertly, unsure whether it went into my vagina in a convex or concave fashion. I tried both ways but could not seem to get the wretched thing to stay in. It kept falling out. I started to sweat and pressed more heavily on it, hoping that I wasn't damaging some essential internal organs. This went on for some time and I became more and more desperate. If the nurse hadn't at that point come back in, I was ready to leave, ready to give up sex altogether. It was not to be. She returned, told me to get up on the bed and then said in a very surprised voice, "You haven't put it in! What have you been doing?" looking at me accusingly. I explained that I didn't know how to keep it in. She could not believe me. She stared at me for a moment, obviously biting back the caustic comments on her lips and then said, "Right! Since you are obviously having difficulties, I'll go and get a model for you to look at." The model duly arrived, a plaster cast of peculiar shape, supposedly the internal organs of the female. I turned it round and round to see how it was going to help me. For the life of me, I couldn't see how it would help. Time ticked away and I dreaded the return of the nurse. I felt sick as well as scared now. She duly returned, saw I was still unsuccessful and with a bad grace ordered me to get up on the bed. "I'll put it in myself and when it's in, you will put your fingers in and feel the position." I was made to feel that I had just failed a very important test. She shoved it in, making me push my fingers in afterwards to extricate it, warning me to see where it had been positioned. After that I tried several times and finally managed it to her satisfaction and I was given a new one covered in a white anti-septic powder and laid in a case, and then I was allowed to leave. I left that establishment hating men and sex and quite prepared to call the engagement off. Stanley couldn't understand what all the fuss was about.

My sister Irene came down from Bristol one weekend to meet Stan. When she saw the small room and the one-bar electric fire, she looked at me sadly and said, "Oh, you poor dear!" I was quite astonished. I really did not know what she was talking about. External surroundings were not impinging on me at all at that time. Of course, Stan's flat was a far cry from her spacious house in Bristol but I didn't care. As with many women, when they have a permanent boyfriend, I began to lose touch with my friends, apart from Shirley. I spent most of my spare time with Stanley, planning our future. All these exciting developments took place in the first five months of my return to England. The Christmas holidays came and Stan went home to Wales to prepare his family for the news that we were to marry. We agreed that I should meet his family after the Christmas festivities. It was then that I realised what a remote place he lived in. I caught the train from Euston to Bangor, and then had to leave the train which was making its way to Holyhead for the ferry to Ireland, and take another local train to Caernarvon, the nearest town to Llanberis. Caernarvon's claim to fame was its castle, where traditionally the eldest son of the reigning monarch was proclaimed Prince of Wales. I remember chatting to a group of men in the compartment of the small, local train. One asked me where I was going and when I said, "Llanberis," the whole group started laughing. I looked at them quizzically and one of them answered, "You'll need a passport to get there." I laughed at the joke, but pondered the significance of the sentence. Was North Wales so foreign? When I arrived at Caernarvon, Stan was there to meet me with his cousin, David. Outside the station, every street was blanketed in thick white snow. The two of them had walked the six miles from Llanberis, because all the buses had been unable to get through the deep snowdrifts. He did manage to persuade a taxi-driver to take us to his home, however. As the taxi crunched noisily over the packed snow, I was able to survey the landscape, now shrouded in white and watch the towering, white bulk of Snowdon appear before us. It looked as if it were guarding the whole area and warning us of its massive power. We struggled with difficulty through what to me was a winter wonderland. No snowploughs had attempted to move this densely packed snow, which obliterated roads and fields alike, blanketing everything in a frozen stillness. The silence seemed to press down on the land. We finally arrived in Llanberis after a long, arduous journey. The village consisted of one main road, with a few substantial houses, but mostly rows of mean terraced houses interspersed with shops and quite a few public houses. On the left, behind the houses, were fields, a lake and then mountains and on the right a few narrow streets, branching off from the main road and clinging mournfully to another side of the mountain range. To me it looked so depressing, with all of its buildings constructed of dark-grey granite with dark, slate roofs, casting a permanent gloom over the village. When it rained as it did almost incessantly, the walls of the houses and the roofs gleamed dark-silver in the gloom. The few big houses only seemed to emphasise the poverty of the small terraced houses flanking them. Even in the summer, it was amazing how much it rained. Many a time, we stood outside Stanley's house in the drizzling rain and looked towards the Isle of Anglesey where the sky was azure blue and we knew that there it would be bathed in sunshine.

    Stan's parents lived in one of those grey, granite, terraced houses, and when we went inside, there was his mother, this diminutive figure with yellow-grey hair, and yellow-stained fingers. She was an inveterate smoker, a cigarette dangling constantly from her lips. I noticed that her legs had purplish, mottled marks on them. Every evening, after supper, she would settle herself in her accustomed chair next to the coal fire, her legs wide apart, a cigarette in her mouth and she would spend the whole evening in this way, staring into the coal fire and throwing out the occasional caustic remark. On that first night, after falling into an exhausted sleep, I woke up suddenly to be confronted by such an intense, impenetrable blackness that I thought I had gone blind. There was no light anywhere, not even in the street outside. I shut my eyes in a panic, longing for the morning to come. When I woke up again to the emerging daylight, relief flooded over me. I nuzzled down into the bed because of the intense cold, and then heard some sort of altercation below. Suddenly Stan arrived with a cup of tea for me. I asked him what the argument had been about. Apparently, his mother was taking exception to the fact that he was waiting on me by bringing me up some tea. With every one of her three children, she tried to put them off marriage. She was adamant that marriage would be a disaster, they would become slaves to the other partner etc. Later in my life, I could understand her ambition for her children, feeling the same way myself, but her manner of trying to achieve what she wanted for them was counter-productive. She turned them all against her. The saddest result of her driven obsessions was that all three of her children did eventually get married in spite of her, but not one of them told their parents that they intended to marry and, even worse, not one of them invited them to their weddings. She had to learn of the news from other people.

We spent most all of our holidays in those first few years in North Wales. I got to know the area very well. One constant topic of conversation was the language problem in Wales. In all the coastal towns of Rhyl, Colwyn Bay, Llandudno, and Prestatyn, English was the predominant language and considered to be the superior one. In the grammar schools, subjects were taught in English and woe betide anyone who tried to speak Welsh. Welsh people who only spoke Welsh were deemed to be inferior. There was a definite form of language apartheid being practised. But a few miles inland from the coast, English was very seldom used except to speak to the occasional 'foreigner'. The villagers in Llanberis considered that Stanley had done very well for himself to bring home an English fiancée, but I had to accustom myself to sitting in the living room with Stan's family, unable to take any part in the conversation, because they all spoke in

Welsh. No one seemed to be concerned about that, presumably because English was that much more difficult for them. Only occasionally, they broke off to speak to me in a halting, sibilant English. But after Germany and France, Wales was definitely more foreign to me. How different it is today, where Welsh is compulsory in all Welsh secondary schools, to the detriment of those pupils, like my grandchildren, whose first language is English. There are all-Welsh-speaking schools, which tend to be superior to the others because of the entrance policy that the parents should be Welsh-speaking. Anyone wanting to obtain a post in the media or in local government has to have a working knowledge of Welsh. The language still splits the country in two, and ancient animosities exist between the Welsh- and the English-speaking areas. This was shown most vividly in the referendum for Welsh devolution. The capital, Cardiff, with other areas in South Wales voted against it, but whole swathes of West and North Wales won the day. Language is still an emotive subject there, almost on a par with rugby.

Stanley wanted to show me all the sights of North Wales. He had managed to save enough money to buy a Lambretta and we toured the whole area. I grew to love the soft Welsh countryside, the green fields against the dark bulk of the mountains and the sparking streams which cascaded down the mountainside like silver ribbons. In summer I would paddle in the small brooks, luxuriating in the cool waters, or sit beside Llanberis lake gazing in wonder at the awesome mountains. Stanley's uncle worked on the Snowdon railway and managed to get us cheap tickets to go up on the small narrow-gage railway to the summit of Snowdon, passing the persil-white lambs gambolling across the tracks as the train chunted wheezily along the track. At the top it was still icily cold with some vestiges of snow clinging to the rocks. All of the North Wales coast lay open below us, the many shining lakes in the valleys and the grey Irish Sea glinting in the distance. We could see Telford's graceful suspension bridge over the Menai Straits and the low-lying green fields of Anglesey. One time, we actually walked up to the summit, along the easy 'pig track', an ancient, stepped flint track hewn out by the quarrymen to help them get to the mines high up in the mountains. The job must have been onerous; they sometimes had to climb for over an hour to reach the mine, then work all day until it was time to wend their way wearily downwards, exhausted and filthy, back to Llanberis. By the time we were there, a shower-block had been installed for them to wash off the grit and dust before going home, but in earlier times, it was only the tin bath at home to welcome them. I began to appreciate why these people were so inarticulate and suspicious of outsiders. When the snows fell every year, each village was totally cut off from the others. The villagers were forced to turn inwards for months at a time, to family and neighbours and for some, to forget the trials of winter in the cheerful sociability of the pubs.

We decided to get married at Easter. This was 1957 and I was twenty-seven years old, quite well-travelled but still very naïve and Stanley was almost two years younger. It was when we were planning all the details of the wedding that I began to have some qualms. Small anxieties and events made me begin to think. One evening, we went for a drink in a pub in Boleyn and Stan began to talk to a man propping up the bar. He mentioned our different backgrounds and how we were planning to get married. I remember the man looking at us gleefully and saying, "Oh, it'll never work! The Welsh and the English never get on, you mark my words." We laughed and assured him that it was not true, but a faint doubt entered my head. Soon afterwards, we went to the pictures to see a film whose title I have forgotten. During the screening, I noticed that Stanley was fidgeting a lot and seemed restive. When we emerged from the cinema he was quite morose, more so than usual and I asked him if anything was wrong. He hesitated for a long time and then said, "I really ought to tell you something." Another long silence. I tried to cheer him up saying, "Come on, spit it out! It can't be such a terrible secret." And then the flood of words. It was a long story and quite a sordid one. He had moved to Birmingham with his cousin David to get a job and they had rented a room in a house. One night they had gone to the pub, as usual, and had met a girl. By the end of the evening, they were all quite drunk and the girl appeared to have no home to go to, so they took her home with them. There was only one bed in the room, a double one, so the girl slept between the two of them. Inevitably, something happened and with hindsight it was inevitable that it was Stanley who made love to her, David being much smaller in stature than Stanley and presumably less highly sexed. OK, so it happens, although a strange woman sharing a bed with two men was somewhat scandalous in those days. Unfortunately, for Stanley, it was not just a 'one night stand'. She became pregnant, and he decided to get as far away from Birmingham and from her, with as much speed as he could. In fact, he left her in the lurch. One could argue that she had it coming to her with her behaviour, and that was Stanley's defence. And what was my reaction? I who had had Roman Catholic morals instilled into me when young? Not what you might think. My reaction was obviously the result of reading too many romantic novels. The story he told me, stumbling over the details, justifying himself by saying that she must have been a prostitute, seemed like something out of a Mills & Boone romance. So I felt sorry for him, sad that he had nursed this secret for so long and had not been able to unburden himself. I rationalised to myself that this had happened in the past, it was now all different, he loved me and I loved him and so on. I told him to forget it and I forgave him. We never mentioned it again. Yet years later, in the 1990s, the past caught up with him. He was living then in Llandudno and was confronted one day by a young woman who had been searching for news of him for years. She had finally put an advert in the local paper and had learned of his whereabouts. She was the daughter of the 'three in the bed' incident. She was *his* daughter, but he did not want to know her. Apparently, she had been adopted by a wealthy couple, had had a comfortable life and had never seen her mother. Now she was happily married with two children. But Stanley would not acknowledge her as his daughter.

So doubts began to fester in my mind. I worried that our only source of entertainment seemed to be the pub, that very few of my friends liked him and certainly not my parents and that he was so quiet. But what began to frighten me most of all was the sheer irrevocability of marriage, living with one person for the rest of one's life. I tried to imagine what this meant, but failed: what if it didn't work out? Divorce would not be an option I would want to consider as a Catholic, albeit a 'lapsed' one and anyway, not easy in those days. I had, almost unconsciously, always allowed myself an escape hatch from difficult situations and yet here I was contemplating marriage, a lifelong relationship with one person. The situation seemed to me what Albert Camus called *sans issu*, there would be no way out. I nursed these feelings over some weeks becoming more and more convinced that I needed a 'breathing space' from this whirlwind romance. As usual, I was too scared to mention it to anyone, because it seemed such a weakness in me. My concerns grew stronger. I thought of the strictures of the man in the pub, Stanley's disclosures of his past, his silences, his predilection for alcohol. I really didn't know him at all, his personality was a complete mystery to me and here I was entrusting my whole future life to him. Finally I summoned up enough courage to talk to him about my concerns. Walking home after school with him one day, I broached the subject in the most devious way possible (what weasel words!) stumbling over them to get them out quickly: "Stan, I've been thinking that we shouldn't rush into marriage like this. We've really only known each other for a few months and I think we should get to know each other a bit better. Can't we postpone the wedding for a while? I don't think I'm quite ready yet. There's no hurry, is there?" He stopped dead in his tracks and I couldn't bear to look at him. There was a tense silence and since he seemed not to know what to say (was that a good sign?). So I continued, persuasively, "We could save up a bit more mo..." He interrupted me viciously, his face white with anger and emotion. "You want me to postpone this wedding? You want *me* to wait around until *you* decide when we should get married? I'll tell you this then. You want to postpone this wedding, then that's the end! In fact, I'll walk away right now if you like." The onslaught was so ferocious, the gauntlet flung down so brutally, that I caught my breath. Fear of his vehement anger, so reminiscent of my father, fears of being alone again made me retract immediately everything that I had said. "Oh, no! Don't be silly! I don't want to lose you. I love you! I only thought it's all a bit quick." The cowardly and feminine reaction seemed to pacify him. I apologised again, soothed his anger with soft words and we resumed our walk home. The die was cast. The subject was never mentioned again and I assuaged my fears with the preparations for the wedding.

Stanley was keen on getting married in a Welsh church and we found one in the City of London, St Benet's guild church at Paul's Wharf, the incumbent being a vicar with the redoubtable name of Enoch Jones. I thought one couldn't get a name more Welsh-sounding than that. Because of the pressing problem of saving up enough money as a deposit on a house, Stanley suggested that we combine our salaries into one account in his name. This was to make sure that neither of us would spend much. I agreed without even thinking about it. Other problems surfaced. He refused to invite any members of his family, which meant that he needed a best man. The only possible person in his very small number of friends was a Welshman whom he had been at college with and whom he had met by chance again at the London Welsh Club. There was only one snag, Gareth refused to act as best man for him. It took all my powers of persuasion finally for him to agree. Neither of us wanted a white wedding, in fact I was just as bored with all the fuss as he was. But I did need a new outfit and found to my annoyance that I had to ask him for some money to buy one. He was not enthusiastic. According to him, I was already breaking into our savings, but when I remonstrated with him, he deigned to give me money for my bridal gown. I bought a pale-green fitted jacket and matching A-line skirt, with which I combined a small white cap, white gloves and black shoes. My wedding flowers were a spray of freesias, but no bouquet. We had no money for a photographer, so had to rely on one of the guests bringing a small Kodak camera, which is why in my photograph album, there are only dark, diminutive photos of the wedding party. The wedding morning dawned. I had to get up very early to buy all the food for the reception, since we had no refrigerator, come back and help Mum make the sandwiches and then rush to get ready myself. We took the bus to the church since Stanley said we could not afford a taxi there and back. The ceremony itself was quite bizarre. No sooner had Enoch started to deliver his words in what seemed to me a particularly 'hammy' way, all drama and sonority, than he discovered that half the congregation had no prayer books. He stopped in full flow, rushed out to the Vestry and then proceeded to hasten down the nave distributing books while Stanley and I were left high and dry standing at the altar. Stanley was very tense and edgy, but I felt as if I were hovering up above the whole proceedings, looking down at some sort of ancient ritual. I do not even remember making my vows, although I was assured later that my voice was loud and clear. It was a really weird experience. The 'reception' continued in this surreal manner. All the guests were from my family and friends except for Gareth, who removed himself rapidly from the spread put on by us. I was chatting happily to all and sundry, but Stanley ensconced himself in a chair by the window and refused to participate in the proceedings, in spite of all blandishments. His behaviour only underlined my parents' opinion of him as a boorish Welshman. A few hours later, we left the party to their own devices and went on our honeymoon to Brighton, of all places. We arrived quite late, and the 'comble' for me was to discover that one of my aunts, with a malicious sense of humour had bribed a hotel staff member to sew up the sheets so that we could not get in them. I was totally exhausted with all the events of the day and to have to sit down and unpick the blasted sheets before we could get into them was almost the last straw. That honour was awarded to what happened once we were in bed. Stanley tried to insist on claiming his conjugal rights. I thought this was absolutely stupid considering my state of exhaustion and the fact that we had been sleeping together for the last few months. We had the most unholy row, a fitting end to a wedding that one could say, with no shade of irony, was quite unusual. That was the inauspicious beginning of our three-day honeymoon. Still, the other days did compensate.

I was gratified to be going back to school as a respectable married woman, now a member of that select band in school who could spend hours discussing their husband's foibles. I was not so pleased to return to the poor lodgings which were now my permanent home. The worst horror to live with was that the only toilet was outside in the garden. Memories of my past homes. To get to it, one had to go downstairs, along the hallway, and through both the living room and kitchen of the owner's portion of the house, finally to arrive at the back door to the garden. This meant running the gamut of any of her friends who were in the house, who stared as I stumbled past them apologising profusely, and who, when they realised where I was heading, sniffed disparagingly at me. We decided at the end of term to seek alternate lodgings and I had the bright idea of advertising in the local paper for a house to rent, not just a flat. We seemed to be in luck. We had one response when we were in Wales and although the house would not be available until September, we decided to take it. We would be in Wales for the whole of the summer anyway. The journey to Wales that year was quite memorable. I clung on to Stanley's back with our luggage perched perilously behind me as he did seventy miles an hour on his little Lambretta. There were no motorways built then so it was the A5 all the way from the south-east of England to the north of Wales, not to be recommended without an overnight stop. Disaster struck us just outside Oswestry, where a car clipped the side of one of our suitcase on a mountain road and the bike veered and we fell off. Luckily we were not hurt, but I was bruised and both of us were shocked. Our luggage was strewn in the middle of the road and suffered another knock as another car passed by. By that time, a kindly resident had come out of his house and took us in for tea and biscuits. It took several days in Llanberis to recover from this episode.

I was looking forward to having our own home, albeit a rented one. When we arrived back from the summer holidays it was early evening. I looked at the house dubiously from the outside. It was very small and with a poor, mean look. Inside was worse; it was dark, damp and minuscule. I have always been affected by the atmospheres in houses. I know instinctively whether I am going to like them or not. I also have a horror of confined spaces. I had deep forebodings about this house, which had seemed to be the answer to our prayers, but which now typified both of my fears. The feelings were crystallised when I went into the bedroom which was so small that in it there was only a four-foot-size bed. I took one look at that bed, imagining having to sleep in it with Stanley, and promptly burst into tears.

"I can't stay here! It's awful. Look at the size of the bed!"

"What are you talking about?" replied Stanley, irritated at these emotions.

"Look at it! We can't sleep in that! It's not even the proper size for a double bed. And it's far too small and dark and horrible!" I shivered in disgust.

"What are we going to do then? We've got nowhere else to go. Let's just get to bed and look at it properly in the morning." A reasonable suggestion which in no way allayed my fears. I knew instinctively that I could not live in this place. Why didn't he understand that? I made a sudden decision.

"I know what I'm going to do. I'm going home to Mum's house, she's got a spare room".

"You can't be serious. We've paid a month's rent in advance for this and your father won't want us staying with him."

"I don't care. I'm leaving now, so don't unpack my things."

Stanley could do nothing with me. He stared at me unsure what to do next. Then, seeing how upset I was, he shrugged his shoulders and quietly began to move our cases out of the odious house. We arrived late and threw ourselves on my mother's mercy. She was very good about it, probably glad to have some company again and also some extra money. We were to stay with my parents for most of that year, while we saved hard for a house. But it was not a happy time. Stanley could not face seeing my parents every evening, so spent most of his time in the pub, while I had to listen to my mother telling me ad nauseum that I had chosen 'a wrong 'un'. I was even reduced to writing pitiful letters, expostulating about his behaviour and putting them on his pillow for him to read when he rolled in at nearly midnight. Such behaviour on his part could have finished our marriage before it had really begun, except for the fact that he exchanged his Lambretta for a cheap car and we spent most weekends scouting around the area looking for houses to buy. We mollified my mother somewhat by taking her with us; she was thrilled at being in a car. We eventually found some new houses being built in Chipping Ongar, (the name intrigued me) about a forty-five minute drive from Plaistow. We were very fortunate to be able to buy the show house at a reduced price. I felt that all our efforts to save had finally been vindicated. It was 1959, I was twenty-nine years old now, a successful teacher who was looking forward to starting a family in our own new, semi-detached three-bedroomed house in a pretty village in Essex. Only Stanley's name was on the mortgage because, being the Maths teacher, he looked after all our finances. I was not worried; the mere fact of moving into my own home seemed to be luxury beyond my wildest dreams.

Chapter 12
Songs of Innocence

The swinging sixties. How many lines of description, eulogy, appraisal have been written about that decade! Yet this tempestuous era did not suddenly occur, a bolt from the blue. There were already signs of change at the end of the 1950s, changing attitudes to authority, to the 'status quo'. It was manifest in a lessening of respect for the familiar norms of society, particularly the class structure, and an increasing scepticism about government. Most people had more disposable income, could even buy a car for the first time. We were included in that, although our 'banger', which was forever breaking down because Stanley saw no point in having it serviced, could hardly equate with Issigonis' revolutionary Mini. For women the greatest boon was the arrival of the contraceptive pill. No more agonising every month before the next period, as I used to. Women rejoiced in their new-found freedom to enjoy sex as much as men and even the wearing of trousers was accepted. Macmillan, the Prime Minister said; "We have never had it so good" and we believed him. In fact sex, sexual stimulants, sexual advertising have all since penetrated the main-stream of our society and there must surely be a backlash in the future.

There were some who were unable to share in the excitement. There were still many people who struggled to make ends meet. Young lower-middle-class people with children (and I could now equate myself with them) did not enjoy all this wealth. Teachers' salaries were still not commensurate with their qualifications, as doctors and solicitors were. True, we were certainly better off than our parents and could now afford washing machines and refrigerators and televisions, but these were now seen as necessities and there was usually little money left over at the end of the month for pleasure. As for me, soon to have children, the permissive society passed me by. I was already too old for miniskirts and pop songs, and our finances were stretched to the limit. On our first night in our own home I became very emotional. The tension of the move and the tearful farewell to my mother, finally caught up with me. After unloading all our belongings, Stan and I walked through the main street in Ongar that evening. There was not a soul to be seen, the road was empty, so different from the busy streets of London. The unaccustomed silence weighed down on me. I felt that I was a continent away from Shirley and our confidences. I even missed my mother's restrictive presence, which used to suffocate me. I thought about the future, my future with Stanley. I was to be bound and alone with Stanley for ever. I was overwhelmed with an intense feeling of loneliness. What Stella Gibbons called "The long monotony of marriage" in *Cold Comfort Farm* was beginning. I stood stock still in the street and burst into tears, unable to explain to Stanley all my mixed-up emotions. He did not understand my mental turmoil and resorted to his time-old strategy of plying me with glasses of sherry in the village pub. But I was apprehensive about our life together and the feeling remained intermittently until it was dissipated in the excitement of setting up home and planning the garden. The choice of a name for the house exercised me. Names have always been important to me. I still clung to a vestige of independence and was secretly quite annoyed once married to be called 'Mrs Jones'. I wanted to cry out, "I am not Mrs Jones, I am Sylvia White!" So when Stan told me that the Welsh word for 'White' was 'Wynne', which I thought much prettier-sounding anyway, we called the house 'Wyndale'. I still have a photograph taken by someone of the two of us together looking down with pride at the roses we had begun to grow in the garden. We were like two lovebirds building a nest together. I gave up the dutch cap and we waited for our first baby. It actually took me nine months to conceive. In the meantime, we settled in to the *train-train de la vie*. I stayed on at school until I was eight months pregnant to have more time with my baby afterwards. When I realised I had conceived, I spent hours reading Dr Spock's *Baby and Child Care*, a very popular book at that time, which purported to help one avoid all the problems of bringing up a baby. Many years later, Dr Spock was discredited, but the damage was done. He was my Bible. I was fully armed for the event. I attended prenatal classes at the weekend, although I couldn't persuade Stan to join me and in the event they proved to be useless. I was so overwhelmed by the whole procedure when I gave birth that I forgot to practise the breathing exercises we had been taught to help relieve the pain.

I remember lying in the bath one evening, watching my tiny baby moving gently in my womb and the skin of my stomach stretching to accommodate its movements. A leg or an elbow would jut out spasmodically and then there would be a rippling action across the whole of my stomach. I imagined the embryo stretching with satisfaction. Then I was suddenly seized with apprehension. This baby *had* to come out! How would I cope with such a seismic event? How painful would it be? Would I be able to bear the pain? Why hadn't my mother explained it all to me, she who had borne eight children, to see four of them die later? Caught up in these fears, I decided I wouldn't mind dying now to avoid such trauma. I remembered David Lodge's comment, "Literature is mostly about having sex and not much about having children. Life is the other way around." How right he was. Perhaps I wasn't meant for motherhood, I should never have married... Such thoughts would race through my brain until the warmth of the bathwater eased my fears. Then a few days later the inevitable happened. I was woken up in the middle of the night with sharp pains in my stomach. Was this it? I was more frightened of waking Stan for a false alarm than concerned about the early pains. Should I let him sleep longer? Then a sudden stronger pain made me dig him in the ribs to take me to the hospital quickly. Fortunately, it was not far to Ongar Cottage Hospital, one of those caring hospitals that have since ceased to exist. Sudden panic; suitcase, car, hospital, only to be examined on arrival and told 'It isn't time yet Mrs Jones'. Stan departed and I was placed in a room on my own, lying on a high trolley like a beached whale. The pains had gone and the silence was awesome. I felt as if my soul was being transported high into the sky, that I was freed from my corporeal self, that ungainly body still tied to the earth, while I was suspended in deep darkness, floating higher and higher in space. I slept fitfully, woken occasionally by a nurse coming to examine me. Morning came with another inspection and then the calm was replaced by excitement and bustle. The birth was not proceeding normally. The placenta, the baby's life nourishment was emerging from my womb before the baby. There was blood spilling out onto my legs and sheets. Tampons were placed to mop up some of the blood and then I was taken off the trolley onto a stretcher, covered with a bright-red blanket, ready to be taken the six miles by ambulance to Epping. I could feel the stretcher being lowered gently and expertly down the winding stairs of the hospital and when I did open my eyes, I saw Stanley's white face swimming into view. He had just arrived, expecting to see a happy mother and child, and I was being taken out on a stretcher. I clung ferociously to his hand as the ambulance sped through the still, silent, dark countryside to St Margaret's Hospital in Epping. Blood was still coursing down my legs, I thought that I would probably die, but that Stan's grip might possibly save me. In the event, all was well and I was finally delivered of a tiny baby boy whom we christened David Wynne Jones. The next day I was conveyed back to the Ongar hospital for two more weeks' rest. But 'rest' was hardly the word to describe what ensued. There were continuing problems. It appeared that my nipples were semi-inverted and David was having trouble sucking on them. I was forced ignominiously to do exercises to try to bring them forward but to no avail. More anxiety. Was he getting enough milk? The hospital staff soothed my fears and gave him extra milk. Each feeding time was such a struggle for him and exhausting for me, that he was eventually fed from a bottle, which relieved me because then I could actually see how much he had taken and compare it with Dr Spock's recommendations. But I felt that I had already failed as a mother. One of the first tests of a good mother was the ability to feed her own child and I had signally failed. I felt this particularly, because a young woman in the opposite bed, whose baby was born the same day, had nipples that stood out like miniature dummies. And her boy sucked very contentedly on them. Her name was Audrey and she became a lifelong friend. She and her husband came from Stratford but, like us, were living in Ongar because the houses were cheaper. He was a husband 'in absentia' most of the time, too busy going to night school to visit his wife in hospital and she had to endure the unpleasant experience of seeing all the other husbands arrive with smiles and flowers while she was most of the time alone. Stanley was marvellous, visiting me every day, thrilled with his new son.

What love we showered on that baby. He allayed all my fears about marriage and childbirth. I was almost overwhelmed both by his beauty and by the responsibility for him. He was so vulnerable. What if I decided not to feed him? He would die. So I made sure that no such thing could happen, by feeding him too much, forcing him to take the required ounces of milk. That may be why he is so fastidious about food now... David and I shared a few contretemps in that early period of his life. A few days after bringing him home, I took him down to the shops in his pram to buy food and left the pram outside the baker's shop. In those days, this was quite normal. What was not so normal was the fact that I came out of the shop and walked home. Only when I unlocked the front door did I realise that I had left him outside the baker's shop! I had completely forgotten about him! Another time, he narrowly avoided an injury in the car. Stanley had to make an emergency stop on our way home from work one time. The carrycot and baby on the back seat were pitched violently forward. If I had not been in the passenger seat, he would have shot through the windscreen. This was before seat belts had even been discussed in Britain, although France had made them compulsory much earlier. I've noticed how we are often years behind France in innovations, even though we have this overweening sense of superiority over the 'Frogs', encouraged as always by the media.

The third, not-so-pleasant event for David and me, occurred when Audrey and I were walking along a deserted country lane and spied a café set back from the roadside. We decided to see if we could get a cup of tea. It was hot and we were thirsty so I offered to see if it was open. The front door was locked and I decided to go to the side entrance round the corner. Stepping under a pretty-looking porch, I was suddenly stopped in my tracks. There, draped across the width of the door, basking in the sunshine was an enormous Alsatian dog eyeing me watchfully. For a split second we stared at each other. I was able to register his amber-yellow eyes before terror took hold of me. I turned on my heels and ran back down the path. Of course, everyone knows that one should never run away from a dog, but we had no experience of animals in our house, both my mother and father agreeing for once that they were dirty, smelly objects. Consequently. I grew up with a fear of dogs, particularly Alsatians. They always seemed to me like wolves (well, they are of the same genetic breed) and I had read too many of *Grimm's Fairy Tales* describing the terror they can inspire in a community. So I acted quite unconsciously and irrationally and the dog, much more rationally, followed suit. He leapt up, barking furiously, raced after me down the path. I managed to get as far as David's pram at the end of it, which appeared to provide me with some sort of protection from the slavering beast. I grabbed the handle and slewed the pram around. David was immediately flung out, coverings and all. It would be better not to dwell on what could have happened then. Suffice to say, the dog's owner had emerged from the house by this time, had surveyed the scene and shrieked at the dog to 'Heel!' I could tell by the panic in her voice that she saw the danger only too clearly. The dog stopped in his tracks and slunk back resentfully, deprived of its prey. Audrey had been watching aghast, David was screaming on the ground while Anthony, Audrey's son, set up his own noisy chorus in sympathy. I had to endure a long diatribe from the woman about behaviour in front of a dog, before we were able to escape. We never did get that cup of tea.

I became more friendly with Audrey. We had already decided that if we had to choose between our husbands or our babies, it would be the men who had to go. A prophetic decision. David was a very quiet baby, seemingly detached from all the bustle around him. When I went out walking with Audrey, he would lie like a pale corpse in his high pram, tightly swaddled in blankets. Anthony was the opposite. Not so securely bandaged as David, he would wave his chubby legs in the air and kick off his coverings, red in the face with his exertions. On our first Christmas with David we bought him lots of little presents, all neatly wrapped up, so that he could have the pleasure of unwrapping them. We sat him in the middle of the carpet and looked at him with expectation as he started to handle the presents. But there was not a glimmer of excitement from him; he sat stolidly, calmly attempting to unwrap all his presents without even a smile on his face. He examined each carefully and then placed them neatly in a pile on the side. And that was that. None of the excitement that we had expected. In fact, he only seemed to laugh properly when he was tired. I threw myself into the part of a real housewife and mother with gusto, inviting neighbours in for coffee, cooking a Sunday roast every Sunday. God! How I hated what D. H. Lawrence called 'the surfeited dreariness of English Sunday afternoons'. I even insisted on cleaning the oven after the roast *every week.* The editor of *Women's Own* would have been very proud of me. I conformed excellently to the stereotype of the loving wife and mother and the super efficient housewife. But it was hard having to juggle career and motherhood, not to mention attending to Stanley's wants in and out of bed when I was dropping with fatigue. Fortunately, there were the long holidays. We took David to Wales, where Stanley's Aunt Buddug, who was childless, went into ecstasies over him. In the Jones family the rumour was rife that she had deliberately refused to have sex with her husband for fear of giving birth. I never found out the truth. David was to be deprived quite soon of his paternal grandparents. Only a few years later, Stanley's father died of cancer, to be followed in quick succession by his mother, and later his brother and sister, all of cancer. In spite of not liking her very much, I grieved for his mother. She was so diminutive, seemingly so frail. She had been burdened for years with a feckless husband and recalcitrant children. I had no opportunity to attend any of their funerals. According to Stanley, women were not permitted at Welsh funerals. How true that was I never attempted to find out, being too preoccupied with my own family. As a result of these early deaths, Stanley began to think that his family suffered from a death wish, but at the present age of seventy he must surely reluctantly concede that such a conceit is now inappropriate. It was one of his stock excuses for avoiding difficulties.

David grew into a very pretty baby with slanting blue eyes and blond curly hair. Where did the curly hair come from? Definitely the Irish family. My mother's brothers both had narrow, slanting eyes and the long, Irish face and we have inherited them. I agonised over David growing up. He crawled later, walked later and talked later than Anthony and I feared he was backward in some way. When a toddler, he would not join in with the other children playing in the park, but preferred to sit by me watching placidly all their boisterous antics. His personality was evident quite early on. I am pleased to say he is not in any way backward and has become very successful academically. But he is still placid and quiet, a very reserved man.

The problem of an unwanted pregnancy still dogged me. I was reluctant to use the contraceptive pill because of any possible health risks. So I had again recourse only to the dutch cap, which was apparently now only 80% safe. And so it transpired; eighteen months after David's birth I fell pregnant again. Stan and I were not too concerned because David gave us so much joy that we wanted another child. It was only seven months into my pregnancy with satisfactory health checks, that I began to swell visibly. I now weighed thirteen stone. Even the staff at school started to comment. My doctor decided I should have an X-ray to see what was happening. When one considers now all the technology surrounding the birth of a baby, with scans, ultra-sound, amniocentis, it seems almost unbelievable that the current belief in the sixties was that X-rays should be avoided unless imperative. Even to arrange it was difficult. Stan had to take David to Mum's house, take a day off work and then drive me to Epping hospital. On a plea from the doctor, we agreed to take another hugely pregnant woman with us to have the same check-up. She gave us a running commentary all the way to Epping hospital, describing in great detail all the women in her family who had had twins. She was quite sure she would also have twins and seemed placidly happy about the possibility. Listening to her, I was suddenly fearful. What if I *were* carrying twins? My mind sheered away in horror at the thought of the consequences. Two of everything would have to be bought. I consoled myself with the thought that no one in either of our families had had twins. My fears were forgotten in the difficulties I had in manoeuvring my huge bulk on to the table for the X-ray. Then we waited for the results. Surprisingly quickly, the nurse came in to the waiting room and said smiling. 'I can confirm that you Mrs Bradford have one big healthy baby, and you Mrs Jones are carrying twins.' The words fell on my ears, but I didn't really understand them. I blurted out, stammering, "You must be mistaken! It's Mrs Bradford who is expecting twins! Could there be a mix-up with the X-rays?" She looked rather vexed for a moment and then smiled again. "Mrs Jones, I can assure you that there has been no mistake. You are carrying two healthy babies. The X-ray results will be sent to your doctor, but I advise you to see her yourself as soon as possible."

In the car I started weeping as the full implications of the news hit me. I turned to Stan, "I can't bear it! I won't be able to cope. It's hard enough for me to manage now." A paroxysm of sobs prevented me from saying any more. I leaned against the car door wishing I were dead. Both Stan and Mrs Bradford tried to cheer me up, saying the news was great, I would have two for the price of one and other such inanities. It was only when I broke the news to my family that it was discovered that my Irish uncle Danny, a very merry man, had been a twin, but the other one had died at birth. And I hadn't even insured against twins. This was the end of my teaching career for the foreseeable future. The doctor confirmed that my blood pressure was raised (no wonder!) and I should try to take life more easily. I went with Stanley and David to stay with my mother during the day, so that she could help out somewhat. The winter of 1962/3 was brutally cold and we had a particularly heavy fall of snow. Two weeks into the new plan of action, I slipped on the snow outside my mother's house, the doctor was called in, my waters had started to break. I was rushed to hospital, where they managed by bed rest to stop the pregnancy from developing, because I was only seven and a half months into it. But there was no suggestion that I should leave the hospital. I was there until the birth. I quite enjoyed that time: no cooking, no cleaning ovens, no teaching. It was hospital policy not to let mothers awaiting a birth see all the newborn babies being fed by their happy mothers, so I had my own single ward. I was happy chatting to the patients in the other ward and then each night returning to the quietness of mine. Stan, bless him, came to visit me every evening, braving the treacherously icy roads. We were shown the X-ray of the twins, one foetus lying horizontally across the top of my womb, the other squeezed into the space below. I would speculate on their differing personalities as I watched their movements. The horizontally-placed foetus seemed to be much quieter than the other, who kicked around vigorously. The fateful day arrived when I went into labour. I had much more attention this time and was given pethidine to dull the pain. But my life has never been simple. On the operating table, I was religiously following instructions to 'Push hard, Mrs Jones!' while grabbing the pethidine inhaler to help me between the labour pangs. The round, brilliant, white light above the delivery table shone down on my labours. I could sense its glare through my closed eyes. Then, suddenly, frighteningly, the light was extinguished. Darkness descended on me. Opening my eyes in sheer terror, I saw nothing but an impenetrable blackness. 'This is it,' I thought. 'This is what comes of wanting more children. You are about to die.' I waited to see my past life flashing by me, but heard only faint noises, whispers, and then gradually more sounds. As startlingly as the light had been cut off, it reappeared again. The theatre was once again bathed in a harsh glare. There had been a power cut and an emergency generator had been brought in. I wasn't dead, after all but still in labour. Finally the first baby arrived with the screwed-up, red face of a little girl. I thought, 'God! How much longer?" The pains ceased and I lay exhausted on the table. Then all was quiet again until a nurse whispered, 'Mrs Jones, you can rest now. Your other baby is not ready to be born yet.' Not ready? That foetus kicking in my womb for so long had decided to have a rest. What an inopportune time to choose, I thought resentfully. Three long hours more I lay on the table before the second baby decided to emerge. Further complications; it was a breech birth, but there was more room for her (yes, it was a girl) and she was delivered quite swiftly and safely. Her bottom came out before her head and I swear to this day, if one looks closely, one can see the difference between the two of them, Kathryn, the eldest one, with a slightly narrower face as she was squeezed through the birth canal, and Valmai with a wider, rounded face as befits someone who slipped out in the passage created by her sister. No one else can see this difference but me.

When we were all cleaned up and ready for visiting hours, Stanley came in with a tale to tell. Apparently, on arrival he had inquired urgently, 'How are they?' and the nurse had replied, 'The three are doing very nicely, Mr Jones.' He was staggered – he thought I had given birth to triplets! The saga of the birth is not yet quite over. I had the same problems with my nipples, second time around, so categorically refused to go through the same worry. I informed the young nurse that I did not want to breastfeed. She refused to accept my decision, believing that I should at least make an effort. I pointed out that my breasts had not changed significantly after two years; if I hadn't been able to feed the first baby, I was hardly likely to be able to feed two. Thereupon she grew nasty and informed me, 'If you don't even try to feed your babies, don't think we shall. They'll starve!" What emotional blackmail, in my weakened state. I could have burst into tears at this cruelty, but decided to appeal to the Matron who, thank goodness, agreed with me. Two days later, the hospital had a gastroenteric bug scare and the whole of the maternity ward was closed. I was thrust out unceremoniously back home with two three-day-old babies. Even my doctor was horrified and offered to lend me her cleaner to do my household chores. With four mouths to feed (I discounted myself), I was down to ten stone in a few weeks because of all the stress. The night feeding was the worst. I was in the main bedroom and Stanley slept in the smaller room. The theory was that I would call him when one of them woke up. Should one then feed that one, get her back to sleep and doze fitfully for the next one to wake up? Or should one wake the other one as well and try to persuade a very sleepy baby to take some food? Even worse, I was so stressed that I could not sleep in the same room as the babies. Every sigh, whimper, light snore that they made had me wake up rigid with fear that it was time to feed them. So I insisted in a tired frenzy that Stan change bedrooms with me, so that I could sleep alone. In this way, I was able to enjoy a few hours' sleep before the dreaded feeding time. Nappy-washing was a real chore. This was before the days of disposable nappies. I hated the messy excreta-filled nappies which had to be cleaned off before being put in the washing machine. With two babies the job was even more disgusting. To feed the twins during the day, I would prop one of them in one arm of the settee while I fed the other, trying not to listen to the other's vociferous complaints. They were much less placid than David, starting up from sleep at the slightest noise. I tried to put them out in their pram in the garden during the day to get some fresh air, but they would have none of that. Even the noise of the birds made them scream like banshees.

Obviously, my health was suffering. I experienced one really frightening moment on a Sunday afternoon. I went up after Sunday lunch to the bedroom to have a rest, slept fitfully, only to wake up to the fact that I could not *see* anything. I believed I had gone blind. I could not get to the stairs to call Stanley, so screamed at him to come up. It was a most horrifying experience and lasted for some hours. The doctor was called and she examined me, pronouncing that it was a fit of nerves and that I should go back to bed straightaway. She sent a nurse in for a day until I recovered. We had left David with my mother for the first week or so, but I wanted him back as soon as possible. Bringing him home from my mother's house was fraught with tension. He had been almost a month with my mother and when Stanley went to get him, he refused to get in the car. Stanley was in no mood for tantrums, so tore him from my mother's grasp as she protested and David bawled out his own dislike of the situation. It would probably have been better if he had stayed longer with my mother for all the attention he received when he came home. He went from being cosseted and given loving attention to being almost ignored. I confess that I do not remember much about him in the house those first few weeks. Even now, he is slightly resentful of the attention that had been given to the twins by everyone, even neighbours in the street who cooed and aahed over them and did not even see him. I do believe he still has a chip on his shoulder as a result...

Audrey had also had two more children by this time, although not twins. What a feat it was to go anywhere with six very young children! The chic middle-class customers in shops would eye us askance as we trooped in to the shops. It was all great fun. Audrey then dropped a bombshell. She was selling up and leaving Ongar because of noisy neighbours. I was bereft. Who would I laugh with? So I persuaded Stanley to do the same. We had made enough profit on the house in Ongar to be able to move back nearer to London and his school. Stanley started to look for another house in Wanstead, a much more salubrious area than Plaistow. It had a pleasantly middle-class atmosphere, little traffic, lots of greenery. We found a house with a huge garden tucked away at the end of a cul-de-sac. It was quite rural. The large back garden included a magnificent weeping ash, its feathery leaves casting dappled shadows on the lawn. There was a front garden as well, but even more interesting was the secret enclosed, communal garden in the front, encircled by the houses. We lived next door to the 'big house' with its lake, which was big enough to sail a small boat on. Once we had moved in and acquainted ourselves with the neighbours, my three children were allowed to use the pond and their garden, playing with their two young children, the youngest of whom was the twins' age. I remember being in this lovely garden one summer's day and hearing a most peculiar creaking sound. It was one of the large trees in the garden of the 'big house'. I watched it and it suddenly started trembling, its small, dainty foliage shaking as if in pain and then suddenly and most gracefully, it began to lean over and finally toppled into the lake, quite dead. It was very sad.

One of the problems in our new house Craigmore, was the fact that there was no central heating, only handsome fireplaces which were totally inadequate for the size of the house. I felt the lack of warmth bitterly. I had only enjoyed such a luxury twice before; at college and in my last, modern house, and was determined to have the same in Craigmore. Stanley said we could not afford it, and since he held the purse strings, I was silenced for a while. But I soon persuaded him to agree to install oil central heating, the cheapest at that time. I can still remember the feeling of perfect bliss as the heating filtered through the rooms like a warm tide flooding the creeks and pools at the seaside. The only drawback was the large oil tank sited in the garden. This was a major enticement for Alistair, the youngest of the children next door. He would steal cupfuls of it to satisfy his craving for lighting fires, egged on, I must say, by the twins. Many years later, we heard that he had been arrested for arson... He would also persuade them to climb out of the window after they had gone to bed to have more secret adventures in the gardens. In the house on the other side of the secret garden lived an Italian woman, Marina Orpin and her husband and young child. She was very elegant and quite charming. I was amused to discover that when entering her house, one had to remove one's shoes and don furry mules, which had the dual purpose of keeping the floor clean and buffing it up at the same time. Together we pulled down the unsightly wire around that secret garden, opening it up. We tended it lovingly, planting new shrubs and mowing the tiny lawn, creating an oasis of tranquillity only a hundred yards from the High Street and the Tube to Central London.

We stayed in Craigmore for twelve years, and the children had an idyllic childhood, safe from traffic and noise. They spent most of their time in the garden getting up to mischief. Poor David had a real job trying to limit the twins' subversive tendencies. A good example of their naughtiness was the Sunday school concert. All three went regularly, but not religiously, to the local Sunday school and even joined the choir. David had a pleasant singing voice and took all the rehearsals seriously. A special concert was arranged in the church hall one time and the children all trooped onto the stage dutifully to sing the songs they had learned. No sooner had the pianist started to play, when Valmai caught the eye of Kathryn and the pair of them dissolved into giggles and couldn't stop. The whole proceedings were interrupted by this sudden outburst of mirth. The pianist ceased playing and marched the two of them firmly off the stage. I was mortified. Apart from such contretemps, I was very happy in Craigmore. When the twins were born, I obviously could not continue full-time teaching for a time, so I was fortunate enough to be able to work three days a week instead. I lost my position as head of department to Thelma my younger colleague, but was not unduly worried, since I had enough at home to keep me occupied. Came the time when East Ham Education Authority decided it could not afford to keep part-timers, so I had to leave Brampton Manor, which was a great wrench for me. I had been very happy and professionally fulfilled there. Luckily, I found another part-time post with Redbridge Education Authority, in Nightingale secondary school in Wanstead. It was a secondary school like Brampton Manor, but the children came from much more affluent parents and it was also a mixed school, so for the first time I would have to teach boys as well as girls. The downside was that since there were more grammar schools in Redbridge than there were in East Ham, the more intelligent pupils had been 'creamed off' and those who were left in the secondary school were mostly not so bright as the Brampton Manor girls I had taught. French was not considered very important in this school, the headmaster was much more into the new mixed ability method of teaching which was very fashionable at this time. Personally, I thought that to lump children of all abilities together regardless of their educational level of attainment was sheer madness. It created huge problems of discipline and preparation for the poor embattled teachers and a lack of motivation both in the brighter pupils and the poorest, with only the middle section of the ability range making any real progress. The Maths and French teachers, trying to teach linear subjects, had even more problems. Eventually even the dogma-driven head realised he had to compromise his egalitarian principles and he 'set' the Maths and French classes into ability ranges, but the rest of the staff had to battle on to conform to his 'modern' educational ideas. He eventually left to become a lecturer in mixed ability teaching and left the school with real problems, which took years to alleviate.

To fill up my timetable, I was also allocated a class of school-leavers who had been turfed out of their own classes for insubordination. They were all boys and I had them for the whole of Friday afternoons, since they no longer had a proper timetable. I might have congratulated myself on my discipline after all these years, but I was no match for this lot. I could not even begin to teach them anything, since they would not listen, so for a time I was content to let them do what they liked as long as they kept quiet. As if to emphasise their rejection by the school establishment, lessons were taken in a mobile classroom in the grounds of the school. To me, at least, this was an advantage. The noise they created could not be heard so easily. The boys played cards, read magazines, did any residual homework (they seemed to have very little) but it was still an uphill task to keep them quiet. I reached the point where I could not sleep the night before I took them, so awful was the experience. Finally I could stand it no longer and went to the headmaster to remonstrate. He was a handsome man with steely-blue eyes that put the fear of God into both children and staff. He listened calmly to my piteous pleas to be relieved of this terrible class and then said, "What you are asking, Miss White is quite impossible. I cannot start tinkering with the timetable just because you have some difficulties of discipline. I am fully aware that this class causes discipline problems, but you must find your own strategies to solve them. You have carte blanche to teach whatever you like as long as it conforms to good educational practice." I had a sudden flash of inspiration, "Would you mind if I take them out of school for a particular project to study?"

"An excellent idea, Mrs Jones! These are intelligent children and would respond to a new initiative. Just keep them occupied and amused.". That was his parting shot, but from then on, there were no more problems for me. The sheer enjoyment both the boys and I had in getting away from the stuffy school atmosphere proved its own worth. I ascertained that most of them knew little of London, its fascinating richness and variety. Many of them had never been to the City of London, although they had frequented the West End for shopping with their parents. We went to the Spitalfield and Billingsgate markets, to the Tower of London, to the Docks and to the great museums and they were model boys. It was an enthralling time for them before they left school and a very salutary one for me, realising that one needs to start from the interest of the children themselves to motivate them.

I used to invite my parents occasionally to Sunday lunch. They were dutifully impressed by our spacious house. My father had become much quieter by that time; retirement and old age were relieving him of some of his earlier frustrations. His temper was still very unpredictable, so one had to be careful not to annoy him. I had no idea how he treated my mother when they were alone, because she would never discuss him. That is until I visited her one day and she suddenly said, 'I don't know whether I can cope with him much longer. I just can't manage him.' I thought she was talking about his uncertain temper, but she was in fact referring to his physical condition. Apparently he had not been well and had gone to see the doctor who diagnosed narrowing of the arteries in the brain. I found out that this was the onset of senile dementia, now called Alzheimer's disease. Eventually the burden became too much for my mother. He had become incontinent and refused to go to bed, so she had to leave him slumped in an armchair in front of the dying embers of the fire. He was taken into Leytonstone hospital in the geriatric wing. I went one day to visit him. I had arrived just as the nurses were changing his sheets. Still in his nightshirt, he had been flung, like a doll, onto the next bed, his legs and bottom quite naked for all to gaze on. It was such a humiliating position that my eyes filled with tears of sadness for him. This was the man who had terrorised us as children, now reduced to the helplessness of a baby. Tucked up once again in clean sheets, his face was as soft and vacant as a newborn child. He didn't even recognise me. When I left the hospital, I was weeping tears of bitterness and anger and sorrow. When he finally died, we were in Wales and I rushed back to the funeral. I saw him for the last time in the mortuary, his face immobile and waxen-white, but he had already gone. The spirit had departed. I could shed no more tears. He had been an awful father and husband and I could not forgive him, but I did begin to understand the frustrations which had caused him to behave so terribly.

Gradually I became disenchanted with part-time work. Since I was the only French teacher, I had to undertake the duties of a head of department, ordering books, preparing pupils for the CSE exam. All this without any extra salary. Also, I never had time to get involved with the full-time staff. Most of my energies were concentrated on my own children and the pleasures they generated. Stanley was never interested in taking the children anywhere. In fact, I was coming to the cruel conclusion that he was a totally unreconstructed male. He would go nowhere with them, except to the sweet shop on Saturday morning to buy them some sweets. In all their childhood he never once pushed their prams anywhere. He believed in a strict division of labour; for him, women were put on this earth to serve men as sex objects, housewives and cooks. His job was to look after the garden (desultorily), do any small repairs (seldom) and occasionally a bit of cooking, when the mood took him. He quite enjoyed taking charge of the kitchen at odd moments and would produce some of the Welsh dishes he grew up with. 'Lobscouse', a sort of Irish stew and 'stoon struden' a mixture of potatoes and swede which were delicious. As far as I can recollect, he never went with me to the supermarket to buy food. When I look at the young men with their wives and children in the supermarkets today, I really envy their wives. Yet his principles were not so firm that he wanted me at home all the time. Oh no! He wanted me out at work to bring in the money, unlike my sisters' husbands who refused to let them work while the children were young. For this I am now grateful, since I had a proper job which gave me financial independence finally, while they found that they were too old for any sort of real job, and consequently have never been able to enjoy a financially secure retirement.

Yet the old yearning for something more began to rise in me again. I missed the friendships I had had at Brampton Manor and the bright children I taught and above all I missed the intellectual stimulation that Shirley was getting at East Ham Grammar School for Girls. She was teaching sixth form French, reading the classic novels with the girls, finding the satisfaction of preparing them for A-levels. She had also now taken a decision to read for a degree. I was thrilled when she told me and began seriously to consider doing the same. But the first hurdle to get over was the lack of Latin, since one could not read for a French degree without it. Shirley started a two-year evening class in Latin and tried to persuade me to join her. I wrestled with my conscience as to what I should do. The job of running a home and bringing up such young children, plus the part-time teaching was totally exhausting and I did not see how I could manage any more work. It took me a whole year to decide and then my thoughts crystallised. I hated teaching French to the less intelligent pupils, most of whom saw no reason to burden their brain with that foreign stuff, and I saw no future for myself in teaching if I continued as I was. Could I do what Shirley was doing? But she had no children or husband and could devote herself much more to her studies. I was galvanised finally into looking for an evening class in Latin for one year only, since I wanted to start the degree with Shirley. In our area of London, the east end, Latin was not high on any college's priority, but serendipity! I found that Walthamstow Technical College ran a one-year course in Latin. Having finally decided, I cajoled Stanley into babysitting on that one night a week (memories of the time spent cajoling my father to give me money for the cinema, when young). This may seem strange, having to persuade my own husband to look after his own children. But that was the position and I had to live with it. Occasionally he baulked, as when his brother came to visit and they wanted to go to the pub and laughed at me for insisting it was my night off for my Latin class, so I had to miss my lecture. I nursed a secret resentment at this male chauvinistic behaviour. On the whole Stanley treated my Latin studies as a harmless pastime, so he was acquiescent most of the time. He scoffed at the idea of a degree though.

The year passed, I was given an A grade in Latin O-level, much to the chagrin of Shirley who after two years study only managed a B grade, but to be fair to her, she was studying Latin literature as well as

Language. I was still not sure about committing myself to a four-year evening course at Birbeck College, which meant reading for a French Honours degree with English subsidiary. I could not even be sure whether I would qualify. We discovered we had to be interviewed as to our suitability for a degree course before we could even be considered for entry to Birkbeck. If this were satisfactory, we would then sit an entrance examination, an oral examination and an interview with the head of the French department before we could be accepted. So, as usual, I decided to attempt all this before I finally made up my mind whether to start a degree or not. The problems this decision would cause with Stanley seemed insurmountable and I was not at all sure where this would lead to in my marriage. But like Scarlett O'Hara in *Gone with the Wind*, I did not need to decide anything yet, for tomorrow was another day.

Chapter 13
Marriage in Freefall

Back in London, Stanley was once again on his familiar stomping ground, able to meet his school pals in pubs more easily. Yet I was content with my life as mother, cook and housewife. The problems of school now took second place. Only the ends of terms were difficult both for Stanley and me, when we were bone tired. We argued incessantly over trivial things, until the exquisite pleasure of reconciliation in bed. External events bothered me little; only the assassination of President Kennedy affected me as it did the whole nation. To watch the scene on television where he was shot and slumped down onto his lovely wife was harrowing and shocking. The other momentous news that cut through my self-induced contentment was when Neil Armstrong and his team set foot on the moon in the space ship Apollo 11. For the first time ever, flickering pictures of the world seen from space appeared on the television; the intense blue sea surrounding the earth was really beautiful; the astronauts bobbed comically across the dust-bowl surface of the moon. I could not really take in the enormity of what had been achieved.

All this cosy family life was soon to change dramatically. After suffering the exigencies of Birkbeck's entrance requirements, I received a letter informing me that I had been accepted to read for a French and English degree. And then I really felt I had no choice as to whether I could manage it or not or even what Stanley would say, because I was so exhilarated at the thought of studying again. Then came the dubious pleasure of telling him the news. I chose an enchanting summer's morning in the garden with Audrey present to explain that I had been offered a place to read for an Honours degree at Birkbeck, that I had decided to accept it and from October, for ten weeks every term, for four years, I would be going to Central London to evening classes. A sudden silence – the peace of the morning was shattered. I realised not for the first time in my life how 'peculiar' I seemed to many of my acquaintances, since the high spot of my week for the last year had been to go to a Latin evening class. Happily Shirley shared my passion, so I was not so alone. But I hadn't bargained for Stanley's reaction. Afterwards on every possible occasion, he would scoff at me saying that a degree meant nothing, and anyway, a French degree would be an easy option, not difficult like Maths. But he never really forgave me.

I made sure that I wouldn't give him any grounds for complaint. Each day after teaching, I would pick up the children, rush back home, cook a meal, sit with them and Stanley to see that they ate it, even wash up, before I rushed off to Tottenham Court Road by six thirty. I was invariably late, sidling in apologetically next to Shirley. I enjoyed the English lectures much more than the French. We had one very good English lecturer, a specialist in Thomas Hardy, who enthused us so much that we both felt we could teach Hardy ourselves. The French course was very traditional with no sop to modern trends of fluency and contemporary social life. We studied Old French which was like a foreign language and gave me almost a nervous breakdown in my efforts to master it, and then we galloped through the centuries from medieval texts such as *Aucassin et Nicolette* and *La Chanson de Roland* right through to twentieth century literature. Interesting as these works were to me intellectually, I felt they were of little use professionally, apart from such twentieth century authors as Sartre and Camus. My spoken French was quite weak; I had not spoken the language since my student days in Paris, but after three years of intensive study for a degree, I could read French with aplomb, but I needed years of visits to France and sixth-form teaching to gain real proficiency. It can be imagined that the amount of study I did at home was minimal, being left mostly to the school holidays. After teaching for four days a week, lectures for four evenings a week and looking after the children, I would be totally exhausted and had no time to give in any work. Not that the college seemed to care; no one questioned my apparent apathy. Having been accepted for the course, one was left to one's own devices until, at the end of four years, one was faced with ten, three-hour examinations in the space of six days. It was 'sink or swim'.

I learned what tiredness was in those hectic days; the feeling of having ants crawling all over me in the train at the end of evening lectures, unable to sit still, shifting my body around to find some relaxation – it was horrendous, the *coup de grace* being that when I arrived home, Stanley would invariably call out, "Are you going to make some coffee?" He was not at all happy to be kept at home forcibly for four evenings a week, and made very sure he had his ration of free time when I wasn't at college. After the third year of this gruelling existence, I suddenly realised that I had had not retained anything really significant in my lectures and reading, because I did not have the time to study anything in depth. The thought of failure after all these efforts was too depressing to contemplate, so I started to panic. Shirley, as usual, suggested a way out. She was also finding the course difficult because she was still teaching full-time and was having problems with her father, who had incipient Alzheimer's disease. She announced that she was going to take the final year off work. Her bank balance was healthier than mine and she reckoned she could manage it. Initially, I was aghast at this news. Not only was I going to fail abysmally, but Shirley would emerge with a first- or second-class degree. What could I do? There was no possibility that Stanley would agree to help me. He was standing on the side waiting to say, "I told you so!" I had recourse only to my poor mother who – bless her! – borrowed money from somewhere (she wouldn't say where) so that I could take a year off. Hand on heart, I must say that it was only her generosity that made it possible for me to succeed.

I enjoyed so much that last year away from teaching. It was such a blessing to have time to study in depth and time to give to my children. I tried hastily to catch up with the last three years of the degree course and almost made myself ill in the process, suffering serious vertigo attacks until I learned to calm down. I remember meeting the twins after school one day, smiling at them and Valmai saying wonderingly, "Mum, why are you always so nice to us now?" I was quite shocked by that remark, suddenly realising that my studying had affected them all. The only other real crisis came when I was in the middle of those final exams. My sister Irene decided to come and stay for a few days, the day before my last two exams. She said she had problems with her husband and wanted to discuss them with me. I really could not say no. We spent the evening discussing her situation and went to bed very late. The next day I felt dreadful, barely able to drag myself to the Tube. I felt sick by lunchtime, could eat nothing and wandered around the students' union building looking for somewhere to lay my head. I found a sofa and immediately fell into a fitful sleep, only to wake up feeling worse. The final exam, one of the most difficult, the French Essay was upon me. I realised I was in trouble when after thirty minutes, I still hadn't decided which question to answer. I rejected them all, because my brain wasn't functioning. Finally, in desperation, I chose one and with turgid, ponderous sentences attempted to make a cogent analysis of the difference between style and form in literature. This type of subject would have been beyond me in normal circumstances, but that day I was pausing every moment trying to think of what to say. Needless to say, my marks for that exam were very poor and cost me the difference between a First Class degree and an Upper Second. To this day, I regret that, although I was pleased that Shirley gained a fully-deserved First. At the end of this four-year slog, Shirley and I met for coffee to mull over the experience. We had always scoffed at the idea that a degree would make any difference to us and, a bit like Stanley, we were slightly contemptuous of degrees, but after that tremendous effort, we realised finally that four years of such discipline and such hard work had altered us in indefinable ways.

Immediately on completing my degree in June 1966, I was surprised to receive a letter from East Ham Education Authority offering me a temporary job until the end of the school year in the prestigious East Ham Boys' Grammar School. How they knew about my degree is still a mystery. But since I needed a job fast to start paying my mother back, I went for an interview with the French Inspector who asked me, somewhat tongue in cheek, I think:

"Don't you think that all your reading of the French eighteenth-century classics like Corneille and Racine was a bit of a waste of time for teaching French today?"

I remember answering in a toe-curlingly embarrassing way, about how important still were the ideals of honour and duty debated in Corneille's plays, how relevant they were to modern society and other such trite statements. He smiled, but seemed swayed more by my enthusiasm than my response. I taught French Literature to some really brilliant sixth form boys, one of whom after a few lessons, said to me in an aggrieved tone, "Mrs Jones, we aren't at university yet, you know!" While at the school, I was informed that there would be a Head of Modern Languages post available in another school in the Borough in September if I cared to apply for it. Would I care! The school was Sarah Bonnell Girls' Grammar School, an ancient establishment founded in the seventeenth century. The building was quite small and tucked away like a secret convent from all the noise and racket of Forest Gate. The headmistress was a small, dynamic Welsh woman, Mrs Thomas, who had divorced her husband and come to London with her young daughter. She was a whirlwind presence around the school. She had her idiosyncracies, a certain neuroticism, an overweening pride in her situation as Headmistress and a huge ego which needed to be massaged regularly by the staff. We got on famously. We were both ambitious for the school and worked very hard together. She would invite me to her house once a week, ostensibly to discuss school matters, but we invariably ended up discussing our lives and emotions. I remember she had a large, original painting on one wall in the lounge, given to her by the grateful staff of a previous school. It was a sea scene, a myriad of intermingling misty greys with just a suggestion of white, rolling surf. I would gaze at it, mesmerised by its power, its space, its suggestion of escape to far-flung lands, while I listened to the gory tales of her messy divorce. I found the teaching at Sarah Bonnell immensely satisfying, particularly at A-level, mainly because the girls were so highly motivated. We read Flaubert, Zola, Maupassant and saw French films together. I also had to develop organisational and leadership skills as Head of the French, German and Spanish departments. After the girls' successes at O- and A-level, I was complimented by the same inspector who had interviewed me before, for running such a vibrant dept.

But there were changes afoot. In two years' time, there would be the great Socialist upheaval of comprehensivisation. I was reminded of a quote by Pope which I had read in an article about comprehensive schools:

With the same cement, ever sure to bind,
We bring to one dead level ev'ry mind

For Sarah Bonnell, with its long history, its unique attraction as a haven of security for working-class girls and its reputation as a beacon of learning, it would be very difficult to amalgamate with West Ham Boys' Grammar and another mixed secondary school. Even the name Sarah Bonnell was lost, being given to a Girls' Comprehensive School in Stratford while we ended up with the prosaic Stratford

Comprehensive School. What would the original Sarah Bonnell have made of that? This so-called 'educational' experiment, but really a social one, was and is still very controversial, malign 'social engineering' with a vengeance, under the guise of social equality. Whole swathes of proven grammar schools disappeared almost overnight and the ladder of opportunity offered to working-class children was suddenly removed. In the last year of Sarah Bonnell as a school, the deputy headship became vacant, as the incumbent was retiring; 'getting out', was a more appropriate phrase, I think. Mrs Thomas encouraged me to apply for the post. It would be a difficult year because of all the changes taking place, but an interesting one. I remember sitting in the evening in our kitchen when Stanley had gone out and the children were in bed, agonising over the decision. I really did not want to take on any more responsibility. Only the thought of having to work under someone younger than myself clinched the argument for me. I applied and was accepted. Under Mrs Thomas' guidance, I undertook the drawing-up of the school timetable and was responsible for staff development. In practice, this meant providing a reassuring presence to the staff in the light of the future changes. They were all very apprehensive about the future merger, since the LEA in its wisdom had decided that every member of the three schools amalgamating would lose their jobs and have to apply for positions in the new school. All the staff feared the change; they feared the thought of facing mixed-sex classes, they feared the loss of a close-knit staff. The rumour went around that the wearing of academic gowns would be banned in the comprehensive school, because of the possible adverse affect on the susceptibilities of the non-graduate staff. This proved to be true and quite ironic for me who had only just thought about buying a gown and wearing it with pride. Consequently, I never had the chance. More worrying still, the news broke that the first round of advertisements for the teaching jobs would be for the pastoral posts. Only when they were filled would the academic posts be advertised. So the academic qualifications of the teaching staff would be secondary to their ability to promote the social development of the pupils. Prestige and power would rest, not with the heads of departments, but with the year heads, responsible for the welfare of the children. Discerning staff realised that to fail at this first hurdle would be very detrimental to their future career, so inevitably, ambitious teachers chose to apply for the Year Head positions first, even though, for some of them, their strengths did not lie in that direction. Shirley was a case in point. She was a gifted teacher but not suited to this type of social work. She applied for a post as year head as I did, but failed to get it. It was the first time she had failed an interview and it was a great shock to her. As a result, she gave in her notice immediately, without waiting for the second 'tranche' of interviews for academic posts. She obtained almost immediately a post in a prestigious girls' grammar school in Putney. Many other good-calibre staff, devoted to academic excellence, suffered the same ignominy and then resigned. Newham, as the education authority was now called, lost a whole swathe of excellent teachers because of its crass system of re-organisation. I was one of the more fortunate ones; I was offered a post as Head of Second Year in the new school, providing pastoral guidance for over two hundred pupils and so I had to learn ever more skills and strategies.

I suddenly surfaced from all this high-powered, intellectual excitement to realise that my marriage was in jeopardy. Stanley had been a Maths teacher at the same Pretoria Boys' Secondary School in West Ham since I met him. It was a rough school in a rough area and although with his tight-lipped mien he had a disciplinary asset, there were days when the teaching must have been very difficult. He hardly ever talked about his school, except for descriptions of particularly obnoxious pupils, but was obviously chafing now to move. He started to apply for senior master or deputy head posts. Secretly, I did not think his strengths lay in that direction; he was an excellent Maths teacher but was not strong on social skills and I could not see him smoothing out the problems of agitated staff, but I kept my counsel. He was finally successful and was offered the Senior Master post at King Harold Boys' Secondary School in Waltham Abbey, about a thirty-minute drive away from Wanstead. His chief responsibility was timetabling, where his mathematical skills would be of good use. But, of course, his workload increased dramatically and he was under greater stress. He began to drink more heavily at the weekends, with another Irish colleague from the school. He spent most of Saturday and Sunday lunchtimes in pubs and during the school holidays, his level of drinking increased dramatically, especially when we were in Wales. We went there in the summer of 1967 to have the twins christened in the Llanberis parish church where David had been christened. There was the usual time-honoured ritual of walking up the village street to the Victoria hotel with Stanley's aunt and uncle, joined this time by his elder brother and wife on holiday. They spent the evening drinking and trying to talk above the noise of the other customers whose conviviality increased as the evening progressed. When 'turning-out' time arrived, the locals poured out, maudlin and intoxicated, raising the roof with their traditional Welsh hymns. Sometimes I enjoyed listening to their deep, pleasant voices, at other times I grew weary of the same routine.

We emerged from the pub on that particular occasion and walked back home under the dark cover of the night, lit only by the bright stars studding the sky. Most of us were in a happy mood, but Stanley had drunk too much and his mood had turned nasty. He turned to me aggressively, "I was watching you eyeing that chap on the next table. What the fucking hell do you think you are playing at? Showing me up in the pub, putting on your superior airs. I know your game, you slut. Keep your eyes off other men, do you hear?"

I kept quiet, knowing it was useless to respond to him, but his brother and uncle began protesting, until he turned on them as well:

"Keep out of my affairs, you two. You've got nothing to do with this."

And so it continued all the way home, his mood becoming increasingly ugly as I remained silent. So incensed was he when we got to our bedroom that he started to push and slap me around and finally began to tear my nightdress off. Whereupon his brother, who had heard the fracas, stormed into the room and a fine fight ensued between the two of them, with Stanley getting the worst of it with a blow to his face which silenced him. Next day, his eye swelled up with black and red bruising, but as usual, he apparently couldn't remember what had happened. He attended the Christening ceremony sporting a black patch over his left eye, giving him a swashbuckling air totally at odds with his lowering countenance. I still have the photograph of the party standing outside the church. These scenes when he drank too much provided a pattern of future 'holidays'. One night after a pub outing, he could not get to the toilet quickly enough and shat all over the bed. I awoke to feel something warm and slippery and heavy against me and when I put on the light, I was nauseated at what I saw. I pushed him out of bed, took off the sheets and tried to turn the mattress so that his mother did not see the yellow-brown stain on it. It was useless. She smelled the sickly smell as soon as she entered the room, although I had surreptitiously removed the sheets to try to wash them myself. I was so ashamed of him and sorry for her to have to witness such disgusting behaviour. She was obviously used to such episodes, however; she just turned on him and cursed him for "being such a bloody fool".

Back in Wanstead, he was still careful about his alcohol input during the week because of the demands of the job, but at weekends, he drank long and steadily. I tried cajoling him, pleading with him, but gave up the task as hopeless after one particularly unpleasant episode. He had been out late on the Saturday evening and had fallen senseless into bed, but on Sunday morning made preparations to go out again. I remonstrated with him. "Stan, don't go out again. There's a good film on television and you've got school tomorrow." He did not reply, but his mood became surly as he started to wash and comb his hair. I followed him around as he moved about the house, complaining more and more bitterly about his behaviour, and determined to have a showdown. Still no reply from him. Increasingly frustrated by his silence, I turned on him like a shrew, threatening that I would leave with the children if he continued like this. I was becoming increasingly concerned about the money he must be spending. I hated him at that moment– hated him for his laziness, his lack of support, his indifference to his children, above all for his drinking. I felt aggrieved and belittled by his evident disregard for all of us and for the house. I continued to follow him around until he finally broke, and turned on me: "You fucking bitch! Get off my back, will you?" he screamed. "YOU WILL NOT TELL ME WHAT TO DO, DO YOU HEAR? I'll do what I like, go where I like and you can go to HELL!" The final word was uttered on a shrieking, breaking note that left me shocked and silent. Then he rushed downstairs, sat with his head in his hands for a moment and then walked out, slamming the door behind him. I sat in the lounge quivering, crying, overwhelmed by his outburst, facing the fact that I had lost the battle. A chasm was opening up in front of me – a chasm down into which our marriage was sliding inexorably. One painful fact stayed in my mind; his need for drink was stronger than our marriage. I sat silent and bereft for what seemed hours, until I went to collect the children from Sunday school.

The next day, I borrowed a spare bed from a neighbour ostensibly because my sister was coming to stay. I had nowhere else to put it except in the bedroom, next to the double bed. When Stanley saw the bed, his face hardened, "What's all this for?"

"What's this for? You might ask! This is for me to get some sleep at night, that's what this is for."

"What are you talking about?"

"I'm talking about you abusing me when you're drunk, so that I can't sleep. And if I can't sleep, I can't do my job properly. I can't see how you can, either, what with all the drink you put inside you. If we had another room, I'd move into it."

He had the grace to be silent, looked at me sheepishly and then turning on his heel he left the house. I decided it was no use attempting to talk to him anymore. We were beyond words now. Yet, I still couldn't will myself to do anything about our marriage apart from going to a marriage counsellor. I decided to try that possibility. That was a waste of time. I had asked Stanley to come with me, but his predictable response was, 'I don't want some nosey parker prying into my affairs.' The interview was quite short. I explained the situation, the drinking, the verbal abuse, and beginnings of physical abuse. She listened carefully to all I had to say, but I remember only one remark she made, "But you chose him, didn't you?"

I gazed at her in complete bewilderment. What on earth was that to do with the situation? Only later, did I realise from my description of his behaviour, that all the signs had already been there when I first knew him. It was just that I was in love then...

Life continued and our marriage bumped along. One day, Stanley came home looking more cheerful than usual to announce that he had been asked to accompany a school party to Brittany. His headmaster, a very pleasant man whom Stanley liked, had also suggested that the whole family come. I could be of help with my French if needed. This would be a free holiday for us, and not Wales for once. The whole party was to be based in a boarding school in St Malo. I was quite keen to go, although I was now becoming wary of being with Stanley in public. I surmised that he would be kept busy with the schoolchildren. We decided that as it was only for a week, we would stay on and camp for a second week. What I did not know was that his drinking partner, the Irishman, would also be going. Such was the hold that alcohol had on him now, however, that after a few days settling in, and dutifully fulfilling their obligations to children and staff, he and the Irishman would disappear after the evening meal and would not return until the early hours of the morning. They made quite a drunken racket on their return, amplified by the echoing, cavernous corridors of the building. I was fearful that they would be reprimanded by the leader. This pattern of behaviour went on for a few days and then they both disappeared, for over twenty-four hours. I had the most unpleasant experience of sitting on the beach watching the children play and hearing the staff who were supervising their children, complaining about the disappearance of the two men. When Stanley almost fell into our room two nights later, he spent most of the night in the toilet being violently sick. Apparently, they had been drinking cheap, red wine like beer… He had alcoholic poisoning and was ill for days. I could not wait to get home.

Stanley now started to take off for a day or two at weekends and holidays, apparently to visit his family or friends in Birmingham. I found it quite a relief to be free from the tension his presence generated in me. The next time he said he was going away for a few days to Wales to see his mother, I asked him to take me and the children with him as far as Newport where my sister, Irene, now lived. It would be a break for the kids and me. He agreed and we drove in almost complete silence for part of the journey, but the rest was fraught with incidents. For some time now, I had been having exceptionally heavy periods, which left me feeling weak and tired. I had started one on that day. Stanley was in his usual mood of sullenness, still recovering from the previous night's drinking. He was anxious to unload us as soon as possible, so didn't intend to stop 'en route'. Suddenly, I began to feel the blood collecting in my sanitary pad. "Can you stop somewhere convenient soon, Stan? I need to go to the toilet. The children could go, too." I didn't mention the need to change my pad, since he had always been squeamish about women's bodily functions.

"I'm not stopping. I want to get to Llanberis as fast as possible. I'll still have a long journey after I've dropped you in Newport."

His tone brooked no argument, so I lapsed into silence, trying to keep as still as possible. It was no use. The slightest movement on my part brought forth more gouts of blood. The sanitary towel now saturated, the blood began to seep into my pants. I tried again, "Stan, you've got to stop! I need to get to a toilet."

There was no response as he drove grim-faced along the road. The situation became desperate. I felt anger and shame sweep over me. I felt that I was no longer in control of my life, nor even my body. A sudden shift of desperation and the blood started to ooze onto my thighs. I was terrified of staining my clothes. Unable to contain myself any longer, I screamed at him, "You've got to stop! I've got blood trickling down my leg!"

He heard the note of panic in my voice, looked at me, was now shocked out of his hangover and pulled quickly onto the side of the road, whereupon I jumped out of the car, blood finally pouring down my legs as I ran for the nearest bush. Crying now, ashamed of my body and the state I was in, anxious that the children should not see me, I was in total distress. I managed to staunch the flow with two towels, cleaned myself as well as I could and was then able to help the children have a pass water. Something broke in me after that incident. I felt I had a stone lodged in my chest, preventing me from breathing. There was more to come. When we arrived in Newport, just outside my sister's house, he helped unload the luggage and then started to get back into the car. I leaned on the car window to speak to him.

"Can I have some money for the few days here? I can't let Irene pay for everything and I need some money for the children."

He frowned and his face darkened. "Haven't you got any money?"

"No, I haven't, or I wouldn't be asking you for some."

"Well, you'll have to borrow from your sister, because I haven't got any to spare, either." And with that he started the car and drove off at speed. I stood there, wrestling with the surge of anger that swept over me. Then my thoughts crystallised. "That's it!" I thought. "It's no longer a question of feelings to worry about. It's a question of hard cash." I vowed to myself that I would never be placed in such a situation again. I would open my own bank account and have my salary transferred. When Stanley found out what I intended to do, it was another nail in the coffin of our marriage. He could not forgive me. From then on, he decided he would pay all the bills, but give me no housekeeping money. I accepted that arrangement, until I found that he was even reneging on that promise. When I had to order more oil for the central heating, I was refused because he had not paid the last bill. This event occurred at a time when he had gone on one of his absences, none of which he ever spoke of. I needed to replenish the oil supply quickly, but had no money to do so. I rang to speak to the manager of his bank and persuaded him to see me. I explained the situation to him and he was justifiably concerned. Although, legally, I could not touch what was after all some of my own money, because the account was only in Stanley's name, the manager agreed to release enough funds to pay for the oil. That was the last of such incidents. My next salary went into my own bank, and I was just that little bit more in control again.

I finally found out one day where he was going during his absences, or rather where he was not going. He took off for another few days saying he needed to visit his sister who was not very well. It was just before Christmas and the weather was quite severe. I worried about him having problems with snow in North Wales, so telephoned his sister's house in the evening to inquire if he had arrived safely. His sister's voice answered, "Stanley? Stanley isn't here and I'm not expecting him. Why do you ask? Am I ill? No, I'm not ill. How are you? And the children?"

I extricated myself from the conversation as soon as was polite and put the phone down. Time stood still for a moment. I could not take in the enormity of what I had heard. Stanley had lied to me, *lied to* me and had gone off where? I remember standing in the hall, breathless with shock. The hard stone lodged in my chest for weeks now suddenly dissolved and I began to weep uncontrollably. The anguish of my pain made me bend over and hold on to the telephone table. I contemplated the hollow mockery of my marriage. I was unable to stop crying. Gasping for breath, I forced myself into the kitchen to look at myself in the mirror, at the picture of misery I presented in order to stop my tears. I phoned Shirley to tell her the news. She added one more piece to the jigsaw of events. She had seen Stanley in the company of a woman in the bar of the Students' Union at Birkbeck. So, not only was he a liar and a drunk, he was a womaniser as well. He was cheating on me. I felt sullied and cast off. When he returned, late that Sunday evening, I had recovered some composure and asked him quietly:

"How is your sister, Stan? Is she recovered?"

And the lies poured forth, until I stopped him and told him what I had learned. I was cold and detached, curious to see his response. He chose aggression. He became extremely angry and belligerent and the swearing started.

"Oh! You've been checking up on me have you, you fucking cow! Spying on me, are you? Well, you mind your own fucking business where I have been. You don't own me. I've told you before, don't try to run my life. I work for the lot of you and that's as far as it goes. You think you are so fucking clever, you and your friend Shirley. Well, let me tell you this. Your so-called French degree isn't worth the paper it's written on. You want to try something really hard and see where it gets you. You couldn't do shit without me and that's your problem. I'll cut you down to size."

I listened to all these profanities with a thudding heart, holding my breath so that he could not hear my gasps. I realised I was faced with a man who had lost all control over himself through his drink and he was therefore dangerous. But before I could say anything he had shambled out of the room and I was left taut, edgy and with my anger unfulfilled.

It seemed that with the breakdown of my marriage, nothing could go right. I had an unexpected day's holiday from school and I decided to go to Leytonstone to buy something I needed. High Street, Leytonstone was always a very busy road, heavy with traffic even at eleven o'clock in the morning. I was in my usual rush to cross the road, and hadn't noticed a car coming up behind another one. I was knocked down, unconscious. When I regained consciousness some time later, I was in Whipps Cross Hospital, with a raging headache, a heavily bandaged leg and an excruciating pain in my shoulder. I was taken to the X-ray department, where it was discovered that although a huge lump of flesh had been gouged from my thigh, there were no bones broken. I asked about the pain in my shoulder which was really bad when I moved. That was also X-rayed, but nothing untoward found. The nurse said it was just heavy bruising causing the pain. I was not allowed to have any painkillers in case I was suffering from concussion. I lay as immobile as I could to keep the pain at bay. So I was feeling very sorry for myself when Stanley appeared at visiting time, dragging the children in with him. He was terrified. I explained about the pain in my shoulder and he went to see the nurse. I remember the words he spoke when he returned, "You've got to stop complaining about your shoulder. It's only bruising, the nurse said. There's nothing wrong with your shoulder. Pull yourself together and stop making a fuss!" For the sake of the children, I kept quiet, but when they had gone, tears oozed from under my eyelids at his unkind words. I felt really wretched. The next day, the headache was somewhat alleviated, but the shoulder pain as bad as ever. For two days, I complained about it and finally I had another X-ray, where it was discovered that I had broken my collar bone. Not that anything could be done about it, apparently, except to immobilise the shoulder as much as possible. But I felt vindicated and when Stanley heard the news, he had the grace to apologise and bring in a bunch of flowers the next day.

It took me a long time to recover from that accident. Fortunately, the summer holidays were soon on us and I refused to go to Wales. Instead, my sister Doreen and I rented a farm cottage in Dorset and took all four of our children and our mother with us. It was a lovely holiday; fresh milk from the cows every morning, with the children dividing their time between swimming in the sea and jumping up and down on the farmer's haystacks. I had to go into the nearest town every day to have my leg dressed and my shoulder was still painful, but it was bliss to be away from Stanley. On my return to Wanstead, I was coldly determined to act. I finally decided I could take no more of his behaviour. I was not the type of woman who could bear unfaithfulness; it diminished me and made me ashamed. I could not cope with the feelings of rejection. I had to survive for the sake of my children and my work. I reasoned that I had three things to cope with; children, work and a useless husband. One had to go and it had to be Stanley. Even when not 'under the influence' he was now permanently tetchy and short-tempered with the children and me. I made an appointment to see the local solicitor. He was not, initially, very helpful. "Have you thought of the effect this divorce will have on the children?"

Had I thought about it! I had been thinking about that very question for the last year. "Are you sure you can cope on your own? Would it not be preferable to wait for a few years?"

Wait for him to hurt me in one of his drunken rages before anything was done? Did this man live in the real world? For one moment, I wavered, consumed with guilt, then I became quite agitated and replied in a high-pitched voice:

"Do you think I really want to do this? I am here only because I can see no other way out of this intolerable situation."

Once the solicitor realised my determination, he became more accommodating, even quite unctuous. "If you are really decided on this divorce, Mrs Jones, I'll see to it that we get rid of him for you, and will make sure that you keep the house."

His volte-face was unpleasant to me. One moment unhelpful, even condescending and the next, a switch to a disagreeable complicity. I emerged from his office confused, upset and feeling sorry for myself. Yet even then I did not have the courage to tell Stanley what I had done. Only at the weekend, when my sister and brother-in-law were staying, did I leave the divorce papers in the kitchen for him to look at. My brother-in-law did not approve of my actions. "Rocking the boat, aren't you?" was his reaction. The fateful moment arrived. Stanley had gone out for his usual pint, Roy having declined to go with him. When he returned, he went into the kitchen. Roy and Irene knew something was likely to happen and the silence was heavy with anxiety and speculation. I waited for the storm to burst. It did. Stanley rushed clumsily into the room, like a juggernaut, grabbed me by the hair and dragged me into the kitchen. My sister and Roy must have judged it safer to stay in the lounge. He was beside himself. He screamed at me, fear and anger in his voice.

"What the fucking hell do you think you are doing to us? I know what your game is. You want this house for yourself, but by God you won't get it without a struggle. I'll sue you for denying me my rights as a husband." And with that he went out again. I lay rigid with fear when I went to bed, dreading his return. But when he returned late at night, although drunk, he was quiet and fell asleep almost immediately.

During the days that followed, I was wracked with doubt and indecision. My courage ebbed away as I thought of all the consequences for the children. How could I manage on my own with only one salary? How would I afford to keep the house going? What would their reactions be? Stanley must have been worried himself, because he moderated his drinking and came in earlier in the evenings. Weeks of strained silences and a tense stalemate followed. Nothing more was done about the divorce. We lived our own separate lives. Then a bombshell. Stanley came in from school one evening and announced that he had applied for a year's school exchange to Canada and his application had been successful. He would be leaving at the end of July. Immediately, fears of coping on my own resurfaced:

"Why do you want to do that? *Canada* of all places."

"I need space. I need to find myself again."

That was the only explanation he gave. I was then curiously relieved. I would have space as well. I would be free of the emotional turmoil I had been enduring for months. I would have time to see whether I really could cope on my own, time to see whether he would return a different man, or whether I would need to divorce him.

Chapter 14
Stalemate

How was my life now that my spouse was thousands of miles away? Quite good, actually. I discovered that I work best on my own, that I no longer had that build-up of resentment that he wouldn't help out. I don't think the children missed him much. Years later when I asked them whether they had missed his presence, they echoed the words of Shirley, "He was never there." He was certainly never around when needed, but I have heard many women make the same remark about their husbands... *Le train-train de la vie* continued; school for us all, Saturdays at Lyons Corner House to meet Shirley (I bought the children ice-cream sundaes to keep them happy) and weekends with Audrey and her children. The only excitement I remember is the change to decimalisation. In one fell swoop, all the tables learned so arduously at school about poles and perches, were thrown into the garbage can. More seriously, the currency change meant we were being tied in more closely with Europe and I was all for that. We kept the children occupied by visits to museums and exhibitions when it was raining and parks and countryside when the weather was fine, especially the lakes in Epping Forest where they swam and cooled off. Then suddenly all the lakes and ponds in the area were out of bounds; a polio germ had been found in one. Polio, commonly known as infantile paralysis, was a scourge at this time, and parents were fearful of their offspring catching it. Fortunately it was not long after, that a vaccine was found by a man called Salk to eradicate this dreadful disease. I had no social life, apart from these two friends and my mother who was very helpful, but I was much calmer and more satisfied with my lot. Stanley wrote long letters from Toronto, describing the house where he was staying, the squirrels in the attic keeping him awake at night and the magnificent colours of the trees in the Canadian 'fall'. He wasn't very happy with Toronto; it was too commercialised and the children were 'lippy'. He must have spent much time on his own because he started painting again; he had taken Art at Teacher Training College. When he returned home at the end of the year, he brought three of his paintings with him; the garden in Toronto covered in snow, and two still life paintings of flowers. I thought they were very good and had them all framed for him. He still has them hanging up in his lounge.

My tranquil life was soon to change. Almost immediately he had left, I noticed that when I went upstairs I would feel giddy and would have to hold on to the banisters for support. This continued and I became weaker, so I had to see the doctor. Tests showed that I was very anaemic (I, who had been congratulated by my doctor in Ongar on the high number of rich red corpuscles in my blood!) It was obviously because I was still losing large amounts of blood when menstruating. I had to see a specialist. I discussed my problem with the school secretary who had had similar problems. She advised me to ask to see a specialist at the Royal Marsden Hospital in Chelsea where she had gone and which had an excellent reputation. When I made this proposition to the doctor he eyed me thoughtfully for a moment and then said, "I don't see why not. It may be sensible." I pondered his reply later, not understanding the inference. I was only when I was at the hospital that I discovered it was a flagship cancer hospital. Could it be that I had cancer? Fear flooded my whole being as I sat in the waiting room. All my thoughts were for my children who would be bereft if I died. The specialist informed me that I had large fibroids in my womb which would have to be removed; I would have to have an operation, a total hysterectomy. I was too scared to broach the question of cancer. I left the hospital in a daze and narrowly missed being run over by a passing bus. I couldn't cope with the enormity of the news. Who would look after the children while I was in hospital? What if the prognosis were poor? Such thoughts whirled around frantically in my brain. A hysterectomy – the word meant nothing to me, with my usual ignorance about anything medical. I started to read about it; about the fears that women had at losing their wombs, the devastating realisation that they could no longer have children, that their sex lives could be affected, that there would be a long convalescence. Old wives' tales abound about hysterectomy and its psychological effects on certain women. Then I looked at the situation pragmatically; as far as the children were concerned, my mother would obviously look after them, and Audrey would rally round at weekends. As for me personally, there was no point in worrying about a possible cancer until I knew the result of the operation; the loss of my womb would, in fact, be a bonus. No more worry about having children and no more debilitating monthly periods. I would almost be a new woman.

I had the operation and – thank God! – the fibroids were found to be benign. I was put in the same ward as cancer patients, where the women were all unfailingly cheerful. I really admired them for their courage. The gravity of cancer was brought home to me forcibly one day during my stay at the hospital. A sudden bustle erupted in the normally quiet ward; there was an organised, efficient removal of a bed almost opposite mine and a large new bed, draped in canopies was wheeled in. Curtains were drawn around it. It proved to be a waterbed, which apparently was very expensive. I had never heard of them. The bed was needed for a young woman who was being rushed down from Blackburn. We never saw the poor creature, who was manoeuvred into the ward very circumspectly on a stretcher, and quickly transferred to the waterbed. We could only guess what was going on behind the curtains, the susurrating whispers, the brisk movements of the nurses and the moans emanating occasionally from behind the drapes. The woman's arrival created a sudden tension in a previously happy atmosphere. Patients spoke in low tones to each other and we were all fearful of what might happen. During the night, the moaning intensified, punctuated sometimes by deep groans. I fell into a fitful sleep but was suddenly woken up by increased activity. More doctors and nurses appeared and disappeared behind the curtains until finally the waterbed with the patient on it was hurriedly wheeled out of the ward. The desperately sick woman had been released from her agony and had died.

I stayed in the Marsden for two weeks. The operation had been a total success, womb and ovaries removed in one fell swoop. I was put on a drip for several days, not being allowed to have any food or drink. Anxiously, I eyed the tube of liquid dripping into my body. I had recently read about embolisms and death from faulty tubes. At times, the liquid stopped dripping and I had to call a nurse, who would fiddle with the tube to start it again. My imagination started to work overtime and I envisaged a blockage occurring during the night and killing me. Eventually, I became so apprehensive that I demanded the removal of the drip in spite of the protestations of the staff. I suffered no ill effects from its removal and was feeling strong enough to enjoy the social life in the ward. The food was good and we were allowed either a glass of wine or Guinness with our meals 'to build us up', which I thought was very advanced thinking on the part of the staff. The only worry I had was the sleeping pills that we were made to take at night to get a good night's sleep. I was terrified of becoming dependent on them. When I did return home, I was unable to sleep properly for days. On the day due for my release, I had a shock to discover that Stanley had arrived to take me home. It was the Christmas holidays and someone (my mother?) must have informed him of my stay in hospital. When he saw me in the hospital, almost his first words were, "Do you know, if it wasn't for you, I could have been in the Bahamas for Christmas." Whether that was a joke or not, I still don't know, but in my weak state, it was tactless in the extreme. He insisted on sharing my bed when we returned, and I was still too weak to argue with him. He was at pains to tell me as we lay in bed in the dark, "You realise you can't have any more children don't you, so you aren't a woman anymore." I brooded over his words and thought to myself, "What a cruel thing to say to a woman recovering from a serious operation." He had clearly heard all the old wives' tales. But I recovered my equilibrium, grateful to be freed from the burden of menstruation, the perennial fear of pregnancy. I welcomed my life as "no longer a woman." Nothing was said by the doctors at the Marsden about oestrogen tablets to replace lost hormones as advised today. I don't appear to have suffered any ill-effects from this. The long convalescence predicted did not occur. I couldn't afford such a luxury, since Stanley had returned to Canada and my school was anxious to see me back again. Mrs Thomas was on the phone most evenings discussing events happening at school. In the end, I decided it was preferable to be back there myself, but I was given a lighter timetable for a few weeks.

July 1972 Stanley returned to the fold, unusually docile and submissive for a while. He even wanted to share our weekends together, taking the children out with me to Epping Forest. But for me time had moved on. He was more of an irrelevance to me now. I could not bear to sleep with him anymore, since I did not know where he was going on his times away and I was scornful of his weakness and his lack of responsibility towards his family. In my mind, he had been weighed in the balance and had been found wanting. I was almost glad when he began to slip into his old routine of drinking at the weekend, and the bouts of aggression were thankfully much less. Now that he had returned, I could start considering some further study. With a demanding post as head of year at Stratford Comprehensive school I decided I needed a wider understanding of educational principles, so I applied to take an advanced diploma at the Institute of Education in London. Surprisingly, Shirley decided to join me. All I asked from Stanley was to babysit for two evenings a week, which he agreed to without comment. I made it clear that I wanted no more debilitating emotional traumas in my life. If he paid the mortgage, that was enough for me. I still received no housekeeping from him, but with my good salary, I was able to cope much better.

One lovely summer's day, I was in the garden reading. The children were in the next-door garden – I could hear their cries and shouts. I was feeling very content at that moment, sprawled out on my front on the lawn. The warmth of the sun and the unaccustomed leisure made me feel sleepy and I dozed for a while. When I woke up, a most peculiar sensation of heat and fullness seemed to suffuse my body. My breasts felt bigger and I noticed my nipples were hard and prominent, sending an urgent message down through my stomach to my vagina. I had never felt such a strange, compelling need which demanded to be assuaged. How? I hadn't had sex for a long time and in my busy life had not noticed any lack of it. The sensation grew stronger, my breasts ached with the exigent signals being sent down my body. I had always been squeamish about my body, a relic of my early Catholic upbringing, I imagine. I had never been able to touch my breasts to examine them as one was exhorted to do regularly. Yet such was the fire in my body, that I walked slowly into the kitchen in a dazed euphoria, almost like an automaton, my brain having temporarily stopped functioning. In slow motion, I went up to my bedroom, grabbed a rough towel, removed my bra and proceeded to rub my nipples with the towel. Violent shudders coursed through me, my fingers went instinctively to my clitoris to massage it, and within minutes, I gasped and held my breath as I had a clitoral orgasm, then another and another. I felt the muscles of my clitoris palpitating urgently. Finally it was over, except for a deep yearning for penetration, which could not be assuaged. My body quietened although a dull ache remained for some time. I was amazed at myself;

I had masturbated. The word was anathema to me. I had never thought of myself as a strongly sexual person, but my body was now telling me that it needed sex.

I didn't tell anyone about this episode, not even Shirley. I felt faintly ashamed of my body. But I said to Audrey that we should start socialising more, go to dances to meet the opposite sex again. She was also going through a marriage breakdown. If anything, her husband was worse than Stanley. He was mentally and physically cruel to her. He would follow her around the house, criticising everything she did, until her nerves were at breaking point. She was glad to get out in the evenings. We found that there were some dances taking place in the hotels around the area we lived. They were much more 'up-market' dances than Ilford Palais, but there were the usual weedy types and misfits and recently divorced men who wanted to bend your ear with their problems. We never had enough money to buy much in the way of alcohol, so would buy a bottle of wine beforehand and drink it in my car, or take a hip flask of whisky, secreted in our handbags to take a surreptitious swig whenever we were not being observed. Audrey was caught out one evening. As I went to the toilet, she was seen by the manager as she swigged her flask. When I returned, she was red-faced and said in a low tone, "We've got to get out of here before we're thrown out. The manager's just caught me and given me a good old rollicking. He's told me not to come back here." Sedately and composedly, we left the bar and once outside collapsed into fits of giggles. We enjoyed the fun, the laughter and the dressing-up more than the actual dances. Once, we both bought enchanting white dresses which were the focus of much attention. I remember another evening which was hilarious. We went to a very charming hotel, the Roebuck in Buckhurst Hill. It had a quiet bar and the men there were pleasant middle-class types. It was almost empty that evening and we ordered drinks and prepared to sit down and have a chat. Suddenly a group of Irishmen surged into the bar and started to talk to us. They made us laugh with their jokes, bought us drinks and probably thought they were on to a good thing. We heard strains of music coming from the function room next door and one chap went to investigate. There was a wedding reception taking place. Emboldened by the drinks and with the support of the Irishmen we 'gate-crashed' the party. Champagne was flowing freely and no one enquired as to who we were. We danced the evening away, and were in full swing when I looked at my watch – it was one o'clock in the morning. Like Cinderella, it was time to leave and speedily. In the haste to get out, I was separated from Audrey and found myself outside the hotel in the pitch-darkness of the field surrounding the hotel. To my astonishment, the Irishman with the lovely soft, Irish brogue who had been talking most of the evening about the Irish problem came up alongside me. He insisted on escorting me to my car. We stumbled over the rough grass and suddenly I fell down into a hidden ditch and had to be hauled back by him. We were laughing uproariously. As we approached my car, I seemed to sober up quickly. I anticipated trouble, and sure enough he climbed into the car with me and proceeded to cover me with wet, soft kisses. I let it ride for a while, but my brain had taken over by this time. As he started fumbling at my dress, I suddenly announced to him in a clear voice, "It's no use, you know. I've got my periods," which was of course, a lie.

"That's OK. Sometimes, it's even better."

Better? Ugh! "No, I'm sorry. We can sit and talk if you like, but that's all. If you try anything, I'll push you out of the car." Brave words, since he was a big, burly man, but he was also educated and pleasant. He agreed and we spent the next hour or so discussing, of all things, the Irish problem. It was a surreal experience. I did not arrive home until about four o'clock in the morning, feeling quite sober, but when seven thirty came, time to get the children up and cook their breakfast, I could not move my head. Stanley shook me vigorously and told me to hurry up, but it was useless. I moaned, "I can't get up – I feel terrible." Whereupon, to my later astonishment, he said no more, got the children ready and they all disappeared. I slept then until early afternoon and then rushed round to Audrey to see how she had fared. She had been given a lift home and had been in bed by two o'clock. How we laughed!

Another potentially serious event which in the end proved to be equally amusing concerned David and Anthony. All of the children were playing in Audrey's garden after school, while we continued our listing of the inadequacies of our husbands, ending with each of us saying, satisfyingly, "God! How I hate him!" We looked up and saw that David and Anthony had disappeared. We jumped up and called to them in a panic. A small brown head appeared at one of the upper windows – it was Anthony.

"We're playing in my bedroom, Mum."

"God, I'll have to get them out of there. Tony has just finished painting the doors." She knew what she would have to suffer if they made any sort of mess.

"Come on down, Ant. You're not to stay up there."

"Oh, Mum, we're not doing anything – just playing."

"Come down, I say! I don't want you messing up the bedroom."

David's blond head appeared at the window.

"Anthony's locked the door," he announced in portentous tones.

Audrey was becoming exasperated.

"Well, unlock it and come out of there. This minute!"

Anthony's head appeared again and a note of panic in his voice.

"I can't unlock it. It's stuck."

"What do you mean, you can't unlock it? Turn the key and come out now!"

Silence for a few moments, then Anthony's face appeared. He was crying.

"I can't open it, Mum. It's stuck." We were suddenly galvanised into action and rushed up the stairs to try the door. Useless. The key was in the lock on the inside. David had by this time realised the situation and began screaming to be let out. Anthony joined in the chorus and there was pandemonium. There was no way we could get them out through the window, since we had no ladder and it was too high anyway. I tried explaining to Anthony gently how he should turn the key in the lock, but Audrey, now frightened herself, started threatening him, which made him cry all the more. His sobs increased and could be heard through the door with David's inharmonious screams as accompaniment. These were so wild and shrill that the hair was beginning to rise on my neck. "We'll have to call the Fire Brigade," I said. "David will be sick if he carries on like this."

Audrey rushed down to phone the Fire Brigade, while I attempted to calm the two boys from the other side of the door with the four girls staring wide-eyed at the proceedings. Then there was a bang on the front door and what seemed like a posse of heavily-booted, helmeted firemen charged up the stairs and without waiting for permission, proceeded to break down the door. Why hadn't they thought of ladders? This method was obviously quicker, but the damage to Tony's newly painted door was extensive. As the door swung open, the two boys emerged sheepishly. Audrey grabbed Anthony and started to hit him while I gathered my mob together and departed. I had problems with David for months after that episode. He would scream every time he was in a room with the door shut. He had to have his bedroom door open all the time. As for Tony's reaction; when I asked Audrey what had happened, her succinct reply was, "He was really angry."

My brother Vic suddenly swam back into my life. Irene had come to stay for a weekend and he rang up to ask us to go and hear him singing in a Plaistow pub. It was the usual scene; a cockney version of the Welsh pubs I had suffered for so long, although thankfully no longer, since I would not go again to Wales with Stanley. The loud voices meant that one couldn't hear oneself speak and one had to drink quite a lot to suffer it. It was pleasant hearing Vic singing, it always made me feel emotional at the opportunities he had missed. There was also a dance taking place in the pub and I danced with a Scotsman who seemed mildly interesting. He was a merchant seaman and told me about all the ports he had visited. We ended the evening in Vic's house, all of us uproariously drunk, and I had the pleasure of having my feet stroked by the Scotsman. Feet are also erogenous, it appears. I was feeling quite sexy and foolishly agreed to meet him again. I drove home with Irene and shot through a red light, narrowly missing a car coming across the other way. That sobered me, and I started berating myself mentally, for agreeing to let the sailor come to my house. I had no idea where he lived, so couldn't phone him to make my excuses. I wasn't worried about Stanley, he would be going out and the children would be in bed. The sailor duly turned up, looking quite smart in a grey suit and we sat talking in the lounge, sharing a bottle of wine between us. In no time at all, we were upstairs and he was in my bed. He was a skilful lover and I luxuriated in feelings long forgotten. We were aroused from our post-coital slumber by the sound of a key being turned in the front door lock. I was electrified and leaped out of the bed to peer out of the window. Our house had a front porch rather like a lych-gate porch in front of a church. I could make out in the darkness the figure of Stanley swaying on his feet and looking perplexed at his keys. He couldn't open the door because I had had the sense to lock it. I heard him try the key again while my partner in crime was throwing clothes onto his body with feverish haste. He whispered to me that he could climb out of the window as long as Stanley wasn't looking. I waited until Stanley vanished into the darkness of the porch and then gestured to the sailor to GO! My heart was thudding against my ribs. It was 'touch and go' whether Stanley would turn around and see him climb out. As it was, he dropped on to the pebbles around the window and one could hear clearly the crunch as his feet made contact. Horrified, I watched Stanley turn round to see what the noise was, but he was befuddled with drink and the Scotsman melted silently into the darkness. Stanley now started banging on the door. I slipped down the stairs, all sleepy innocence and let him in. "What's going on here?" he said thickly. "Why have you locked the door?"

"I heard some noises outside and was frightened," I replied. His brain was too dull to reason. He shouldered past me and fell into his bed. "*Quelle chance!*" I murmured, feeling no compunction at having cuckolded him. That wasn't the end of the Scotsman. A few days later, having left the children playing in the garden while I went to get something from the shops, I returned to find they were not to be seen and the house was empty. Before I could begin to worry, the neighbour from 'Pond House' came out saying that all the children were with her. She had called the police because a man had been seen prowling round the 'secret garden'. By the time the police had appeared, the man had disappeared, but I had to listen to the story of how frightened they all had been... The Scotsman even wrote to me from his ship and sent the letters to my school. I must have received about ten and the staff were becoming suspicious, at seeing tatty-looking letters addressed to Sylvia Jones in an uneducated handwriting. Fortunately, they then ceased.

I tried another attempt at socialisation. I joined a social club in central London, called the Black Cat Club. It was for singles who met in the upstairs room of a pub in Oxford St for dances and conversation. This group was much more respectable, middle-class types with failed histories who were trying to make a go of life again. It was a place where I could get away from Stanley and could dress up. On my first night there, I bolstered my confidence with a quarter bottle of whisky before I went in. I was quite terrified to be on my own. I looked around at the small group of people; they looked like accountants or solicitors or obviously teachers. Some were dancing desultorily while others were in earnest conversation. My heart failed me. Then I spied a burly man who was dancing with a very slim, elegant woman. They were seemingly a couple, but I liked the look of him and spent some time eyeing him. I have a theory (with no proof whatsoever) that a woman who is sexually mature, and I count myself in that even though I had been celibate, on and off for some time, sends out unconscious messages to which men respond. How else can I explain my success that evening, when I had spent countless hours against the wall in the Ilford Palais longing for someone to ask me to dance? He came over and asked if I would like to dance with him. We danced the whole evening together. He seemed to forget his companion. He made me laugh and he attracted me sexually. He was strong and sturdy, of medium height, with light-brown, curly hair and deep-brown eyes. He was unfailingly courteous, had a deep, resonant voice, which thrilled me and an accent which showed he was from a good background. I promptly fell in love with him, my third and regrettably my last *coup de foudre* and he seemed equally affected. I was in seventh heaven when he asked to see me again, although he had a girlfriend of long standing whom he finished with. And so a relationship started that lasted for about eight years. He had an exquisite sense of humour and was so kind that I later invited him home to meet my children, who loved him. He played with them and joked with them and a house which had been grimly silent for many months suddenly came alive again. I never made the mistake again of letting him stay the night, so for a time he was more of a friend than a lover, but there was no doubt of the sexual attraction. He paid me compliments, brought me flowers and presents for the children and courted me assiduously. I was entranced. It was like being back in Germany when Gordon was so sweet to me. He came often to the house, at weekends when Stanley was away, but never attempted to abuse my hospitality. Stanley must have known something was going on, but since I was never out at night, presumably discounted any 'shenanigans'. We racked our brains as to how we could sleep together. Finally, I gathered up courage to ask my sister Doreen to have the children to stay with her one night while we stayed in a hotel in Stevenage. She met Keith and did not demur. I still don't know why. Perhaps she could see my happiness and was glad for me.

Our first night together, free from the fears of Stanley returning or of the children waking up, was wonderful. I expanded physically and mentally. He watched me with his dark-brown eyes as I undressed. He said he loved my slanting eyes, my full breasts and my strong thighs. He was proud of his own masculinity and marched around the room naked and uninhibited. I was thrilled. Once we were together in bed, we started to kiss each other passionately, our tongues touching tentatively at first and then thrusting greedily into our mouths, each of us trying to take possession of the other. He said he loved the taste of my cool lips and the scent of my hair. Our embraces quickened and my body came alive as he stroked me, murmuring words of endearment. Finally, my body responded to his passion and we came together. The hackneyed phrase: 'time stood still' came into my mind as I thought about it afterwards. We slept like babies after the exhaustion of our lovemaking. When morning came, we made love again, even more satisfyingly as we discovered new delights in our bodies. When we went down to breakfast, I still yearned for him and felt faintly sick at the force of my desire. But we soon had to pick up the children and the window of love closed down again. Eventually, Keith became a kind of surrogate father to my children. They were delighted when he appeared. Whenever I could, I arranged a night away somewhere, to continue our lovemaking. Once it was even Stanley who stayed at home to look after the children.

I was fortunate to have Keith's friendship to bolster me because life was pretty grim otherwise. In 1970, the Conservatives won the election with Edward Heath as Prime Minister, the first grammar-school boy in such a post, with a brief to try to control the trade unions. His attempts to do this led to a confrontation with the TUC and the miners, a battle he lost. There were numerous strikes and stoppages reminiscent of the 1926 General Strike, race riots in Notting Hill, Bristol and Liverpool and 'sit-ins' in the universities. Unemployment was rife and inflation galloping upwards. Britain discovered that she had fallen behind France and Germany and had become 'the sick man of Europe'. A new, nasty phenomenon of 'flying pickets' appeared; miners who were bussed around the country to intimidate any other miners attempting to go to work. Very successful they were too. Arthur Scargill the miners' leader, called it a class war, saying, "We wished to paralyse the nation's economy." The miners started an overtime ban and to make matters worse, the price of petrol quadrupled because of an Arab embargo on oil shipments to the West, the result of the Arab-Israeli War. In December 1973, Heath cut energy production back to three days a week. I had to queue for over an hour in the mornings to get enough petrol to get us to school and we couldn't travel at more than fifty mph. We had no electricity or gas on certain days so I had to try to boil a kettle and cook on the fire, and there was a cut in TV hours and street lighting. It was almost total breakdown and Stanley was nowhere to be seen. I felt so alone in this crisis and looked forward to the weekends when Keith would arrive to cheer us up. Because of the crisis, Heath decided to call a snap election, on the question of "Who governs Britain?" He lost. He had totally misjudged the public mood. His only achievement was to take Britain into the Common Market, after trying twice before and being humiliated with a 'No!' vote from De Gaulle. I was profoundly grateful when we were allowed in. The closer we were to the culture of Europe, the happier I was. A Labour government was formed. The three-day week restriction was thankfully lifted in March 1974 and we began to breathe again.

Stanley then dropped his second bombshell. He informed me that he had applied for a post in Wellington, New Zealand and not for one year, but forever. He was going through immigration procedures in order to get a free passage. Leaving England for good. Just cheerio and that's that? Disappear? That was his intention but his plans were foiled at the last minute by the school in New Zealand insisting that if they accepted him he would need to bring his wife and family with him. So he asked me to go with him. I was completely nonplussed. I had put off the thought of divorce only temporarily, but knew in my heart that I would have to gather the courage to start proceedings again one day. I was reminded of what William Maxwell said in his book, *Time Will Darken It*, "Women are never ready to let go of love at the point where men are satisfied... It is a fault of timing that affects the whole human race." It was not simply a matter of love however. That had already gone. It was all the problems that women have to face as single parents, lack of money, lack of support and the burden of bringing up children alone. All these fears, compounded by the fact that I had been brought up in the Roman Catholic Church, which does not recognise divorce, and I was most reluctant yet to make the break. This new offer from Stanley could help to solve all these problems. I rationalised to myself that this move to a completely new country and a new job for Stanley could possibly save our marriage. He would perhaps change, in a less stressful environment. That was one thought I wanted to cling on to. But what an agonising decision to have to make in a short time. I remember sitting at the kitchen table noting down all the pros and cons. It would mean that I did not have to consider divorce, that the children would still have a father. The downside was all that I would be leaving Keith, my house and my school, which I would leave in the lurch, since there was no time for the statutory three-month resignation period. I would even have to forgo money owing to me from Newham Education Authority for the costs of my course. The children's schooling would be disrupted, especially as David had recently won a scholarship to Buckhurst Hill Grammar School, one of the few still left in the area. Even more important I would be losing my independence. I mooned about the house for weeks, unable to make a decision. I consulted all my family and friends, most advising me not to go. The lone voice expressing a different opinion was Shirley. It had to be Shirley with her different outlook on life from other people. She was very excited for me, saying how wonderful it would be to go to New Zealand. And as she mentioned this, the old-familiar ache for new scenes took hold of me. I agreed with her; it would be wonderful to see a new country and live a different life. So I said, "Yes" to Stanley, not without misgiving. Once I had made that decision, I was re-invigorated. We sold the house in record time, took the children from their schools, I bought myself a new winter coat (*a winter coat? In Wellington?*) and boarded a plane for a twenty-three hour flight to an strange, far-away country. It was a leap into the unknown.

Chapter 15
Vistas new

Our precise destination in New Zealand was Chilton St James, a private girls' school in Lower Hutt, a suburb of Wellington, with a wide, silver-flashing river flowing alongside it down the coast to the Tasman Sea. The river was named after the English MP Sir William Hutt, who had been the director of the New Zealand Company which was formed in 1830 to promote immigration to New Zealand. Further upriver is another township, Upper Hutt. We flew with Air New Zealand in a massive Jumbo jet. The flight was over twenty-six hours long, but we stopped to refuel in Havana. I still remember the blast of hot air that greeted us as we left the plane and the sight of the policemen in the airport lounge, big burly men in sunglasses, with powerful guns in their holsters and looking as if they had stepped out of an American gangster film. I was concerned about the children's sleep but fortunately there were spare places in the plane and the air stewardess allowed me several extra seats for them to lie down. We finally arrived in Auckland and transferred almost immediately to an internal flight to Wellington. I was keen to see the countryside as we flew down the North Island. It looked almost empty compared with England, with green fields stretching into the distance and a long chain of bush-covered hills. As we approached Wellington, small, neat bungalows could be seen sporadically and then there was a proliferation of them. From my vantage point, they looked so pretty with pink, blue and green coloured roofs. The shock was immense when the plane landed and they proved to be painted in coloured corrugated iron. Suddenly the place seemed so primitive. I was forcibly reminded that I was no longer living in England with its long rich civilisation. Stanley had forewarned me that he would have jetlag and would therefore need a few days to recover when we arrived. This proved to be the case, mainly because he met a like-minded passenger during the flight and they both proceeded to take advantage of the cheap alcohol on board. He was certainly in a bad way when we arrived at Chilton St James. I was also very tired, having been too keyed-up to relax sufficiently. But Stanley had misjudged the determination of the deputy head who insisted that he start teaching the day after. The girls were all back at school and were ready and waiting. This did not improve Stanley's temper.

He must have been very apprehensive about this new post; he had been appointed mainly as a sixth form teacher of Maths, a level at which he had never taught before. Consequently, he had to spend every evening during the week preparing minutely for his classes, to the detriment of his temper, which caused fear in the children, who were made to understand in no uncertain terms that they had to be quiet in the evenings. In fact the head of the school was very kind to us. We were allowed to live in one of the bungalows on the campus, rent-free, so that we would have time to settle in before looking for accommodation and Stanley could thus concentrate on his teaching. We also paid reduced fees for the twins since they were siblings and Stanley was a teacher at the school. This did not prevent me from indulging in my usual emotional outburst on the first evening. I sobbed as I realised that we now had no home to call our own.

Chilton St James was like a toy village with its orderly, detached, single-storeyed buildings and neat paths. I would watch the birds strutting around on its well-manicured lawns and once saw a magnificent black and white one, which I assumed must be peculiar to the southern hemisphere, since I had never seen it before. Only later did I discover that it was a magpie. So much for my ornithological knowledge! From our window, I could see a range of hills on the horizon, but they were not the soft, green, rounded hills of England; they were scrub-like, covered in short, tough, grey-green bushes. Ugly white scars, running vertically from the summits, ravaged the hills from top to bottom. They proved to be firebreaks. Fire was an ever-present danger in an island where the summers are hot and the winters mild. Even the rose bushes in the garden around the bungalow, planted in mathematical rows, seemed to have a pale, faded beauty; the petals broke apart when touched lightly. They had none of the vigour of English roses. They flowered all year and seemed exhausted at the effort.

The twins settled in remarkably quickly, making friends with these middle-class girls of consummate assurance. Their classmates were charmed at meeting identical twins, both of whom took full advantage of the interest in them, especially when they pretended to be each other, to the amusement of their friends and the consternation of the staff. There were two open-air swimming pools in the grounds where they spent time every day after classes. They were soon being invited out to swimming parties and barbecue parties – it was one social round for them. David, as usual, suffered the change more intensely. He had always been a quiet, withdrawn child and had taken time to become adjusted to Buckhurst Hill Grammar School. In fact we had received a letter from the head concerned about his introverted behaviour. Now, just as he was beginning to make friends, he had been wrenched from one environment to another, one that differed in every aspect. He went from a small boys' grammar school to a large mixed comprehensive. For the twins, the school was on the doorstep, but he had to take a bus to school. I had difficulty in persuading him to go to school on the first day, because the school rules insisted on boys wearing shorts. This was normal in a country where all the men also wore shorts. In England, no one in state school wore shorts when they reached secondary school. He was adamant that he would not wear them. So he went to school in his long trousers. I went with him on that first journey and stayed at the school gates until he entered the school grounds, a tall, lonely figure. I waited with apprehension for his return. When I asked, "How did you get on?" he replied tersely, "I'm going to wear shorts tomorrow." He never divulged what happened on that first day, but he must have been mocked mercilessly.

A few weeks after we had arrived, the deputy head called in to 'have a chat'. This was partly to ensure that we had no problems, but partly to tell us quite bluntly that although he knew I had had a successful teaching career in England, he would advise me not to consider any sort of teaching for the first year, so that I could support my husband in his new job. Words failed me at the temerity of the man with his old-fashioned 'mores'. Stanley had never asked for support and would not take it kindly if I offered to help in any way now. He dropped occasional hints as to the problems he was having – one particular girl, very intelligent, had caught him out in a mistake already. The stress on him must have been intense, but he would brook no interference or help; all I could do was perform my usual duties as wife and mother. In any case, it was not long before we discovered that our finances were in a parlous state and that I would have to find some sort of job, even part-time. Because he had to work so hard during the week, it was not long before he began to relieve the stress by drinking heavily at the weekends. Since we did not have a car, we had to take a local train in to Wellington on Saturdays. It was a very pleasant journey, as the train ran along the side of the coast and we could look out on the blue waters of the Tasman Sea. The civic area of Wellington had some very fine classical and Victorian buildings which reminded me wistfully of London and there were some very attractive suburbs, with tree-lined avenues, but the centre of the town was a disappointment. It seemed to me to be provincial in the extreme. The shops had raised wooden platforms with wooden roofs over them, presumably to protect the customers from rain or sun. But I was irresistibly reminded of the Wild West hick towns one sees in cowboy films. They all seemed so primitive and depressing in their lack of sophistication. We would start out on Saturday afternoons wandering around the shops with Stanley in front. Then he became progressively more distant and refused to walk with either the children or myself. He was like an Asian overlord trailing his family behind him. I could hear him cursing the place and the school. I was reminded of Montaigne: "In marriage a man becomes slack and selfish and undergoes fatty degeneration of his moral being." I don't know whether Stanley had ever had any morals. I was not too concerned about his behaviour now; it was more agreeable to chat to the children. Then he would say he was going off for a pint and would disappear into one of the primitive pubs in the area, where many of the Maoris gathered. I can't imagine he liked that very much. We would be left to our own devices. We went once to a 'fleapit' of a cinema, more like a wooden shack, to see Robert Redford and Paul Newman in *The Sting*. I was so tense most of the time in Wellington I did not really concentrate on the film, so that when we emerged from the cinema, blinking in the dazzling sunlight, I hadn't even understood what the 'sting' was. I imagine the children understood even less, but we passed a few hours away. Then we would meet Stanley in a pre-arranged place in the early evening. He left the pub early, before closing time which was at about 6.30 p.m. New Zealand had very strict licensing laws mainly because of the drunkenness on the streets. Very few whites seemed to go into the pubs, but at the end of the evening, the Maoris and a few whites would emerge, wrecked with drink, staggering into the middle of the road, fighting and swearing.

We were really frightened. We had very little contact with the Maoris in the fastness of Chilton St James, except for the occasional cleaner. It wasn't long before we left Stanley to go into Wellington on his own. I pined to see other parts of New Zealand, Auckland at the top of the North Island and the hot springs in the South Island. But Stanley said we couldn't afford to go anywhere.

The twins had made friends with the children of the school cook. He was a plump, jolly man, the epitome of a cook, but quite perceptive. He had summed up our difficult situation. He became a good friend to us and would take us for picnics at the weekends, and I had the opportunity of seeing the beauty of the countryside, the fast flowing rivers, and sparkling waterfalls catching the sunlight like diamonds and breaking up into a myriad of colours. I marvelled at the silence, eerie at times and the strange emptiness of this new world. When we went up towards the hills, the immensity of the space and the unbroken silence surrounding us almost frightened me, accustomed as I was to crowded London. We walked through settlements of widely spaced bungalows, each with a neat garden, but separated from one another by fences which would then peter out suddenly and then there was nothing but the bush, the dark-green, ragged bush, although the air was perfumed with a pungent spiciness. This was a primeval landscape of high eucalyptus trees; their tall, slender barks of grey, brown and cream bore smooth grey-green leaves that were rounded on the lower branches but which became long and very narrow and pointed as they grew on the crown. We saw the remains of the bush fires; the stumps of the gum trees, the ground covered with the dead leaves, called 'débris', which were copper-brown and papery in texture. I read that the eucalyptus trees, compared to other trees, were especially flammable because of their high oil content, but had evolved to survive the raging forest fires, with new growth appearing from their charred trunks. Walking through this devastation wrought by the fires, what struck me most was the eerie silence. Everything seemed dead.

The need to increase our finances became more urgent, so I decided to ignore the deputy head's advice and start looking in the local paper for a teaching job. I tackled this chore avidly; I was already becoming bored with just being a housewife. Having always led a busy life, the unaccustomed leisure irked me. I occupied most of my time listening to the radio programmes, provincial in the extreme, which were punctuated with local advertising and description of local events. Yet they were national programmes. I missed the culture and excitement of London, I missed my friends and family. I missed the overpopulated, crowded countries of Europe. I would spend time looking at an atlas, noting the isolation of New Zealand. It was so far from anywhere, its nearest neighbours being Fiji and Australia, thousands of miles away. To pass some of the time, I learned to type by writing discursive letters to Shirley, describing aspects of New Zealand and my feelings towards it. It was not long after I had started applying for teaching posts that I was asked to go to an interview for a French post at a prestigious, private girls' school in Wellington. It was in one of those dignified, residential parts of the town and I was quite fearful as I passed through the wrought-iron gates into the imposing building. The headmistress was most pleasant. She asked me what I did with my leisure time. As it happened, I had just been reading a biography of Virginia Woolf, one of my favourite writers, describing the differing sexual relationships she and her 'Bloomsbury' group went in for. Deprived of any form of intellectual conversation for so long, I launched enthusiastically into a description of these experiments and her character and personality. The head was most intrigued and I'm sure I was offered the job on the strength of my outburst. I would not be able to start teaching, however, until the spring term, so I needed some temporary work until then.

I landed a post in Upper Hutt. It was a boys' high school where I tried to teach English to the Upper School boys, since French was not on the curriculum. Although I was by now an experienced teacher, I had some initial difficulties with these boys. They were mostly tall and since they all wore shorts, I was confronted by a plethora of huge, muscular, bronzed thighs. I was reminded irresistibly of D H Lawrence's comment about Australians seeming to run to legs. The set texts of English literature did not appeal to them in the least. There was also a definite lack of interest in history, apart from their own. To me, they appeared to have no genuine culture, preferring to discourse at length on all aspects of sport rather than showing any interest in European culture. They were full of arrogance and were quite sure that New Zealand was the greatest country in the world. I tried to suggest that they had no criteria to measure that belief by, since they had never experienced any other country. They ignored that fact. Their chauvinism, their brashness and their naïveté appalled me, as did their harsh, whining accents. To compound my difficulties, they never seemed to stop talking. Verbal diarrhoea, I commented acidly to myself. I had great difficulty in getting any teaching done.

During the lunch hour, relieved to be able to get away from the noise, I would leave the school and walk down to the river nearby. It was crystalline in its purity and as it fell over the rocks it was refracted into a myriad of colours in the warm sun. The surrounding green fields were a fitting backdrop to its gleaming beauty. I could only gaze in wonder at its pristine freshness. Unfortunately, its beauty was marred by the litter scattered over the banks; tin cans, old rubber tyres, broken boxes and paper everywhere. There seemed to be a complete disregard for the environment.

Christmas was approaching and I began to worry about accommodation. We needed to find somewhere in Lower Hutt for the sake of the children, but I could not even begin to talk to Stanley about it. He was apparently not concerned. I understood why a few weeks later, when he announced that he was going back home at Christmas. For one moment, my brain raced as I tried to understand why he would want to spend Christmas in Britain. Then he explained. He had had enough of 'this God-forsaken place', and was returning home for good and he intended to do it secretly, not informing the school of his departure. "Don't you dare mention this to the children or anyone else." The unspoken question of what would happen to us lay heavily between us. He answered it himself, "You can stay here. You've got a job lined up. You'll be OK." Stay here? No home, a new job and now no husband? The enormity of what he was suggesting took my breath away. *I* would be left to face the wrath of the headmaster. *I* would be left with the three children and nowhere to live. The same pattern of behaviour was being repeated. I exploded, "How dare you suggest that I stay here to face the mess you'll leave behind! Can you imagine the effect on the twins when their school friends come back? They'll be the laughing stock of the school. And our name will be mud! And where do you think we are going to live, after you have 'swanned off'? Don't you even *care?* Don't these children mean *anything* to you?" He stepped back at this unexpected onslaught, stared at me without saying anything. What could he say? He knew very well that what he was intending to do was shocking in the extreme. So he resorted to his usual tactic – turned on his heel and went out. As soon as he had gone, the enormity of what was ahead of us hit me. I had to get back to England. I could not stay here in a strange country, without friends or family, with no prospect of a roof over our head. *I had to get away, too!* I geared myself up to facing him when he returned. No matter how, the children and I had to return. He could not yet abdicate his responsibilities. That could come when we were back in England. There I could cope with it. He was quiet and subdued when he returned and listened quietly to my explanation of the impossibility of remaining alone in New Zealand. He finally accepted my argument and together we tried to plan how we could leave, even though my stomach churned at the thought of what we were doing. We had all our belongings with us, so the children and I would have to return to the UK by boat. Stanley insisted on going back by aeroplane. That way he could leave the school as soon as it broke up for the Christmas holidays and I could follow afterwards. The dreadful secret had to be kept from the children and the school. The only person who eventually guessed something was up was the cook, although he did not really know what was happening. Stanley told him that we were returning home for Christmas, which he obviously did not believe since we would be taking all our belongings as well. But he was so good to me. Once Stanley had finally left, taking his own luggage and our hopes of a new life in New Zealand with him, the cook offered to drive us to Wellington with all our luggage to pick up the boat. Our farewells at the quayside were very tearful. The twins cried and I had tears in my eyes as we waved him goodbye for ever. Having very little money, all I could buy as a keepsake were two small, wooden Maori gods and a green mother-of-pearl brooch, made by the Maoris. The experiment had failed. The move had not saved my marriage; in fact it now underlined the absolute necessity for me to leave Stanley and try to pick up the pieces of my life again.

The ship which took us home belonged to a Greek company. It sat in the water like a huge, white whale as we boarded it with all our paraphernalia. And in spite of my tearfulness, my heart began to lift at the prospect of adventure ahead. We would be on the boat for three weeks, before we transferred to a plane for the final leg of the journey to London. The ship was staffed by swarthy, bulky Greeks who were very good with the children. The food was Greek and very tasty, specially the salads. Rather like a school, a ship on the ocean is a closed world, a microcosm and I looked forward to some lessening of the tension now that Stanley was not around. I began to relax and became less stressed. Our cabin was in the bowels of the ship, but that did not matter. The children delighted in the fact that there was a lift which they proceeded to use constantly. In order to create a sense of community, passengers were sat together at mealtimes on large round tables. I looked forward to meeting some interesting people. Unfortunately, because we were a family unit, the purser had decided that we should sit at our own table, apart from the other passengers. I was appalled. I was quite happy to have breakfast and lunch with the children, but in the evening, I needed more adult company. For two evenings running, we sat together mostly in silence as we listened to the chatter from the next table which increased gradually as the meal wore on. To try to make polite conversation with my glowering adolescents was a real strain. I decided I did not like this solitary confinement, but was hesitant about asking the steward to let us join the rest of the company. I became increasingly concerned. How would I cope with three weeks like this? After the third evening, I decided the only way I could meet anyone was to go to the bar and hope to get into conversation with someone. As usual I was most apprehensive, but consoled myself with the thought that a few drinks would give me courage to start a conversation. So I went to the bar. In my apprehension, I went too early. I was the only person there. I sat on a stool at the bar, talking to the bar steward. Soon, more people drifted in, but proceeded to sit at small tables dotted around. My heart sank. I was so conscious of being a woman on my own, particularly as I had probably been noticed with my 'brood' around me. Then, one of the men in a group came up to the bar and said to me:

"Can I offer you a drink? I see you're drinking gin and tonic. Would you like another one?" I was saved! I could have flung my arms around his neck in gratitude. I looked up at him. He was in his early thirties, a tall, rangy individual with a pronounced tan and deep lines etched on his thin face. He also had a strong Liverpudlian accent. I decided he wasn't my type, but I could not be too choosy in the circumstances. When the ship docked for the passengers to get off and explore the area, I would be on my own with the children. I didn't even know whether I would have the courage to leave the ship and then I would miss all the exotic locations. So I needed some sort of escort, if I could get one and he could perhaps fit the bill. He was with a group, but I surmised that they might be friendly and let us come with them. As it happened, the group were passengers he had just met. He was alone. He had been working in Perth, had now finished his contract and was returning home. We became friends and inevitably lovers, a classic shipboard romance. Once again, I was drawn into a relationship which I did not really want but it was preferable to total isolation. My confidence increased as a result. I even asked the Captain if we could join a group on another table, which he readily agreed to. The rest of the cruise was very pleasurable. Whenever we docked, Tom came with us. I remember one night, we docked in the late evening. It was warm, even sultry. There were swarms of boat-hands milling around the ship, loading material. The atmosphere was electric with excitement and bustle, reminding me of stories I had read about great ocean liners docking in India and coolies running on agile feet around the crowds. I felt that I was one of the characters in those novels. There was also the excitement of crossing the date-line. The Australian and New Zealand passengers sprayed champagne over everyone and screams filled the air. When we reached the Panama Canal and the ship slowly glided through, it was another memorable occasion.

I was invited one evening to dinner at the Captain's table and enjoyed some really stimulating conversation. Mealtimes were often quite exciting, given over to different culinary experiences, Thai, Chinese, Mexican. The children loved these times; the dishes were on a buffet and one took one's selection on trays out onto the deck, sat in the deckchairs, savouring delicious flavours, gazing out over the calm, blue sea, and watching a blood-red sun sink slowly into its azure depths, the whole sky suffused then with a myriad of pinks and reds and purple. Another time, a rumour pervaded the ship that we were about to enter into a period of stormy weather. I was really apprehensive, knowing my tendency to seasickness. I had been invited with others for preprandial drinks that evening, so before that I took a seasickness pill to avoid any possibility of sea-sickness But I reckoned without the combination of pills and alcohol. After one or two gin and tonics, I suddenly felt so sleepy. I managed to tell the children that I was going back to my cabin, stumbled woozily down into our cabin and collapsed on the bed, out like a light. I did not wake up until lunchtime the next day. The children had already had breakfast and were joining in the organised games for that day, so they had not been concerned. But the episode made me very wary of sea-sickness pills again. The most important social event of the cruise was the Captain's dance. Everyone was invited. For some reason, my new friend, Tom, was averse to escorting me to the party, although he acknowledged gracefully that he was keen to dance with me. He said he didn't want us to be seen as a 'couple'. Did I mind if we went to the dance separately? Did I mind? As it happened, I *did* mind. I knew I would be terrified entering the room alone. But my pride kicked in, as usual. So I feigned nonchalance and said that it was fine by me. Secretly, I was seething and resolved to pay him back for this rejection. The children and I had great fun putting on our best apparel, the twins giggling excitedly and David smiling. I wore a long, cream sheath dress, which set off my tan perfectly, Valmai wore a primrose yellow blouse with a frilly, spotted pinafore over it, Kathryn wore a dainty, pink and white check dress which made her look deceptively demure and David wore a fetching beige polo-necked jumper with a maroon and beige checked pullover on top. We all looked splendid. I tanked up with some gin and tonic and we sallied forth. The minute we arrived in the room, the children vanished somewhere and I was left on my own. I eyed the company; all in small groups, heads bent forward, deep in conversation. I took a long breath, heaved up my bosom, metaphorically speaking, and barged into the nearest group, with some sort of opening quip. The group parted somewhat and all eyes focussed on me rather suspiciously. Then I made some sort of joke, they all laughed and the ice was broken. I had a wonderful evening, dancing with all and sundry and had the malicious pleasure in telling Tom, who was now in my ambit and who asked me to dance, that I was already booked for that dance. He backed away sheepishly. Later, he tried again and I relented. Some time during the cruise, Tom and I had decided that our romance was to be just a 'ship romance' with no strings attached and had agreed not to try to contact each other again when we arrived back in England. This suited me well. On arrival at home, I would have enough worries; no home, no job and no husband it would seem. He had his own problems of finding a job and re-integrating himself in Liverpudlian society after such a long time. So our lovemaking was untrammelled by any kind of emotional baggage. I learned several new methods of lovemaking which aroused in me completely new sensations.

    Another leisure occupation which I indulged in was Greek dancing at which I became quite adept. I also took a constitutional walk every morning around the ship, skirting the young Antipodeans who were sunning and sporting themselves in the pool, like young porpoises. They were determined to have a really good tan before arriving in the UK. To their chagrin, they discovered that their tans reached a peak of intensity and then proceeded slowly to fade, as if their skins were saying, "Hey! This is enough!" On one of these tours around the deck, I walked under a ladder propped up against the side of the ship. Even as I bent to go under it, one of my mother's sayings entered into my head, "Never walk under a ladder!" She had a predilection for such warnings against fate. I shook myself metaphorically for believing such old wives' tales, but the moment I was walking through it, a sudden clatter on the rungs made me look up and cascading towards me was a pot of white paint. It duly landed on me, spilling its white, glutinous contents over my bust. Following hard on the tin came a dark-complexioned, beefy Greek sailor. A stream of Greek issued from his lips which was incomprehensible to me, and then he proceeded to dab ineffectually at the sticky mess coagulating rapidly on my neck and front. I tried to push him aside, embarrassed and uneasy at this contretemps but he would have none of it, making signs that I should follow him below deck. Still shocked, I allowed myself to be propelled to a cabin. Here, he took a towel and proceeded with evident enjoyment to rub slowly and voluptuously at my throat and breasts. Finally recognising the futility of this method as a way of removing the paint, he made gestures to the effect that I should remove the offending garment. Now, thoroughly alarmed at his temerity and fearful of possible consequences, I regained some of my composure, pushed him roughly aside and escaped to the corridor. I suppose I could have sued the company for the accident, or even received reimbursement for my clothes, but this was not yet the litigation era. I settled for having the dress cleaned.

  The ship disembarked us in Haiti and we boarded a plane, stopping only to refuel in Boston, which lay peaceful and quiet under a blanket of snow, looking unfamiliar after so much sun. Arrival at Gatwick was tiring, what with three exhausted children and a mass of luggage. But there, at the arrival lounge, was Keith to greet us. After I had written to him of our impending arrival, he had said he would be there but I didn't really believe him. He was kindness itself, ushering us out of the airport to a nearby hotel where he had booked two rooms for us to save us journeying to my mother's house. I kissed him gratefully and passionately. We slept together in a double bed, but recognising my exhaustion, he merely held me close as I fell asleep. The next day, I was uneasy at the thought of my mother's reaction to our arrival at her cramped flat. In fact, she was very happy to see us. There were no recriminations from her, only a fatalistic acceptance of the turn of events. Stanley had said he would meet me at the flat, but I was sceptical, thinking he would take this opportunity to disappear forever. But he duly appeared, saying that since the contracts between us and the buyer of Craigmore had not yet been signed, we could stay there a few weeks, which would give us time to find other accommodation. Was it really only four months since we left there? The house seemed already to belong to the past. We just had time to get the children back into their schools and to find temporary teaching posts in Waltham Forest (I didn't dare apply to Newham). With the posts offered to us, came the possibility of a teachers' flat, a flat twenty-three storeys up in a high-rise block in Leyton. So we had to take it. I remember nothing of that teaching post, only spending the evenings feverishly perusing the *Times Educational Supplement* for teaching vacancies. I was looking for a deputy headship, having decided that I may have been brought down financially and emotionally, but I would not lower my professional sights. I had finally decided just to leave Stanley as soon as I had found a post. Unfortunately, the day when we finally did leave Craigmore, was also the day when I had been offered an interview for a deputy headship in a girls' comprehensive school in Bromley. So while Stanley and the children finally decamped from Craigmore taking my mother with them to help out, I was on my way to what I knew would be a rigorous interview. Given the circumstances on that fateful day, it would have been most surprising if I had been offered the post. I was like Banquo's ghost at the party, there in body and miles away in spirit. I failed to get the job, and drove back dispiritedly to the high-rise block in Leyton. I dreaded even going in there. Just after I left the Dartford Tunnel, I felt so ill that I almost collapsed. I pulled in at a roadside café and broke down in a flood of tears. I could not stop crying, almost retching in my grief and despair. To calm myself for the ordeal ahead, I bought a quarter bottle of whisky and proceeded to drink it, coughing and spluttering as the fiery liquid reached my throat. Still upset, I arrived at the flat and at the sight of my mother and the children waiting anxiously for me, I broke down again, weeping uncontrollably. My mother was galvanised. She leaped to her feet, shouting at me, "How dare you come in here in this state of self-pity? Coming in here smelling of drink, you ought to be ashamed of yourself! Look at the state you are in. You don't deserve all the work we've done today to get this place clean and tidy. You've made your bed, now lie on it!" There was an astounded silence in the room, she glaring at me furiously, with the children silent in awe and wonder. She had never shouted at me like that before. She must have been beside herself with worry and anxiety. But how could I begin to explain to her my own utter desolation? My reluctance to divorce because of her Catholic strictures? But her outburst had the effect of sobering me up immediately.

Still frantically looking for a job, I vowed to myself that I would take the first post offered me no matter where it was. And so it proved. I was finally offered the post of senior mistress in Brynmawr Mixed Comprehensive School in South Wales. I needed to look it up on the map to find it. Quite ruthless now, indifferent to Stanley's plans, I decided to go for the interview. I was amazed that I had even got that far, since Wales is notorious for 'looking after its own'. It must have been my name. I borrowed our one 'banger', took my sister Doreen with me for company and braved the wintry landscape of Wales. On nearing Brynmawr we went through a winter wonderland. The fields were covered in a thick blanket of snow and sparkling icicles hung from fir trees masquerading as Christmas trees. It was breathtakingly beautiful. The interview was a success, I was offered the post of Senior Mistress of a 900-pupil school at the top of the main roads, known locally as the 'Heads of the Valleys'. The school's main claim to fame was that it was the highest school in England and Wales, perched on the top of a hill outside Brynmawr, a town where many of the miners in the local mines had their homes. When we arrived back in London and Stanley heard that I had accepted the post, he could not believe it. He thought I was joking. When the truth sunk in, he went very quiet; he was obviously shocked. Then he just said, "Well, you'll do whatever you like, whatever," and went out.

The next six months living in that ghastly tower block affected us all deeply. Stanley almost did a disappearing act, the twins, normally so confident and outgoing became neurotic and David turned in on himself. I realised the enormous shock this move was for them; one moment in the wide-open spaces of New Zealand and the next cooped up in this hell. The lifts which stank of urine broke down regularly, the twins were terrified that they wouldn't be able to get out if there were a fire. Every time we heard a fire engine's whine, which was often, they dissolved into paroxysms of screams and tears. I doused the flat in disinfectant but still found black insects crawling around. I even found one, once, in a pot of parmesan cheese. The only relief from the agony were tennis courts at the bottom of the block where the children could play tennis and seeing Keith every weekend, who came to take us out in his car. Yet there were moments of relief; sitting under a tree in the adjacent park on a summer's evening listening to the band playing and looking up at the clear blue sky through the latticework of branches. Interestingly, Stanley now started to give me housekeeping money. Apparently, a pub friend had said to him it would not look good if I sued for divorce and he had never supported us properly. For the first time in my life, I had money to spare, to buy two beautiful rosewood bookcases and a second-hand car. Those last few nights before the children and I went to Wales, I would lie in my bed, unable to sleep properly, listening to the mournful howl of the dogs in the neighbourhood, feeling as if I were suspended in limbo in this flat, waiting to come down to earth in another environment. I would finally be rid of Stanley and all would be well.

Chapter 16
Country Life

All was not well, even before the move to Wales. I was thrown into confusion several months before we were due to shake the dust of Leyton from our feet. A letter arrived offering me a deputy headship in Chingford even without an interview. Presumably good reports had been sent out from the LEA from the school I was teaching in temporarily. Once again, the old doubts surfaced; was I right to move away? To deprive the children of a father even though, by no stretch of the imagination, could he be considered an ideal father. How could I renege on my decision to take the new teaching post? A move by Stanley decided my fate. Now that he was facing the prospect of my imminent move, he stirred himself sufficiently to prevent that, by attempting to find a house for us in London, since I had the offer of a job nearby. We actually went looking for one together and found an attractive three-storey high town house on the edge of Chingford Plain. He started the necessary negotiations to buy it, but he was often so sozzled that he missed all the deadlines to reply to correspondence and we lost the house. So the die was finally cast. I went house-hunting in Wales during the Easter holidays and, with my brother-in-law Roy, started scouring the area around Brynmawr. Although still quite disapproving of my separation from Stanley, he was a great help. Apart from the small county town of Abergavenny, there were only very small villages in this rural part of Wales. Eventually I found a new estate going up in Gilwern, with only one main street to its name, about three miles equidistant from Brynmawr and Abergavenny. Then I had a stroke of luck; the show house was being sold cheaper than the rest. My finances were stretched to the limit. Stanley, in a last moment's burst of generosity and perhaps repentance, pressed £200 pounds into my hand and said, "Here, you can have this. It's all I've got left from the house." Which raised the interesting question, "Had some of the money from the sale of our house remained on deposit in

London or did he take it all to New Zealand?" I never knew how much money was left to us after the sale of Craigmore, which is another proof of my financial ignorance. But I bought the house in Gilwern. I don't like estates, because they are nests of gossip, but decided I could not let such an irrational thought dissuade me. The house looked lovely from the outside, built of warm red brick with a slate roof and a white-painted front door. It was detached, with a garden front and back and very light with huge windows. But the inside was poorly constructed; the walls consisted of paper-thin plasterboard. To try to bang a nail into a wall for a mirror or a picture was a feat in itself. One needed a certain type of fitment, a butterfly screw it was called, which opened out like a butterfly's wings once it had penetrated the wall to anchor it. But the house suited me; the price range was within my budget. Now that I had sole responsibility for the children and all our finances, I had to be careful. The children could have a bedroom each and the main bedroom was large enough to accommodate easily my huge antique desk, as well as the normal bedroom furniture. I sallied forth to the Abbey National Building Society in Cwmbran, a ghastly new town near Newport, buoyed up by the thought that I was now financially independent. Not so. The building society was adamant that they could not give a mortgage to a woman alone, particularly as I was not even legally separated. Stanley's name must also be on the mortgage deeds. When one considers how today banks and building societies are throwing money at young people, one can only be amazed at such antiquated rules. It was too late to look elsewhere, so it had to be. Naturally, Stanley was delighted.

Gilwern was as undistinguished a village as one could ever find; it had a main street with a butcher's, a baker's, an all-encompassing grocers-cum-sweetshop, a hairdresser's, a Baptist church and two pubs. Just about everything one needed for survival, but nothing to raise the spirits. Indeed when it rained and the slate roofs glistened darkly, and the granite walls of the buildings looked even grimmer, one's spirits moved in the opposite direction. Its saving grace was the Brecon-Newport canal that ran near the village. This was built in the eighteenth century to haul coal and iron from the mining villages to the docks at Newport. It was a haven of wildlife, with very attractive, seventeenth-century arched bridges, spanning the canal. I spent some of my happiest days walking along the canalside.

My feelings when I finally left that cursed flat can be imagined.

Yet, we almost did not make the move on the day designated, because when I looked for my car in the car park around the block, I could not find it. It had been stolen that very morning! Was this an ill omen? Plans had to be altered rapidly. Stanley lent me his car and stayed behind to deal with the police, and we followed the removal van. The Cockney song:

> *My old man said, 'Follow the van*
> *And don't dilly-dally on the way.*

sprang into my mind as we departed, laughing gaily as though we were on holiday. My first problem when I arrived was where to send the children to school. There were only two choices, King Henry Eighth School in Abergavenny, which had been a good grammar school but was now fully comprehensive or my own school at Brynmawr. I did not want the children in my school for various reasons, not least the fact that I could be placed in the invidious position of having to discipline them; not much of a consideration with David, but definitely possible with the twins. So it was King Henry Eighth Comprehensive School for them. With hindsight, not a wise choice. David complained. He had always prided himself on his mastery of Maths, but was placed in the second set at the school because he had followed a different syllabus in London. It took him a year to catch up and to be moved into the top set. He was also put into the second set for English until I went to the school to complain. The twins were in second sets for Maths and French, but were together in mixed-ability classes for the rest. I queried putting them together, but was fobbed off with some jargon about organisational needs. They settled in quickly in their inimitable fashion, causing havoc at times by resorting to their old practice of pretending to be each other. They became part of a 'gang' at school with predictably deleterious results. Gangs were a feature of this fairly remote area. Groups of boys from Brynmawr would descend on Abergavenny, evenings and weekends, and fight with the locals. The twins' talk was all about someone 'beating up' someone else. It was all so alien to me. One evening a policeman knocked at my door enquiring if Valmai Jones lived there. I was horrified. What had she done? Apparently she had dropped some litter in the High Street of Abergavenny, which is against the law. How I wish such a law was so rigorously implemented in London today! He stayed to chat and I still remember the words he spoke to me, "You may think Abergavenny is a pleasant place to live in and it is in the daytime, but it becomes a totally different place in the evening." It was the usual tale of drunken fights and brawls after closing time. The twins came back one day from walking on the canal, burst in noisily to tell me that a man had 'flashed' at them. They were agog with excitement. "What God-forsaken place have we come to?" I thought. Certainly not the idyllic peaceful countryside I had envisaged. I bought a dog to compensate the children for the absence of Stanley, but he proved as much a handful as the twins, even though I took him religiously to a training school. The problem was the telephone. He became alert to the pandemonium that ensued when the phone rang and the twins vied as to which one of them could answer it first. The dog joined in the game, rushing madly forward, barking furiously. The poor animal became paranoid about the telephone. He also wasn't too happy at seeing the outline of the postman through the front glass door and would throw himself at the glass, succeeding one day in crashing right through it. The postman disappeared in a flash.

The toll of the move, my job, the children, began to tell on me. Within weeks of starting my new post, I developed a cold sore on my lip which I insisted upon calling 'facial herpes' much to the amusement of my family. I went to the doctor for medication, which had an adverse effect on my skin. My face billowed. I phoned the headmaster to tell him that I could not possibly face the staff looking so grotesque. He was initially sympathetic, but within a few days suggested that I come into school and work 'incommunicado' in the fastness of my study. Perhaps he thought I was malingering, since he did not know me yet. If so, he was quickly disabused when he saw me. So I returned to work but it was hopeless. There was always someone knocking at my door for help or advice. At least I was able to avoid the comments on my appearance in the staff rooms. Note the plural. The separate male and female staffrooms at which I expressed surprise initially, was in the time-hallowed tradition in Wales of keeping the sexes separate except for procreational purposes. I suggested quite early on that this was detrimental to the smooth running of the school, hindering departmental staff from discussing problems. But the men were adamant that this situation suited them and the women quite passively condoned this blatant manifestation of the division of the sexes. So of course, there was a bigger staffroom for the men and the ladies had to be satisfied with a smaller pokier room next door. I vowed to do something about it. It took all my energy and determination to persuade the headmaster of the benefits of one staff room, not the least advantage of which would be a much larger, lighter staff room. But it was even more of a battle to overcome the prejudice of the older men. Fortunately, I had the support of almost all of the women staff and most of the younger men, who objected to this separation at breaks and lunchtimes. I still have the photograph of me wielding a hammer to administer the first blow to the dividing wall. I was to encounter more male chauvinism later at our first school function, where I met the chairman of the governors, amongst other Welsh worthies. This corpulent individual with a pronounced 'valley' accent loomed up before me saying with a knowing leer on his face, "So you are the senior mistress, are you? A *senior* mistress! It's an appropriate title if you would allow me, you are looking very elegant." I tried to mould my face into a poker-like stare, but it did not seem to disturb him. Worse male chauvinism was to affect me later.

The school was built in the 1950s and was typical of that period with its flimsy fabric and huge plate-glass windows in every classroom, so that one roasted in summer and froze in winter, in spite of the central heating. Whichever Welsh architects decided to site it on the top of a hill just outside the town needed their heads examined. It stood on a high promontory above the town, perched precariously like an eagle's lair. It was closed regularly for days in winter because the steep path leading to the school was made impassable by the heavy falls of snow. Some of the other women staff and I came to dread the winters; the need to drive up to the top of the path, with frozen snow lying on it so that one's car slithered and skidded across it, was a constant problem. My greatest fear was the possibility of the brakes failing to grasp the glistening, freezing tarmacadam, so that the car would slide helplessly to the bottom where a road was running past. This occurred once to a male member of staff but fortunately for him there was no traffic passing at the time, as the car slid effortlessly and rapidly down the path and came to a halt below. If we were lucky, the snow would already have fallen before we arrived at school and we could leave our cars in the town and plough through the snow on foot. If we were unlucky, the snow would fall in the daytime. We would watch helplessly from the huge plate-glass window of the classroom to see it fall lightly and silently on the fields below. In no time, it seemed, the flakes became bigger and thicker, increasing in intensity, rapidly obliterating the countryside around. There was then meant to be an orderly dispersal of children from the building. Most of the time it was a rout, with the staff as eager to get their cars down the slope as the pupils were to avoid lessons. Once, when the school had been closed for days, the headmaster became quite concerned about the students who would soon be sitting their end of school exams. He wanted to arrange for them to have their lessons in Brynmawr itself, but needed to consult with some staff beforehand about the organisation of the move, so suggested that we should all meet in the school itself. I did not think this was a wise decision to make and neither did the other staff involved, who had to struggle even to get to Brynmawr. Arriving at the bottom of the school, some of us saw him standing on a high bank of snow, a tiny, black solitary creature waving to us in encouragement. Then suddenly he was gone. He had completely disappeared from our sight. He must have fallen into a snowdrift. Two brave members of staff struggled up the mountain and managed to rescue him. They brought him down, bruised and shaken. The other staff were now demurring at the task ahead. "This is above the call of duty", was the prevalent thought. Welsh teachers are on the whole a belligerent lot. A tacit decision was made to abandon any attempt to get into the school.

The worst times were when there was black ice on the roads, which could not be seen until one's foot or car was on it. It was really treacherous. I remember my car sliding helplessly from side to side on a main road, quite out of control. Even when rain was the only problem, there were dangers. The Clydach Gorge ran alongside the three-lane Heads of the Valley road towards Gilwern, and when it had been raining heavily for some time, the volume of water was so great that it spilled out hazardously across the road and one needed the sangfroid of a racing driver to attempt it. I would inch forward at about ten miles an hour and feel years older when I arrived home. One year, the rain fell continuously for days until finally the River Usk, which ran through Abergavenny and the surrounding village of Crickhowell, finally gave up the ghost and burst its banks. Abergavenny and Crickhowell were both cut off. We stood at the window at home, watching the rain falling and listened to the local radio reporting more and more destruction of properties. When the rain finally did stop, we went to look at the narrow, side road that connects Gilwern and Abergavenny and saw that the force of the river had torn up the road and punched a great hole in it. I grew to fear more and more the onset of winter. The summer obviously compensated for these hazardous times, in fact the next summer we had the great drought, the hottest, driest and longest summer on record. I had recently bought a lovely flowering cherry tree and had planted it in the front garden, to soften the grid-like appearance of the estate. It soon began to droop because of the weather and I thought that I would lose it, so I had all the family out in the front garden every day, pouring buckets of water on it.

My main responsibility as senior mistress was vaguely phrased as 'responsibility for the welfare of the girls'. In practice it meant disciplining any recalcitrant female pupil. One incident which affected me quite early on was the case of a fifteen-year-old girl. She was pretty but came from a poor home and was not very intelligent. One day she went home from school and never returned. We learned the story soon afterwards. She was apparently pregnant but was too scared to tell her parents, so continued with the pregnancy. Come the day when she began to go into labour, she went down to the bottom of her garden behind some bushes and was delivered of the baby alone. She even bit the umbilical cord with her teeth to separate the baby. After suffering the pains of childbirth, she then went back into the house, leaving the baby behind. Luckily, it was discovered quite soon. The ensuing reactions of her parents can only be imagined. I don't know what happened to her and the baby after that, but I was really shocked at this news. Apparently teenage pregnancies were a fact of life in this area, as I learned later in a much more shocking way.

With so little real responsibility at school, I spent days sitting in my room waiting for something to happen. The only work I did was some French teaching. The pupils seemed very slow on the uptake after the quickness of London children, but I learned that this was because of the slow pace of life and found that some were very intelligent and hard-working. But as usual when one starts a new school there is always some wit who tries to test your discipline. This time it was a fourteen-year-old boy. I said something to the class and immediately he repeated what I had said in his imitation of my London accent. I am sensitive about accents and I was furious that he dared to mock me in front of the class. What I should have done was to turn the insult aside by making an amusing response, but I was caught off guard and threw the full weight of my position in the school at him. "How dare you speak to me like that! Get out of this room now and wait outside my office. You will be caned for such insolence." I glared so ferociously at him, that he slunk out of the room immediately. He was probably already regretting his attempt at causing a laugh. At the end of the lesson, I went back to my office and he was standing outside looking much more sheepish. "You will stay here until I call you in." Once inside my room, I deliberated what I should do. I had already regretted mentioning the cane which I have never used. I was suddenly reminded of a boy many years ago who raised his fist to strike me and I had then realised that I had not dealt wisely with the situation. It seemed I was still making the same mistakes. I had to cane him because I had said I would. There was a cane in the cupboard which I took out gingerly and swished around feebly for a few moments, trying to gather up courage to use it properly. When I did finally call him in, I don't know which of us was the more nervous. I administered a light tap on his hand with the cane, then said: "Don't let me catch you trying to imitate my voice again, do you understand?" He nodded weakly, he was almost in tears. "Right, now you can go." I had no trouble with him after that, nor with any other pupils. My fame went before me. With very little to do, I threw all my energies into enthusing my classes. I realised that France was so far away for them that they needed to learn more about the country. I began to organise school exchanges, eventually finding an excellent school in the Champagne area with whom we continued to exchange pupils for years. Each time I stayed with the headmistress who was very kind, but insisted that we take tea *à l'anglais* every afternoon. This ritual involved sitting on an uncomfortable Louis IV chair and drinking Earl Grey tea with lemon. I loathed it, but did not dare say so. I became friends with this headmistress and would regularly stay with her during the exchange, speaking so much French that I dreamed in French. She had a large, luxurious flat in Juan-les-Pins on the Côte d'Azur and invited me to bring the children there as well. They loved it. Usually, I would take another member of the French department with me to help, but one year the local vicar, whom I had met on various school occasions asked if he could come. I was rather nonplussed but felt I couldn't refuse him. The French headmistress was delighted to have a real English vicar with the group and invited him to stay in her flat as well. I noticed she gave me some very enigmatic looks at times, because the vicar was very funny and made me laugh. She could see we got on famously. He was not a typical vicar. In fact he behaved quite outrageously at times such as jumping the queue to the restaurant on board ship, knowing full well that with his dog-collar on, no one would remonstrate with him. After a few days in France, he became so friendly with me that I began to fear that he had designs on me! I was most concerned. With my Roman Catholic background, the very thought of any liaison with someone of the cloth was anathema to me. But we were placed in a very close association at the head teacher's flat. He would appear in the evening in his dressing gown and sometimes knock on my door when I was in bed to ask for something. When we finally arrived home in England, he told a friend that I was inhibited! Fortunately, he moved to another vicarage soon after but, to this day, I don't know what his intentions were. The parents of my French pupils were very supportive, especially as their offspring would bring home presents of bottles of champagne from the host families. This was totally illegal, but in spite of dire warnings, they managed it just the same. Two of my star pupils read French at university and one even went there for a holiday and stayed to marry a Frenchman. I was accosted one day in Abergavenny by her irate mother who accused me of being instrumental in depriving her of a daughter. It was all my fault.

To relieve my boredom at school with so little responsibility, although I was being very well paid, I started to read for an M.Ed (Master of Education) at Cardiff University. The bonus was leave of absence one day a week to attend lectures. One of our theses was to study our own school and suggest ways of improving it. Since I was fairly new to the school, my first impressions were still sharp and I was able to see clearly both its strengths and its faults, and the old-fashioned practices still obtaining. This clarity of viewpoint tends to diminish as one becomes enmeshed in any organisation, so I was lucky to start this M.Ed. when I did. I received a distinction for this effort, and Mr Archer, the headmaster, a pleasant but rather ineffective man, who seemed more interested in his vast garden than the school, decided to use my dissertation as a blueprint for change. He agreed to work with me to try to implement some of my recommendations. From that time, school was much more interesting and we persuaded the staff to accept some radical alterations to the school organisation.

Some were quite mundane, such as carpeting all the rooms and corridors, which usually echoed noisily to the tramp of feet. But the results of the carpet being laid were nothing short of miraculous – it cut the noise by half and even reduced the speed with which the pupils walked from classroom to classroom. We also increased the size and importance of the Design and Technology department which had been somewhat of a Cinderella subject in the curriculum. My main thesis for the M.Ed. was on the comparison between mixed and single-sex schooling. I was becoming quite a feminist! I think it is now accepted and league tables confirm, that girls tend to do better academically in a single-sex school but conversely boys do better in mixed schools. However, at that time such an opinion was held by only a few educationists. As part of the course, I was also sent to exotic places like Llandudno with other heads and deputy heads to study curriculum development in comprehensive schools. I have to confess that one of these weeks was hilarious. The group of which I was the only female member never really stopped laughing. When one of our exercises was to devise a new curriculum for an imaginary school, we really decided on some revolutionary decisions, which I don't think were very practical. If they were, they were certainly too advanced to be implemented.

At home we were always on a tight budget. Stanley's contribution to our finances was erratic in the extreme and I could never depend on it. So foreign holidays were out and we had recourse to youth hostels for our holidays. We had fun though. I remember taking my seventy-year-old mother with us to Kent where we stayed in a very pleasant youth hostel. After registering and sorting out sleeping arrangements, we walked down to the village and went into a pub for a few drinks. My mother's favourite tipple was Guinness. The fun started when we went back and prepared for bed. My mother climbed onto her bunk and tried to get into the sleeping bag, which seemingly had no opening. I can still see her lying on the bunk, legs kicking wildly in the air, desperately trying to find the opening. She couldn't manage it and collapsed on the bunk in giggles. That set us all laughing uproariously, tears streaming down our faces. Finally, when we had all recovered from our mirth, David helped her into the sleeping bag. I was really proud of her that night. To endure the rigours of youth hostelling in one's seventies is quite a feat. I had discovered that since the death of my father, she had reverted to the person she must have been when young, so different from the stern person I knew when my father was alive. She was funny and witty and really enjoyed life. She had that marvellous trait of being at home in any company and her warmth was very attractive. The children adored her. I used to take them at least once a month to see her in her little flat on the eighteenth floor of a block of flats, where she had moved when my father died. I would drive along the M4 straight after school, which was quite hazardous because I was so tired on Fridays. It was even worse in winter driving in the darkness. Her flat had underfloor central heating and the children, who had to sleep on the floor, would regularly complain of being roasted alive, so hot was the floor when the heating came on in the night. I would lie on the floor beside her bed, having long conversations with her, none of which I now remember. I grew very close to my mother at this time and wanted her to come to Gilwern to live. Wisely she declined.

I took up other country pursuits; walking the dog along the canal, making homemade wine; and walking the surrounding hills with one of the staff, who lived in Gilwern. We climbed Sugar Loaf, the highest hill in England and Wales and gazed appreciatively at the landscape spread out below us, with tiny villages nestling in the folds of the soft, green hills. Doreen and her son, Robert came to stay with us once and we took them up onto the moorland, high above Brynmawr, one windy day to fly his new kite. It was a wild, beautiful place where bands of wild ponies roamed freely. Robert launched the kite rather hesitantly; it trailed for a while a few feet above the ground, when out of the blue one of the ponies came galloping by, caught his legs in the string and, terrified, began to gallop away. Robert started crying while we tried to retrieve the kite by racing after the pony. The scene must have looked really comical as we sped after the horse now festooned with the multi-coloured kite… My speed was hampered by the bursts of laughter issuing from my lungs. I was irresistibly reminded of Mr Hulot running after the plastic sausages being churned out of the machine in *Les Vacances de Monsieur Hulot*, a famous French film. We never recovered the kite but all except Robert enjoyed the episode.

One day I was asked by the headmaster to give special attention to one of the female staff. This was Kate Treharne who later became a good friend. I gathered from the head that her husband had left her for another woman and she had started to drink heavily. I was quite taken aback by his request; I really didn't see myself in the guise of counsellor, particularly in view of my own lack of success in the marital stakes. I agreed to do what I could although I did not know her at all, had never even spoken to her. She was an amazing-looking woman, heavily built, much taller, stronger than most women, with jet-black hair, deep-brown eyes and a high colour. She was a real beauty. She also held strong opinions, and was quite promiscuous. She was English; her parents worked on the land in Hereford and she had two brawny powerful-looking brothers. I was irresistibly reminded of Eustacia Vye in Thomas Hardy's *Return of the Native*. She had the same smouldering looks. She was very artistic and creative, interested in literature but also knowledgeable about many things, animals, gardening, geography and even mechanical, technical things at which I am hopeless. She was also an excellent cook and I learned much from her in this field. I suppose being brought up in a family who all worked on the land, she had developed the same toughness. Yet underneath all this toughness she was a lost soul, unsure of herself, aware that she didn't fit in anywhere. She was not particularly popular with the staff, seen by the women as a threat, and a challenge to the men with her combination of beauty and masculine strength. I felt that she had fought hard against her background and had managed to escape to training college where she trained as a primary school teacher, but her level of education was not high. She was also quite odd in some ways; she had this habit of pausing for a long time before she answered a question, which I found most off-putting. Yet she strove constantly to improve herself. With misgiving at first, I invited her to dinner and she seemed to enjoy herself and the family liked her. Kate taught me how to make homemade wine, since I couldn't afford to buy commercial ones. We would wander by the River Gavenny through the open meadows, which were a sea of yellow dandelions in spring, to pick bunches of the pungent-smelling flowers for the wine. We also picked the sweet-smelling elderflowers, balanced delicately like small, creamy-white saucers on the branches and from them made a heady, perfumed, white wine. In autumn we would return to the same elder tree to collect the luscious-looking, ruby-red berries hanging heavily on the tree, to make a potent elderberry wine reminiscent of port. When Kate came round in the evenings to see me, which she did regularly, she would bring a demijohn of wine which had recently been made and we would become pleasantly hazy as we talked. She drank much more than I did; I think she even drank her own wine while it was still fermenting. But if I did help and support her in some way, she certainly helped me. The children had someone else to talk to and instead of working every evening, I was able to relax when she came and just enjoy a desultory conversation, making me less tense. When not with me, she was often seen at the small pub at the bottom of the road, chatting up the men and sometimes leaving the pub with them. One evening at about midnight, there was a bang at the front door. Alarmed, I got up but could see only a dark shape slumped on the ground. I opened the door and Kate literally fell in. She had been drinking with some man, was unable to drive home, so walked. She was practically unconscious. Another time, she appeared with a nasty-looking burn on her forearm. Apparently, she had drunk so much that she had fallen asleep with her arm touching the radiator and had not been conscious of the pain. I really don't know how she managed to keep on teaching after such escapades, but she was as strong as an ox. The alcohol finally got to her. The platelets in her blood began to malfunction and she was hospitalised for some time. She was warned she must give up alcohol, so she became a teetotaller, a health-food fanatic and a hypochondriac. She also became less interesting and quite neurotic. She eventually took early retirement.

Since my sister Irene and Roy now lived quite near in Newport, the children and I would enjoy some pleasant days out with them and their youngest son, Simon, visiting stately homes and estates. I also joined the Newport Home-Made Wine Club with Roy and I would make the monthly journey to Newport, clutching my own version of a wine and sampling the somewhat dubious attempts at wine-making of other members. Some were excellent and others were execrable, but it was a pleasant social occasion. Then would come the hazardous drive back to Gilwern. Fortunately, the road to our village was a dark, unlit, minor one with very little traffic on it at night. I would drive dreamily along, enveloped in the dark silence of the countryside, glad to be away from the noise and glitter of the town. I remember once realising that I had almost fallen asleep at the wheel and had been driving in the middle of the road, but fortunately encountered no dangers. Most of the people in the club were couples, all happily married it seemed. Most were not my types, but after a few glasses of wine, one sees others from a different perspective. I met one Welshman, unattached, who seemed to like me. He was plump, with dark hair and eyebrows and long sideboards and looked just like a Victorian gentleman. He was painfully shy, but as the evening wore on obviously became less so. He invited me to his flat one Saturday and ever curious I went. I was ushered into his bedroom in double-quick time, where I noted with unease a single, virginal-looking bed with all white bedclothes on it, which had probably never witnessed any passion or consummation. I hate single beds. He was paralysed with timidity as we lay down side by side, on the narrow bed. We lay there silently for a few moments and then I suddenly decided I had made a serious mistake in coming. I was most disagreeably aware that in the cold light of day, I felt nothing but repulsion for his fat stomach, heavy jowls and long sideboards. I was concerned how I could extricate myself but I needn't have worried. He probably regretted the invitation himself. We continued to lie there in total silence for a few moments longer and then, as though we had communicated intuitively, both of us got up off the bed. I departed and never saw him again. I had a few more liaisons: all quite harmless. I was taken out for a meal once in Brecon by a publican. That was a godforsaken place, drear and dismal. I remember being invited back to his pub in Abergavenny and deciding that I would try all the liqueurs on the shelf, since they were free. We had a convivial time together but I fell off the barstool before I could taste them all.

After a brief period of silence from Stanley, he surfaced once again telephoning me to say that he was coming down for the weekend to see the children and have a look at 'his' house. I'm sure this was meant as a witticism on his part, but it left me uneasy. He contributed nothing to the mortgage, so I was always short of money. The children were now adolescents and consequently demanding more pocket money. I made them earn it by doing some chores to help out in the house. I initially had a cleaner when we first moved in, but the children messed up the place so quickly afterwards, that I gave it up as a bad job. I had to take a loan out with the Lombard Bank at a prohibitive interest rate once because I needed money so badly. It was only after the publication of the Clegg report in 1979, which advocated an increase up to 25% for public sector workers, which Margaret Thatcher had reluctantly accepted, that my finances eased. Stanley had not changed his job as a temporary teacher in Waltham Forest, which gave him the freedom to take days off when he felt like it to recover from a particularly boisterous evening. He eventually took early retirement on medical grounds, having found an impressionable doctor in Llandudno to certify that he was unfit for work. He visited us, about once every three months. On the first occasion, he was on his best behaviour, but predictably, he could not sustain this and reverted to his former ways, spending the evening in a local pub and coming home the worse for drink. The gossip on the estate saw him as my 'fancy man', until I disabused them. One time, after he had come in the worse for drink, I heard the sound of his heavy steps stumbling on the stairs. I lay rigid with fear that he might try to come into my bedroom. David must have heard him as well, because I heard him talking to Stanley. Suddenly it became an altercation.

"Get out of my way, you idiot," Stanley said in slurred tones.

"She doesn't want you in there," I heard David's quietly determined voice.

"I don't care what she wants. She's my wife and don't think you can stop me, you little sod."

"I've told you, Dad. She doesn't want you in her bedroom and I'm not going to let you go in."

"You bloody fool, what's it got to do with you?"

I feared the worst. I strained to hear what was being said, but their voices receded and then there was silence. I relaxed thankfully, mentally praising my timid son for standing up to his father. I learned from the twins the next morning, recounted to me in tones of great glee, that David had actually stood at my door with both arms outstretched to prevent Stanley coming in. They had been peeping fearfully from their bedroom door at the exciting scene unfolding before them.

The problem of future scenes like this began to worry me. There was also the worry about his name on the mortgage deeds. I decided to consult a solicitor. He took all my details and then said in quiet tones, "It appears from what you say, Mrs Jones, that you are in quite a difficult position."

"What do you mean?"

"If as you say, your husband is earning less than you, not only can he claim half of the value of the house, but he can also claim maintenance from you when your children have left home."

I gazed at him in complete astonishment.

"Surely this can't be? He couldn't do that?"

"Whether he would or not is immaterial. That is the legal

position. My advice to you is not to wait until this possibility transpires, but to divorce him as soon as possible." Against all my instincts, I realised that he was right. I had to make a final break with Stanley. I instructed the solicitor to start proceedings against him. I anticipated trouble from Stanley even though we had been separated for some time, but as it happened, as soon as he had the first intimation of my intentions, he decided to counter claim for divorce. So I let him go ahead. At least, it meant I did not have to appear in court. Within a couple of months I was a divorced woman, a position, which I still feel keenly, as some sort of disgrace, as if it is my fault. I kept my married name for the sake of my job and the children and now feel that the title of Mrs Jones is part of me.

Keith came down regularly to see me. As ever the soul of discretion, he stayed in a hotel in Abergavenny where we were able to enjoy each other's company unencumbered. In order to forestall any gossip, I made sure he did not come to the house. I was almost paranoid about my reputation in Brynmawr school, which could have easily been destroyed by malicious tongues, the lifeblood of the village. The school secretary who had friends in Gilwern would report on the gossip, so I knew I was closely monitored, being a single woman with a family. We would take the children out with us during the day on Saturday and Sunday, and once again spent most of the time laughing. Keith tried to get a job in the area to be nearer to me, but was unsuccessful, coming up against the Welsh wall of prejudice against 'foreigners'. Even I and other 'foreign' families in the village were never accepted by the locals. Once, during the holidays, I took the children to stay with my mother while I had a weekend with Keith in Eastbourne. In spite of my affection for him and his evident dog-like devotion to me, the weekend was not a success. I had grown up and moved on emotionally, with all my efforts now concentrated on bringing up the children and doing my work properly. Even the sex was unsatisfactory. In the middle of our lovemaking, he would complain of a pain in his back. I wondered what was wrong with him. I learned of the gravity of his health a few weeks later, when his mother telephoned me at school to tell me he had been taken into hospital, diagnosed as having stomach cancer. I left the children with Irene and Roy for the weekend and rushed up to see him. It was pitiful to see the transformation in him; he was gaunt and grey, a shadow of his former self. I could see the hand of death already on him and was devastated. He was unaware of his condition and talked cheerfully of coming back to Gilwern, but weeks later he was dead. I received the telephone call during a staff meeting. I knew I would have great difficulty in finding someone to look after the children during the week if I wanted to go to his funeral and it would be a problem for the school. But really, I could not face it. I now bitterly regret my cowardly decision. I should have gone to his graveside and thanked him for all the joy and laughter he had brought into our lives. My life was poorer as a result of his death.

Although I threw myself with great enthusiasm into country pursuits, I gradually became rather bored with living on an estate. I would stand at the kitchen window washing up and look at the young couples working together in their gardens, and felt that I was so different from them as a middle-aged, single parent. I longed for the anonymity of London and wearied of the distances one had to travel to find any form of cultural life. To get to a concert or the opera in Cardiff was a major event, involving an hour's journey there and the same amount of time travelling back in the dark. It was quite exhausting. So it was very pleasant when my friend Audrey re-appeared in my life. I had lost touch with her since I left London and then a call came one day from her. She was living in Monmouth, not that far away. I grabbed the children and we went to visit her and her family. She had divorced and remarried a man called Bill Bales, who was a typical East End 'entrepreneur', a charitable way of glossing over some of his shadier dealings. He was a builder who earned enough money to buy run-down properties, do them up and rent them out. This gave him a steady income. According to Audrey, she was already quite disenchanted with him. He had several bank accounts in different names and juggled them all with consummate skill. Their house was in quite a remote situation. It was situated on three acres of land and a small river ran along the bottom of the fields. It was extremely dilapidated and while he was working on it, she had to live in a caravan for over a year with her three children, another one on the way, and look after the goats that they had bought as well. Her life was hard, difficult, and in bad weather downright disagreeable. But by the time we met again, her house was completed and was beautiful with its stone-flagged kitchen and generously proportioned rooms. We fell into the pattern of seeing each other on a regular basis, which pleased the children since they could spend time with their old friends.

One day my brother Vic also got in touch with me, saying he would like to see me. He was in his fifties now and perhaps slightly nostalgic about his past. I invited him down for the weekend and decided to invite Audrey as well to a meal. I fancied my culinary skills after all the lessons I had had from Kate. To say the evening was amusing would be an understatement – it was very entertaining. After some wine Vic was in full flow about his life and his loves. He had a very good sense of humour and kept us all laughing. I could see him looking at Audrey who was dressed very sexily. She had an eye for the men. When the children left the table, we carried on drinking, eventually singing all the old songs he had sung when younger. When it was time for Audrey's departure, I started moving dishes into the kitchen and when I returned, they both announced that he was going to spend the night with her.

"What, you're going back with Audrey?" I was nonplussed.

"Yeah, if that's OK with you?"

"But what about Bill, Audrey?"

"Oh, he's away for the weekend on business."

"But should you drive home tonight? You've had a lot to drink," said I in my best teacher's voice.

"Oh, I'll be all right. I know the road. It's very quiet at night."

And so they departed in spite of my concerns. I was already in bed fast asleep, when I was woken up from my sleep by a loud banging on the door. I looked at the clock; it was 1.15 a.m. Who could it be? When I opened it, there was Vic leaning on the doorframe breathing heavily and looking the worse for wear. "What an earth's happened to you? Have you had an accident? And where's Audrey?"

"I'll tell you tomorrow. I've got to get to bed, I'm whacked."

So I had to contain my curiosity until the morning. The sorry tale was told by Vic in a very bitter voice. He could not forgive Audrey for what she had done. She had driven a short way past Abergavenny and was on the local road to Monmouth when they realised that the car had developed a puncture. Vic, in no state to start fiddling around with the tyre, persuaded her to carry on driving, until the car was bumping along so badly that they were forced to stop. Both of them were very drunk, but Audrey, in imperious mode, ordered him to get out of the car and fix the puncture. All thoughts of good cheer and bonhomie now vanished as Vic, cursing, climbed out of the car. A light drizzle was beginning to fall. At that moment, a police car drove by, saw the car and stopped to enquire what was happening. Terrified of being breathalysed, Audrey used all the charm she possessed, said Vic had everything in hand, thanked them profusely from the comparative safety of the interior of the car and said they were able to manage, thank you. The police must have suspected that they had been drinking, but it was late and they were probably not in the mood to pursue the matter, so they drove off. This left Vic bending down by the tyre with Audrey still in the car. Both couldn't believe their luck. Then suddenly, Audrey started up the engine and leaning out of the window, shouted out, "I'm off before they come back!" She then drove off at speed in spite of the condition of the tyre. Poor Vic was left stranded and had to walk back to Gilwern. I draw a veil over the comments he made about my friend the next morning.

Audrey had another brush with the police some time later, though the result was not so satisfactory for her this time. One weekend, I decided I would like to go to France for the weekend with Roy and a group from the wine club, so I asked my mother if she would look after the children for me. She was only too glad to help; she thought I worked too hard anyway. We were going to France by coach, which would not leave until ten p.m., so I arranged to meet Audrey in Newport earlier in the evening for a meal in a restaurant in Cardiff. We had a really pleasant evening. I was in high spirits at the prospect of a weekend away. The trouble started when Audrey decided that she would round off the meal with a couple of brandies. This, after having consumed a half bottle of wine. I declined, envisaging the long coach journey to France. We left the restaurant, which was in a cul-de-sac just after nine. Instead of turning left to get out of the road, she turned right.

"What are you doing, Aud?"

"There's a short cut at the end of the road, which I know. I come here often with Bill."

When we arrived at the end of the road, to my horror the road was blocked by a short stretch of pavement.

"Audrey! You can't go there, there's the pavement!"

"I know but it's only a narrow bit, I'll be over it in seconds."

Unfortunately, just as she manoeuvred the car over the pavement, we saw a policeman standing there looking at us. "That's that!" I thought, "We're in for it now." But to our complete astonishment, he let us go without making any attempt to stop us. We could not believe our luck. Soon we were on the motorway to Newport. When I saw the junction for the turn-off to Cwmbran, I directed Audrey to the right-hand lane to avoid any cars trying to get on to the left-hand side to turn off. She turned the wheel really sharply and the car swerved ominously. Immediately, it seemed, we heard the wail of a police car. It drew up beside us and a loud voice shouted to us, "Get onto the hard shoulder!" We were both petrified. Within minutes, Audrey was breathalysed, and before I could comprehend what was happening, she was told to get into the police car. I was left in her car and then a second policeman got into the driving seat. I was terrified I would lose the coach. I turned to him and in a trembling voice said, "Officer, do I have to go to the police station as well? I'm supposed to be going to France tonight and the coach leaves Newport at ten. Will I be able to get on it?" He was helpfulness itself. He assured me that since I was not driving I didn't have to report to the police station, in fact he would drive me to the coach himself. Which he did. What Roy thought when he saw me turn up with a policeman I couldn't imagine, but he didn't say anything. He was only relieved that I was there. So there we were on our way to France with Audrey somewhere in a police station. I was reminded of my own experiences in such places. I felt bad about leaving her to her fate, but there was little I could do to help her. She had to spend most of the night in a prison cell until she sobered up. Then, later, she had a large fine to pay and was disqualified from driving for a year. It was a severe blow to her and she learned a hard lesson that night. Her marriage was also going badly at that time. The combination of marital problems, plus the ban on driving, finally made her decide to leave Bill in Monmouth and return to London. So I lost sight of her again for a few years. She had been like a turbulent wind rushing through my life, but I missed the excitement she generated.

  I had more problems pressing in at home. The children were adolescents now, David was approaching eighteen, had done well in his GCSE exams and was studying Maths, Geography and Biology in the sixth form. I was concerned that the range of subjects was too narrow, because he had always had an affinity for literature. He had immersed himself in books from a very early age and also the Marvel comics, which he collected religiously. He built up quite a library of them and sells some of them gradually for profit when the need arises. He still retains the best of them however. His other love was television; he would annoy me intensely on Saturday mornings watching *Thunderbirds* and other futuristic programmes, which I thought were fantasy rubbish. I even threatened to take away the TV set but didn't. Otherwise he was a model son, quiet and well-behaved. When he went into the sixth form, David wanted to take English but was prevented by his sixth form tutor who said that taking four A-levels was frowned upon in the school. He was forced to drop English, which he regretted bitterly later in life. Such was the 'dumbing-down' effect of many comprehensive schools. My main problems, as can be guessed, were the twins. They had always had a rebellious streak in their characters, secure in their 'twin-ness', and as they approached adolescence this trait became more pronounced. They were a magnet for a certain type of pupil at King Henry School. Valmai was particularly headstrong. Their schoolwork began to suffer. I insisted that they do their homework every night, but they seemed to have a pitifully small amount to do. Consequently they were moved down to lower sets and became friends with some quite rough girls. Why the school allowed them to stay together in the same classes, I shall never know. Gradually they acquired a reputation as troublemakers, although to be fair to Kathryn she was led more by Valmai. I was summoned time and again to the school to discuss their behaviour. What made any solution difficult for me was the fact that they were no trouble at home at all. As time went on, adolescent boys appeared at the house asking for them. Since they would only be going around Gilwern, I felt I couldn't refuse. One day they came home from school and asked if they could go camping with friends for the weekend in one of the villages near Abergavenny. I made exhaustive enquiries of the friends' families, but all seemed innocent enough, so I agreed. Unfortunately for them, I decided to check that they were all right on the Saturday and spent fruitless hours looking for them. They were obviously not where they had said they would be. They duly reappeared at the time I had stipulated, looking quite innocent. When I asked them where they had been, a look of caution came on their faces.

"We've been in Mr James' field as we said!" said Valmai.

"You little liar! I've been looking for you for over an hour and there was no way you've been where you said you were." Valmai tried another tack. "Oh, yes! We found that the field was too damp, so went to Llangybbi where there is a proper campsite. That was OK wasn't it? We didn't think you would mind."

"You're still lying! I looked in all those villages around and you weren't anywhere to be seen." A look of mutinous apathy appeared on their faces as I started castigating them for their deceitfulness and they stood silently listening to my tirade and then went to their rooms. I was left feeling totally drained and helpless before their antipathy. Sometimes, I had the feeling that the three of them were 'ganging up' on me and it wasn't a pleasant sensation. On another occasion, I felt even more under siege. My mother was going to celebrate her eightieth birthday with a gathering of her family. I intended to take all the children, but the twins made a fuss about going, so I took only David with me since he wanted to come. I considered that the twins, now sixteen, were old enough to act sensibly. The neighbour next door agreed to keep an eye on them. Her daughter was the same age and friendly with the twins. I also alerted Roy to the fact that I would be away just for the night. My mother's birthday party was a great success. She had her favourite brother Danny there who made everyone laugh and Vic entertained with his singing. David and I had intended staying with Mum for the night, but late in the evening, there was a telephone call from Roy telling me to get back home immediately. The neighbour had seen youths going into the house and had telephoned to tell him. He had rushed to Gilwern and found these boys hiding in the wardrobes. The twins had seen his car draw up and hidden them. Well, there was an almighty row, and he made them both go back with him to Newport for the night.

I was absolutely incandescent with rage when I faced them. I couldn't find the words to explain my feelings, how betrayed I felt by them. I had trusted them and they had betrayed my trust. This had been the only time they had been left on their own and they had shamed me. They had let me down so badly. I kept repeating, "How could you do it? How could you do it to me? The shame you have brought on me." Kathryn burst into tears and rushed up to her room. Valmai stood looking at me with the same mutinous face she always had when reprimanded. She showed no remorse whatsoever. I was so determined to get some sort of response from her that I hit her several times, whereupon she rushed out of the house. It blew over, of course, but not before Roy and the neighbour had given me their views about the twins' behaviour. Another time they both came home with tattoos on their arms. With a group of girls they all decided it would be fun to have a tattoo. Since they had no money for professional tattooing, they thought it would be just as easy to scratch indelible ink into their arms. Where Kathryn had a very small design on her upper arm, Valmai had blatantly scratched the name 'Timmy' all along her forearm. It was hideous. The ink had gone in so deep that it was impossible to remove. Years later Valmai had to pay dearly to have it removed with laser treatment. This 'Timmy' proved also to be a twin. He had an identical brother. They were seventeen years old and came from a working-class family in a poor part of Abergavenny. And my daughter had become mixed up with this 'Timmy'! They never came to my house, so the twins could only have seen them at school-times. Yet the bombshell, when it came, left me completely unprepared. A younger married woman on our estate called on me one day and asked if she could talk to me. I was quite astonished since I did not know her very well, although I knew the twins were used to going to her house for tea. She started hesitantly, "I'm sorry, I don't think you know anything about what I've come to say." I stared at her mystified as to what she meant.

"What's the matter? You look so serious."

"Well, the twins look on me as a friend and confide a lot in me, as perhaps they wouldn't to you as their mother."

That was for sure. They were like clams with me.

"The fact is, Val has just told me that's she's pregnant and I thought I had better tell you straight away."

She looked at me anxiously as I tried to take in the enormity of what she had said. How? Where? I remember little of the ensuing conversation. She was probably glad to get away from a situation that was embarrassing for her. Left alone, I still could not believe what she had told me. How could this be when Valmai was at home every evening? How naïve I was! When finally Valmai came home, sheepish and silent with the look of mutiny absent from her face for once, I looked at her and had a moment of pure, blinding rage. Not at her, she was barely sixteen and seemed quite innocent to me. No, I was furious with this Timmy for what he had done to her.

That evening, I drove by myself to his house to confront him and his family. I wanted them to see the enormity of what he had done to my daughter. I spoke of the gossip that would rage around her and us, about the fact that she was too young physically and emotionally to bear a child. I said that she would have to have an abortion and they would have to pay for it. All the while the family stood in silence, listening to me, but at the mention of money, they were only too eager to make reparations. The bigger problem was Valmai herself. She didn't want an abortion, she wanted to keep the baby. Kate was very helpful in persuading her of the consequences, so she finally agreed. Kate also knew of a doctor at the French hospital in Bristol who would agree to carry out the abortion. I made an appointment for the Saturday, trying to keep some semblance of normality in our lives. I couldn't find out from Valmai how advanced the pregnancy was. Her replies were evasive and unsatisfactory. I'm not even sure she knew herself. The drive to Bristol was not very pleasant. The atmosphere between us was fraught with unspoken questions. She was probably terrified and I was really anxious myself. I tried to reassure her that the operation would be quite short and that we could go home in a couple of hours. She didn't respond. Her interview with the doctor was indeed very short. When he came out, he said quite severely, "Mrs Jones, I don't know why you brought your daughter to see me. I am afraid I cannot terminate this pregnancy. It is too advanced for me to attempt it."

For the second time in a few days, I was at a loss for words. The journey home was even more unpleasant than when we came. I was out of my mind with worry. My mind raced as to what we should do now. I felt so weighed down by the problem that I could not face school on the Monday and pretended to be ill. Valmai seemed unperturbed. She had expressed no emotion at all, not even crying, but she surely must have had feelings of guilt and fear. If so, I was not party to her feelings. More consultations with Kate who told me that a woman gynaecologist lived on the next estate and perhaps I should have a talk with her. She generously agreed to examine Valmai and then called me in afterwards. Her words were not what I expected.

"Mrs Jones, there is little I can do for your daughter if she wants to keep the baby. She is sixteen years old, an age when she is able to make her own decision about such a serious matter. I would undertake the abortion. She is still within the term to do so, but it would have to be with her approval."

How could I begin to make this single, unmarried woman understand what the consequences would be for Valmai and for all of us? I wanted to cry out to her:

"How would *you* know that? She isn't old enough to make this decision. She is still a child herself. Have you any idea what havoc a newborn baby in the house would cause? Another child to bring up on my own with no financial help from anyone? Can you imagine the gossip? Can you imagine the rage of her father? What do *you* understand about life?" Wisely, I choked all this back, but mentioned the fact that I didn't want my daughter to be saddled so young with a baby, that I did not want her enduring the poverty-stricken life of the Hyder family. Eventually my passion must have touched her and she agreed to do the abortion if Valmai gave her consent. Surprisingly, Valmai agreed. Perhaps she had had time to consider her position. In no time at all, she had had the abortion. She would not talk to me at all about it, merely resumed her life as if nothing had happened. I, on the other hand, was racked with guilt and remorse. Had I done the right thing? But Valmai eventually had her revenge. About six months later, when life had settled down again, I was in bed when the telephone rang. It was Timmy. I could just about hear his words above the noise in the pub where he was. "Mrs Jones, Valmai has asked me to tell you. She is pregnant again and we're going to keep the baby this time." So all the worry, the anxiety about her was of no use. She must have been determined to have a baby, so let it be. I gave up. She would live with the Hyders and in my mother's prophetic words, "She had made her bed and would now lie on it." But the agony of that time was prolonged more than I had anticipated.

When she was only six months' pregnant, she went into labour and was taken to hospital and put on a drip to arrest the birth. This succeeded, but within the month the same thing happened. Again she was in hospital and the birth was again stopped. This happened one more time, when she now began to look ill with all the drugs being pumped into her. By the seventh month, when she started labour pains again, I refused to let the hospital doctor try to stop the birth. Suddenly I had to face the opposition of the medical establishment. I was threatened that if the treatment was stopped, we ran the risk of the baby being born not fully formed. I would not listen. Valmai was now terrified at having the drip put in her and would burst into paroxysms of tears every time it was suggested, becoming almost paranoid with fear. She agreed with me that she wanted the birth to continue, in spite of the doctor's threats. So this time the birth was allowed to continue, much to the disapproval of all the medical staff. I sat in the waiting room with Timmy for what seemed hours. Then we heard that there were complications, that her blood pressure was rising rapidly and she would have to have a Caesarean operation. More hours later, we were still waiting for news. Then Timmy was sent for. He came out from the bedroom she was in and gave me some garbled information; the baby had been born quite healthy, a little boy, but Valmai had had a fit (it proved to be an eclamptic fit) and it was very serious. A nurse then appeared and said that there was no point in our waiting, Valmai was seriously ill, could lose her life, but that they would do everything possible to help her. Totally distraught, I went home and told the other two. Immediately the word got around and my friends, Kate and Audrey and the neighbour came in to give their support, while we waited for the telephone to ring. I never want to experience a time like that again. Eventually we heard that she was out of danger, had recovered from the fit and now both mother and baby were doing fine. I went to bed that night seeing a bleak future ahead of me. Although Valmai would live with the Hyders, I was not happy about it, nor that her new baby would be brought up there. He was my grandson and even before I had seen him, I felt some responsibility for him. In my exhausted state, I wondered whether I could cope any more. His arrival in the world had changed all our lives.

Chapter 17
Changing Times

After the trauma of Leigh's birth, I felt I needed a period of relative calm to concentrate on my school work. Surprisingly, I soon found that I could have it. David went off to university, Kathryn moved to Cardiff to start training as a nurse and Valmai and Leigh, as I thought, were safely ensconced with Timmy's family. I also had more freedom and some more money during the holidays, so Doreen and I decided to go to Paris for a week. I don't know what it is about France, but I always seem to get into some sort of scrape or other. This time, however, it really was Doreen's fault. Because we both like good food, we decided to go to a better restaurant than those we normally frequented. We chose one which was called 'À L'Alsacienne'. I can't remember what we ordered but what appeared were great, clumsy chunks of a dark-brown meat accompanied by some sort of pale-green mush bearing a slight resemblance to cabbage. We were not impressed and even less so when we tasted the mush, which had a bitter-sweet taste that we thought revolting. Obviously, it was sauerkraut, but we did not recognise it as such at the time. Even today, I dislike it. Doreen refused to eat it, and suggested we try something else. I called over the waiter, a burly, surly-looking individual and in my best French asked if we could choose something else. He was very awkward, saying that we had chosen it and he could not replace it with another dish. Doreen, aware that something was amiss, in her usual impatience said, "Oh, let's go! There's nothing we like here anyway. But we aren't paying the bill! We aren't paying for something we haven't eaten." I duly translated what she had said to the waiter. His face darkened, he looked quite threatening and in a great volume of French said something to the effect that if we did not pay, he would call the police. Of course, we did not believe him and prepared to leave, but he called another waiter over to stand by our table and then disappeared. So we sat there, like dumb animals, too scared by this time to try to leave. With what seemed lightning speed, a French *agent de police* surged into view and in no time we were arrested and taken in a Black Maria (again!) to the local police station. There we faced the same experience as I had suffered in Paris before. Our passports were taken away, we were put in a cage with prostitutes and sat there for over an hour and a half, deafened by the cacophonous noise of the *prostituées*. Then our passports were returned to us and we were told that we had to appear before a court on the following Monday. We were thrown out into the darkness and had to run as fast as we could through the dark, silent streets to get to the hotel before it shut. Doreen ended up running barefoot because of her high heels. The next morning, she was all for returning to England straightaway, but I wanted to stay at least a couple more days. Events then overtook us. I telephoned home to make sure that everything was OK only to hear that my mother, who had been visiting Irene, had had a stroke and was in hospital. So we left Paris immediately.

Roy told us the bad news. They had gone out for a run in the car, my mother sitting next to him in the front, when she suddenly slumped forward silently. It was her first stroke. She was rushed to hospital but never spoke again. When I visited her there, she was unable to move, only her blue eyes stared at me mutely as if pleading with me to get her out of this useless body. Within two weeks, she had her second stroke and died soon after. I could not bear to look at her corpse at that time. I regret that now. Irene and I had intended to give her a quiet funeral in Wales, but the Irish contingency in London, my aunts and uncles, rose up in force to claim their own again. They insisted that she be returned to London for a Requiem Mass. This I had to organise. I stayed alone in her flat the night before the funeral, surrounded by the familiar trappings of her life. It was as if she had just popped out and would soon return. The next day, Doreen and I went to visit the coffin in St Margaret's Church. It was a magnificent one of burnished oak, covered in flowers. I was able to pay for such a magnificent coffin, because Mother had paid a small insurance all her life, so that the family was spared the expense of a funeral. Doreen and I stood each side of the coffin gazing at each other mutely, and then we both broke down in floods of tears, heart-wrenching sobs which shook our bodies. We stretched out to each other, hands intertwined as if to find someone still alive to hold on to in our grief. It is a moment I shall never forget. More trauma was to follow. We went to see the Irish contingent all gathered together in my Uncle Dan's small front room and were suddenly faced with a hostile barrage of criticisms. My Aunt Mag, always the most shrewish of the family started the onslaught, "It's your fault she died in Wales! Always wanting to drag her down there to help you. She was too old for all that. You took her away from us for your own selfish ends!" Julie, the turncoat, who had often enjoyed my hospitality when she visited with my mother, joined in, "And you wanted to keep her down there. You didn't even want her to have a Christian burial. Trying to keep her away from us. You never took her to church there. You didn't want her to go to church. You and your father always hated the Catholics." Then turning on Doreen, "You're just as bad! You didn't care about your mother. How many times did you come and visit her?"

Such recriminations at a time of immense grief left us aghast. I can only presume that it was their own way of dealing with their loss, but it was very hurtful. They were so angry with us that they refused to sit with us in the church or join the funeral cortège. They deliberately walked to the cemetery. We were confronted with the sight of them, a black, menacing group advancing towards the grave, isolated and recriminatory. We never saw them again.

Living for so long now in Wales, I grew to know something about their culture. There was less overt class consciousness than in England, but there was both a linguistic split and a cultural split among the Welsh. There were the puritanical, nonconformist sections of the population, often speaking Welsh, concerned about hard work and good education and then the rugby-supporting, beer-swilling types. There was also a definite sexism running through both sections of the community, a sexism much more overt than in London. I had a most unpleasant brush with an extreme form of it. Brynmawr Comprehensive School was expanding, taking in more of the middle-class pupils in the Gilwern area. I like to think it was because of the higher esteem the school now enjoyed. Mr Archer and I had accomplished many changes, including amalgamating various departments under one head and so creating a layer of senior staff who were able to contribute to the organisation and development of the school. It was finally agreed that we now needed to dispense with my title of senior mistress for which I was most thankful and a second post of deputy head should be created. Although the two deputies would have different responsibilities, one would be senior to the other.

Naturally, I expected to become the senior deputy but found I had to have an interview to apply for my new post. The other candidate was a young man hot out of Oxford University who had just completed a postgraduate certificate in education, but who otherwise had little experience. He was a 'native' of the area, having been born in one of the villages around. I met him before the interviews to show him round the school and found him to be of keen intellect but somewhat of a 'bumbler'. I discovered that our headmaster was on the interviewing panel of school governors for the young man's interview, but not on mine. I queried the reason for this. He said that since he knew me in a professional capacity, he had been asked not to attend the interview. I considered this rather strange, believing that his description of the work I had achieved would count in my favour. But it had been a decision of the governors and I had to accept it. When I went into the interviewing room, six men sat facing me, heavyset men for the most part with florid faces denoting their predilection for beer. There were no women. Most of them were very pleasant and asked me standard questions which were easy to answer. Towards the end, however, one man sitting quite near me suddenly leaned forward with what looked suspiciously like a leer on his face and said, "Mrs Jones, I would like you to tell us what response you would make to an adolescent boy who urinated up your leg?" There was an uncomfortable silence in the room as I tried to digest this unexpected question. With hindsight, I should have said: "Mr----, I find this question highly inappropriate and quite irrelevant. I have never experienced such an incident before, nor do I expect it."

What I did instead was to try to answer the question as truthfully as I could, fumbling with my words in order to make some sort of cogent response. And that was the end of the interview. I left the room, my face flaming with embarrassment and my heart raging even more. I sat with the other candidate waiting for the decision, and asked him if he had been asked such a question. He said, "No!" and expressed astonishment. He was then called back in to the room and I realised he was to be offered the senior position. All my experience and work in the school had been as naught. I complained bitterly to the headmaster and even considered appealing against the decision on the grounds of sexual harassment. He was surprised at the turn of events and said that he would support my complaint. He added, perhaps to comfort me, that the status of the deputy heads was arbitrary and inconsequential, it would make no difference to his regard for me, and my work would continue as before. I went home unconvinced. But the thought of going through all the procedure of a formal complaint was not very enticing. I thought to myself bitterly: "What a bastion of male chauvinism Wales is!" I had already been made aware that it was a male-dominated society, but in my naïveté, had assumed that the teaching profession would be exempt from such prejudice.

What I saw as a demotion continued to rankle with me and I surveyed my situation. I really had only myself now to consider. Valmai had come back home quite soon because she could not stand the rows between all the Hyders, nor the lack of support from Timmy, who continued his life as he had always done, frequenting the pub most of the weekends. I was not sorry to see them split up but felt they were really no longer my responsibility. Leigh was proving to be quite a delight, bright, cheerful and a good baby. I decided to try for another post in London. I really could not come to terms with what I saw as a slur on my capabilities. Quite soon, I was offered an interview for the post of senior mistress (again!) in Chingford, a leafy middle-class area not far from Wanstead. Interviews at this level were quite exhausting events; the morning would be spent being shown around the school and meeting senior staff and after a short lunch the stringent interview would proceed. Having spent so long in Brynmawr studying its weaknesses and strengths, I was surprised at how soon on my rounds of the school I saw where improvements needed to be made. The headmaster had a shock of ginger hair and, I gathered from some staff, a temper to match. The rumour was that he was in thrall to his dominant wife. I sailed through the interview with ease and found that one of my responsibilities, if I were successful, would be curriculum development. I was pleased at that. I was finally offered the post and accepted it eagerly. This would be something for the Brynmawr Governors to consider. By the time all this was over, the school day had finished and there were very few staff left around. The headmaster went home soon afterwards. Just as I was about to depart, the outgoing senior mistress asked me into her office. I thought she would be giving me a few more details of the job. She seemed a very efficient, capable woman and I assumed she would be moving on to a headship. But no sooner was her door closed than she seemed unable to contain herself. She burst out, "I couldn't say this before because of professional etiquette, but I think I ought to warn you of one of the most important duties you will have to undertake as Senior Mistress, more important than any other."

I was intrigued by her tone of suppressed anger. What on earth was she about to divulge? She exploded, "Do you know what your first duty will be every day? To bolster that little shit up every morning." I recoiled as if I had been struck. "What do you mean?"

"You will be expected to listen to his moans about the latest argument he had with his wife; you will be expected to commiserate with him, massage his ego, cosset him and generally act as his nursemaid before he faces the staff. He is a weak, inadequate and vindictive man, and I can't wait to get away from him."

I was staggered at this turn of events, my mind reeling with its implications. She continued, "I've had more than enough of him and his moods and snivelling weaknesses. I can't cope any more. After building his ego up every morning, I'm then expected to take on the responsibility of the school. It's too much for me and so I'm leaving." She then turned to look at me, relaxing somewhat. "But I felt it my duty to tell you what you are letting yourself in for." I left that school, my stomach churning, my head whirling at these revelations. I began to remember other staff making vague remarks about the headmaster's moods. What should I do? I wanted to leave Brynmawr because of the outrageous sexism of the governors and I was about to be cast into an even nastier situation. I brooded as I drove back to Gilwern. I was the last person to act as counsellor and confidante to a weak man. If I were to have a good working partnership with anyone, I would have to respect that person and work on an equal basis with him. By no stretch of the imagination could I see myself as a surrogate mother. I had had enough of the joys and miseries of motherhood! By the time I had turned into the drive of my house, I had made up my mind. The next morning, I waited impatiently for Mr Archer to arrive, told him of the weird turn of events and then, embarrassed and ashamed, I said, "I've accepted this post, but I found out it was on a false basis. I know it is completely unprofessional, but I'm going to write immediately and withdraw my acceptance." I stared at him as I said this, preparing for his reaction. He was shocked and suddenly, so was I. This was a heinous thing to do in the teaching profession. All the time and money spent on advertising the post, short-listing the candidates and interviewing them would be as naught. The whole procedure would have to start again. As for me, it could spell the end of my teaching career. I could be 'blackballed' and find it difficult to get another job. Sure enough, after I had written my letter of refusal, Waltham Forest Education Authority threatened me with legal action. I showed the letter to Mr Archer, who promised to write a letter in my defence. I never saw the letter, but it worked and I heard no more from them.

I was still adamant, however, that I would leave Brynmawr and I continued my search for another post. This meant looking at London house prices. It was going to be difficult financially to move back to London, even though I now enjoyed a very good salary for a teacher. The sheer grind of completing application forms, writing a letter stating why one wanted this job, what qualities one would bring to it and one's views on education, is quite onerous. *N'importe*! It had to be done. It was hardly the most propitious time to be contemplating a return to London. The country had suffered 'the winter of discontent' when it seemed as if it were becoming ungovernable. There were so many strikes! Even the gravediggers walked out, as did the local authority staff, so that the rats had a field day with uncollected household rubbish. James Callaghan, the Labour Prime Minister was forced to resign and new elections were called. The Conservatives won with a landslide and brought onto the political scene our first woman Prime Minister, Margaret Thatcher. She was a real radical who promised change; change from the sterling crises besetting the country, the balance of payments deficit and the constant 'boom and bust' of inflation and recession. Her first few years at trying to change society were quite disastrous. There were increases in petrol duty, a 15% increase in VAT and cuts in public expenditure, all very unpopular. There was a new IRA campaign of bombing on the mainland. The fear it caused was reminiscent of the fear of the V1s and V2s during the last war. There were more race riots in London, a miners' strike (again!) which lasted a year and caused the closure of many pits and a legacy of bitterness in the mining villages. But Margaret Thatcher resolved not to give in and the strikers were eventually defeated. The press had a field day denigrating her. Sexism reared its head in the form of criticisms of her appearance, voice and manner. Apparently, her voice was too shrill, her clothes dowdy, her manner strident. So the vituperation continued. She polarised society, but she was undeterred. The tide of opposition to her turned with the Falkland War. Suddenly, Britain was 'great' again, defending one of her tiny, far-away islands from a greedy Argentina. We won that war and everything began to change. Britain became more confident, there was increased prosperity, mainly because of the new, burgeoning service industries. Equally undeterred, I continued to look for a new job and eventually I went for an interview for the deputy headship of Langdon School, the largest comprehensive school in Newham.

Newham made its debut in the world with the amalgamation of East and West Ham, where scenes of my early life had been acted out. It was like coming home... The school was the result of one of the most ambitious schemes of comprehensivisation in any borough, a startling indication of the strength of the Labour Party in Newham. West Ham, where I had been born, had only ever sent a Labour MP to Westminster since the foundation of the Labour Party in 1906. The school was purpose-built on a forty-four acre site just east of East Ham with over eighteen hundred pupils ominously drawn from East Ham Boys' Grammar School and two mixed secondary modern schools. One can only imagine the initial teething problems of the amalgamation. The grammar school staff viewed the other teachers with suspicion if not downright hostility, while they, in return, considered the others old-fashioned 'fuddy-duddies'. By the time I arrived there in 1981 it had settled down somewhat and had a very able headmaster, a Mr Gabert, who was a Sudetan German. His family had fled to Britain when the Nazis invaded the Sudetanland. So he brought an interestingly different perspective to the school ethos. Typically, he was very concerned with detail, was extremely hard-working and had a deep concern for the welfare of the pupils. Staff were rather in awe of him as he often appeared cold and detached. I managed to get on the final shortlist for this quite prestigious position of deputy head which carried with it an excellent salary. My rival, if one can put it that way, was a young man in his early thirties. He was quite short but very self-assured. His conversation was peppered with all the necessary terminology for success in the teaching profession. I was quite dismayed. On the day of the interview, we were taken on a tour of the Upper and Lower Schools which were so big that it took some time to encompass them. The headmaster escorted us himself which I thought was a very friendly gesture. At lunchtime my competitor and I decided to leave the site and have lunch in *The Spotted Dog*, an old seventeenth-century inn in West Ham. He was talking excitedly, supremely confident of getting the job and privately,

I agreed with him since I was now fifty-one years old and could be considered too old to change jobs. At my interview, which was very searching, the headmaster asked me directly, "Which ability range do you consider to be in need of the most attention in a comprehensive school?"

I knew that the acceptable answer in this most egalitarian of authorities was that the weakest ability range should be given the most help and support, since the middle- and upper-ability ranges were considered to be able to cope better, and the whole ethos of the comprehensive ideal was to try to make the pupils equal. But I had become increasingly concerned about the upper-ability range in schools, many of whom were bored and under-stretched by staff who found it easiest to teach to the middle section of ability. So I waffled on about the needs of the weakest being of great importance but not to the detriment of the most academic pupils who also needed extra support and encouragement. Standard stuff but he seemed satisfied and settled back in his chair again. After the interview, the tense waiting period ensued. I had always thought it a cruel system to keep applicants together waiting for the 'coup de grace'. Normally, the successful applicant would be called in first, so one knew that all one's efforts had been in vain and afterwards the unsuccessful candidates would be asked back into the room, to listen to encouraging phrases such as, "You should not feel disappointed at not being successful this time. The fact that you have got this far shows your undoubted ability but unfortunately, only one person can be successful." These attempts were doomed to disappointment and never softened the blow. This time, to my amazement, I was called back in first and offered the post. I imagine it must have been not only because of my wide experience at teaching in all types of schools, but also because I had always kept abreast of new developments in education, many of which I privately disagreed with. This was still the time when the word 'elite' was unacceptable to the vast range of staff in comprehensive schools. I had seen the result of such a 'levelling' with my own daughters who left school hating any form of learning. I remember the deputy head of King Henry Eighth School calling me into her study when the twins were leaving to say, "Mrs Jones, I must apologise to you. We have failed your daughters." And I agreed, but it was too late for them. Now, attempts are being made to bring some form of specialisation into comprehensive schools by creating 'centres of excellence', city technological schools and the like. I heard with pleasure a few weeks ago that Langdon is now one of the 'centres of excellence' because of its sports facilities, which has improved the academic standards of the school as well.

The senior team in Langdon consisted of the headmaster and two deputies, myself and a woman with a degree in Business Studies, who was responsible for curriculum organisation. She was quite short and rotund and reminded me somewhat of my friend Shirley, but there the resemblance ended. She had a most disconcerting habit of closing her eyes when talking to anyone. I suppose it was an innate shyness but did she but know it, it was very useful tool in reducing the interlocutor to a state of deep unease. During my time at the school I found her to be bigoted and humourless. Most of the staff disliked her intensely and were somewhat afraid of her. However, as the person responsible for timetabling, she virtually controlled most of the teaching activity in the school. Fortunately, while I was based in the Lower School, I saw very little of her except during the regular meetings with the head to discuss problems arising. My duties were quite onerous. I would virtually be the headmistress of the Lower School, consisting of just under a thousand pupils from eleven to fourteen. In addition, I would be teaching Sixth form French which pleased me. I had my own large office, overlooking the pleasant lawns and my own en suite toilet. I even had my own deputy head, a young male who was pleasant and ambitious but somewhat indolent at times. We worked well together. Then there were the many staff under my supervision, who on the whole gave little trouble, apart from a hot-headed Irishman named O'Leary who was not at all keen on my new plans and was extremely rude to me. I threatened him with a formal complaint and he subsided. The Upper School staff were of a different calibre, some of them being quite militant teachers of trade-union hue. We had some difficult children. I remember one angel-faced boy, with dark, curly hair who came into school one morning brandishing a lethal-looking knife. He was soon divested of it, but a nasty incident could have occurred. When I questioned him about possession of the knife, he flatly denied ever having it, although he had been seen by many of the other pupils. He was a pathological liar, constantly in trouble and finally had to be excluded from school for his antisocial behaviour. To look at his pretty, blank face and hear the tissue of lies issuing from his lips gave me a frisson of fear. He was a childish version of a psychopath, showing no remorse for his aggressive behaviour to others. We also had a large Moslem population who were constantly fighting with a rival band of Sikhs from a neighbouring school. They would turn up at the school gates at the end of school waiting for our pupils to emerge. I was often out among them with my deputy trying to separate and pacify the rival gangs.

One of the attractions of the job was that I had a subsidised flat at my disposal. It was in Forest Gate which has many large, substantially built eighteenth- and nineteenth-century houses, once the pride and joy of the rich merchants who worked in the City of London. They were now the refuge for what seemed like vast families of Asians. The block of flats was small, only four flats on the first floor with the ground floor used for garages. But at the back of the garages were our bedrooms, looking out onto a square of garden. One had the novel experience of going downstairs to the bedroom. My neighbours were a motley lot. The woman next door was Chinese; she spoke no English but still insisted somehow in dragging me into her flat to offer me some nettle-like plants which I understood were the Chinese form of lettuce which she grew in the back garden. The advantage of living in the flat was that I could keep the house in Gilwern for Valmai to live in with Leigh. With Kate living near to help her, I was happy that she would be able to cope. I drove every weekend to Wales on a Friday after school to see them, regardless of the weather or my fatigue. Once it was so windy, I was terrified of crossing the Severn Bridge, which swayed ominously when the winds were strong. I had heard stories of lorries being blown over the bridge into the Severn Estuary. So I stopped just before I had to get on it and took a couple of swigs of whisky to steady my nerves for the ordeal of the car being buffeted by the gale.

It was not long, however, before Valmai grew tired of her quiet life in Gilwern, and came to London with Leigh to look for a job. So my quiet, studious life in the flat was soon disrupted. Living with Valmai, now with a young child, I discovered hidden strengths of determination in her. She enrolled at a commercial college to study for a secretarial course, but at the same time would get up every morning at six o'clock and cycle to clean a doctor's surgery to earn some extra money. After a year, she was proficient enough to get a good job in the City. Leigh was nearly three now and I managed to wangle a place for him in a state nursery school near me. He and I would jog around

West Ham Park every morning (the same park where I had experienced seeing Doreen falling in the pond when I was about ten years old). We would look at the flowers and trees and talk about his school. Then we would come back to the flat for about half an hour to practice his reading. I was thrilled that he was so interested in books, just like David had been, but not unfortunately the twins. It was a lovely time for both of us.

With her munificent salary, Valmai wanted to thank me for all my help, so she offered to pay my fare to visit Shirley in Mauritius. After the death of her father, Shirley had married a Mauritian Asian. I hadn't been able to afford to go to Mauritius to visit her in her new habitat. So when the summer holidays came, I decided to take up her offer. Mauritius was a shocking revelation to me in many ways. The flight was bearable except for the piercing screams of Asian babies and toddlers as their ears were affected by the changes in air pressure in the cabin. There was pandemonium on arrival as the aeroplane disgorged its myriad number of different races returning to visit their families. I was checked carefully by passport control because I was an unusual tourist, one who was not staying in one of the luxurious hotels on the coast. In my confusion, I went through the 'Something to declare' exit to find myself in a vast shed reverberating with the wails and protestations of the passengers. I saw customs officers roughly tipping the whole contents of large suitcases on to the tables, examining everything in minute detail even down to the heels of shoes. Fortunately, they soon realised I was in the wrong area and I escaped unscathed. Outside the airport, it was flat scrubland but in the distance, the central mountain range could be glimpsed through the early morning mist. Shirley and Bengs were there to meet me in their battered old Toyota. I grew accustomed to seeing really old 'bangers' on the roads; even the buses were ancient, creaking death-traps. All new vehicles had to be imported and therefore were horrendously expensive. We drove through sugar plantations, their tall, feathery plumes waving restlessly in the breeze. Indian women wearing colourful, wide-brimmed hats and baggy clothes toiled in the increasing heat. The scene reminded me of my old Geography textbooks. Cars drove recklessly in the middle of the pot-holed roads, narrowly missing the African peasants sauntering along languidly. Gaudy advertising signs along the route sped us on our way uphill towards the middle of the island. We passed small villages consisting of nothing but crumbling, dilapidated wooden shacks with unpainted, broken, corrugated iron roofs infinitely more ramshackle than those in New Zealand. Many of them had sagging wooden verandas, with naked children squatting among the mounds of rubbish. The poverty was appalling. And yet all along the beautiful coral-rimmed coastline, with its sparkling white beaches, hotels had been built, magnificent in their opulence, offering jaded tourists a respite from their labours. Once past the hovels and dirt roads, we climbed up higher to the cooler, mountainous area where the wealthier Mauritians lived. In their own grounds stood colonial-looking villas festooned with the riotous colour of bougainvillea and vivid red poinsettias. In their gardens grew bananas, paw-paws and lemon trees, pervading the air with their perfumes. Shirley and Bengs lived in Vacoas in the central western part of the island, near to Curepipe which was the highest-situated town and where it rained constantly. Vacoas was small, and quite poor; the main road had been an old railway line and was several feet below the rest of the area. It was like walking in an uncovered tunnel. Bengs had had the bungalow built to his own specifications, with only two bedrooms, one of which he used as his study. There was a small veranda meant for sitting on to enjoy the Mauritian sunsets, but on which they seldom ventured because of the mosquitoes. They had also had an 'intendance' built in the grounds for the servant they employed initially, but which was now empty because Bengs said they could not afford such a luxury. I stayed in the 'intendance', which consisted of a simple whitewashed bedroom and a shower room. The main disadvantage to this plain dwelling, in which I would sleep for two weeks, was that they had a dog named Jo-Jo, a vicious mongrel who bit me on the second day of my arrival. Like all the dogs in the neighbourhood, he was chained up during the day, and released at night to guard the property. Consequently, once I was inside the 'intendance', I was virtually marooned until the morning when Shirley emerged from the main building to chain up the dog and set me free. There was no way I could communicate with her, so there were no pleasant strolls for me to enjoy in the early morning. I spent the time, perforce, in reading. I would lie in the big double bed with silence all around me broken by the mournful howls of the dogs roaming around. I had the same sensation of isolation and loneliness as I had experienced in the flat in Leyton.

The markets were the most fascinating aspects of Mauritius for me especially the one in the capital, Port Louis. It was in an opensided shed and all kinds of exotic fish of myriad colours glinted in the sunshine. Nearby were all different-sized boxes filled with spices, herbs and vegetables, including such exotic fruit as mangoes, pawpaws, coconuts and sweet potatoes. Men were standing around ready to wield their knives with a deft, curling motion to slice off the pineapple skins for the tourists. I would eat it like an ice-cream, with its rich, sweet juices trickling down my chin. The noise inside the shed was horrendous as the excitable accents of French, English, Chinese, Indian and Creole reverberated against the iron roof. It was just as one had imagined an Eastern bazaar. In Mauritius, darkness fell at 6 p.m. in winter and 7 p.m. in summer. This meant that evening life was quite restricted, unless one was staying in the big hotels. The more affluent classes risked their lives going to the clubs to drink because, apparently, it was the custom of the local youths to place rubber tyres across the middle of the roads, so ensuring that the car owners would stop and then they would rob them. Most of the poorer inhabitants stayed in their homes. No one seemed to walk anywhere at night except Bengs who would take his 'constitutional' armed with a sturdy stick to ward off the marauding dogs.

I was soon made aware of the tensions in the island. Most female Europeans weren't allowed to work, except in positions where they were most needed and many feared that they would be raped if they ventured forth alone. Unemployment was rife; I gained the impression of a divided society, the 'haves' and the 'have-nots' equally suspicious of each other. The wife's possessions were transferred to the husband on marriage and Mauritius rupees could not be taken out of the country. This meant that Shirley was financially dependent on Bengs, apart from her part-time job as an English teacher at the Loretta convent school. She had sold her flat in London to move to Mauritius and was now in difficulty financially. From being an interesting, lively intellectual, she had been transformed into a submissive Asian wife. Bengs' behaviour to her was abominable; he shouted, criticised and belittled her in front of other people. It was painful for me to watch. He insisted on doing all the cooking, saying she was useless. He would then take hours to prepare a meal, shouting demands at her to provide the necessary equipment, cursing if some ingredient was not available. He was so economy-conscious that she was made to measure out the quantity of water needed to be boiled for tea before pouring it in the kettle. They washed up in cold water, so that the plates had a film of grease left on them. The washing machine was a cold-water one, so that the clothes emerged from the machine with the same stains as they went in and only disappeared when the hot sun shone on them in the garden. I was reminded of my own experience at college when a red inkstain on my best dress miraculously disappeared. We were allowed to shower only once a week (in that heat!). Life was quite grim for both of us as we tried to placate him and prevent him from falling into one of his ungovernable rages. Once he even cut up some of her underwear in an explosion of temper. I decided that he was basically an uncouth peasant, with a thin veneer of civilization. He had spent his early life working on the sugar plantations, but was intelligent enough to have overcome this disadvantage, and had gone to London to take a French degree, and teach, before returning with Shirley to Mauritius. I thought he was primitive in his character and his emotions, in spite of his education. I urged Shirley to think of going back to England, but she replied, "To what? I have no money of my own now, and my family have ostracised me – it's impossible." She added sadly, "He was a great lover, you know, but he's a terrible husband." So after two weeks, I left Shirley in Bengs' clutches, full of pity for her, finding it almost impossible to imagine how she had managed to get herself into such a dire situation. I also left with a memory of Mauritius as a land of extreme contrasts; a land of riches and poverty, of sun and rain, of sea and mountains, of heart-rending beauty.

On my return to England, and back in work, I had a succession of family members coming to visit me. Stanley appeared one evening, trying to 'bed' me but with little success. Yet he was pleased to be able to drop in every so often and I tolerated him. Then Timmy turned up like a bad penny and Stanley was generous enough to give Valmai and him the money for a deposit on a small house in South Woodford. Not long after that, Doreen deposited herself on my doorstep. She had left her husband and this time she said it was for good. Since I had a spare bedroom it was fine while David was at university but somewhat crowded when he came home for vacations. We would spend most evenings having a meal and sharing a bottle of wine, to the detriment of my teaching preparation. We had what one could euphemistically call 'stimulating' conversations, which often became quite heated. She stayed with me for about six months working as a civil servant in London, and then quite suddenly, she said that she was going to Monte Carlo. I couldn't believe my ears. She had discovered that her husband was going there to meet her son, Robert, and she saw this as a way of moving back into the family home. I felt a malicious pleasure in imagining her husband's face when he saw her in Monte Carlo. But her many disappearances had finally affected him and he had found another woman. When she found out, she was totally distraught and started divorce proceedings almost immediately.

Once more alone in the flat, I was soon to benefit from one of Margaret Thatcher's innovations. In 1981, she had managed to get a law passed through the Commons allowing council tenants to buy their flats or houses if they had been resident in them for three years. The properties would be offered to them at a third of the normal price. This was a hugely popular move on her part. Five hundred thousand council properties were sold in three years. Thatcher spoke of a "property-owning democracy". One snag was that the LEA were not allowed to use the proceeds of the sales for future house building, since their record of maintenance was appalling. 'Housing Trusts' were formed instead to take over run-down local authority housing. The result of that legislation has meant that the number of local authority rental is now only about one in five, whereas the property-owning class increased dramatically. One of the most beneficial aspects of the legislation was that ex-council tenants now started to take a pride in their properties and would often renovate and embellish them, not always very tastefully. But they transformed some of the run-down areas that I had known when young. I decided to avail myself of this opportunity, so that David could have his own home when he came down from university to start working. He took some time to do this, reading for an M.Sc (Master's Degree in Science) first and then taking a PGCE (Postgraduate Certificate in Education) to start teaching. I decided to sell the house in Gilwern and buy a house in London. I spent days feverishly looking at all sorts of properties and evenings trying to work out what I could afford. I finally found a bargain. It was a beautiful, Edwardian corner house in Wanstead. At the end of its road was the Wanstead Flats, the green belt of land around London and the site of some of my earlier adventures. The house was really spacious; it had four bedrooms, two reception rooms, a `morning room and a kitchen. It even had a conservatory looking out onto a large garden. When I went to view it, it was occupied by an old educated couple who had obviously not been able to renovate it. I was startled to see covering one whole wall, a large banner posing the question:

> *When Adam delved and Eve span*
> *Who was then the gentleman?*

I knew the text had something to do with certain socialist ideas, which seemed to sit oddly on this charming old couple. I looked up the quotation when I went home. It was adapted from an earlier text, but was used by John Ball in his revolutionary sermon at the beginning of the Peasants' Revolt in 1381. The house had no central heating, so that was to be my first job and later I had a new bathroom, kitchen and a downstairs toilet installed. David and I started on the redecoration of the rooms and I was suddenly aware at how huge they were, with really high ceilings. We had one disaster when the plaster came away with the old wallpaper in one room and we had to call in a plasterer. I liked to imagine an Edwardian family living there in such a beautiful house, and mused how pleasant it would be for all my family to come and visit. The years spent there were happy ones for me. I grew exotic plants and vegetables in the conservatory and enjoyed the weekends planning the garden. One memorable occasion was in 1987 when the hurricane arrived in Wanstead. I was woken up in the middle of the night to the sound of a terrible wind rushing around the house. It was so strong that I felt quite frightened. I decided to get up and look outside and found David also standing at the door. The trees along the road were bent almost double and then there was an almighty CRACK and my fence went down dragging with it an old tree. We ducked instinctively, although sheltered by our porch. Wanstead suffered badly. The line of what had been ancient trees along the school path to David's Church school was a devastating sight. Every tree had been felled. It cost me quite a lot to repair our own damage, but fortunately new trees were planted very quickly at his school.

Kathryn came up to stay with her husband and two children on another occasion and I invited Valmai, Timmy, Leigh and David to join us for a meal. It was a convivial occasion until the telephone rang. When I picked up the receiver, I heard Shirley's voice. I had not seen her for a few years, not since the holiday in France which had almost destroyed our friendship. We had always corresponded regularly but hearing her voice, I suddenly realised that I had not received a letter from her for some time, which was strange since she loved writing letters. Her news was shocking; she had developed ovarian cancer and had come back to England for treatment. My happy mood was instantly dissipated. I was very concerned for her. I saw her the next day and heard her harrowing tale, but will leave the details till later. We were both to be affected by her cancer.

Changes were afoot at Langdon. Mr Gabert decided to take early retirement. He had been disenchanted for some time at the lack of support from the LEA and its 'trendy' philosophies. I was sorry to see him go; he was an intellectual who stood out from the rest of the staff. A young woman replaced him; she was in her thirties, very modern and quite sexy. She also shared those modern ideas and the senior staff did not approve of her. She was so different from Mr Gabert. She liked what I was doing in the Lower School and said that I now needed more challenging responsibilities (!). So she made me head of Upper School with special responsibility for staff development. This was the time when the idea of 'study days' was just taking root. This meant that I had to organise in-service training days for the staff, which included lectures by visiting experts, and practical sessions on any subject that members of staff decided they were interested in. It really needed someone full-time for three months to organise. I had to do it around my job as head of school. I threw myself into the task with my usual gusto and thoroughly enjoyed all the planning and organisation. But it meant working every evening and weekends and even getting up very early in the morning to organise everything. I had been able to take my deputy in the Lower School into the Upper School with me and he was a tower of strength. Some of the Upper School staff viewed me with distrust. They would have preferred a man to be Upper School head, but we managed and they grew used to me. Our biggest problem was how to get rid of really poor staff. The local authority would not counsel their being sacked, but suggested we should send them off on re-training sessions, which they enjoyed. One Maths teacher was absolutely hopeless, couldn't keep any discipline, so that his classes often rioted. We also found out that another very intelligent man who taught German would say to his new fourth year pupils, "Who isn't going to take O-levels?" (as opposed to the easier CSE exam). When the boys, they were always boys, put up their hands he said, "Right! You can sit at the back of the class and do any work of your own as long as you keep quiet." This meant that these boys would be in the class for nearly two years learning nothing. We knew that this was happening, but in spite of all our efforts we could not get him removed from the school. It was most frustrating.

Shirley came to stay with me while she was having her cancer treatment. Her whole family had turned their backs on her for marrying a Moslem. So my life became very difficult, what with picking up Leigh to take him to school, keeping him amused afterwards until Valmai came home and trying to keep up Shirley's spirits, I became progressively more tired and began to think seriously of early retirement. But could I really afford to retire? Thinking about it, I finally decided that the educational scene had come full circle and I wanted a change in my life. I had been teaching continuously since 1952, had taught in all the different types of school; senior, secondary modern, grammar and private schools. I had seen the traditional methods overthrown and 'progressive' methods replacing them and I wanted a change in my life. I wrote to the Education Office at the Department of Education and explained that I was becoming increasingly tired and worried that I would not be able to continue with my duties to my own satisfaction. Would I be allowed to take early retirement at the end of the year? The strategy worked and in July 1989 I retired from full-time teaching and contemplated with some satisfaction the prospect of having some leisure time, something I had never had before.

"But what will you do with yourself?" friends asked. That remained to be seen.

Chapter 18
Retiring Pleasures

The bone-penetrating fatigue that hit me when I finally stopped full-time teaching lasted for months. Every day, after lunch, my head would feel dizzy, my eyelids would droop and I would fall asleep for at least an hour. Yet I was still able to sleep at night. When I finally emerged from this semi-comatose state, I was like a chrysalis, newly-born, cleansed, in a way purged of all the worrisome burden and responsibilities of teaching. I reclaimed my weekends again, and felt full of energy. The opposite side to this feeling of satisfaction was the realisation that one's income is very much reduced. I pondered on this problem for some time. The ritual closing of all the windows in the house at night then reminded me that it was obviously too big for me. I rattled like a pea in a pod. So I decided to sell that beautiful, Edwardian house and find somewhere smaller. The housing market was booming and I received a good price for the property, a compensation for all the work I had put into it. I was pleased that a young couple with a family bought it and imagined it resounding with the cries of young children, racing through the rooms. I bought a flat in Snaresbrook in a delightful enclave nestling in a corner of Epping Forest. It was called, appropriately enough, Forest Court and was built in the 1930s in the 'Arts and Crafts' style, with bronze-red tiles between the storeys and ornamental brick bands on the outside walls. It was in a conservation area so there were no fears of further development. The garden, in summer, was a profusion of flowers, protected by ancient oak and ash trees. I fell in love with it immediately. My bedroom overlooked the primeval forest, a sea of vibrant green trees swaying in the breeze. In the autumn, it was a riotous colour of yellow, bronze, and deep red. When I woke up in the mornings, I luxuriated on its ever-changing aspect. One winter we had snow and when I pulled back the curtains, I gasped at the brilliant white scene before my eyes, a fairyland of glinting, scintillating snow.

I soon bought a pair of binoculars and looked closely at the many birds flittering through the trees and the squirrels scampering nimbly from branch to branch, not to mention the red-brown fox slinking by in the evenings.

I had enough money left over from the sale of my house to contemplate doing something with it. Not for me stocks and shares or unit trusts, I wanted my money to provide me with some pleasure. But no sooner had I settled in the flat than I was asked to do a term's part-time teaching at Forest School, the private school nearby. I don't know how they found my name and telephone number, but they enticed me with the proposal that if I worked for the summer term, I would be paid for the whole of the summer holidays, eight weeks to be precise. It was an offer I could not refuse. I found the same problems of disaffected youths there as in other schools, although it was a joy to teach French to some of the very clever ones. I was also asked to teach the sixth form at Ilford County High School for Boys, a prestigious state school in Redbridge that kept some form of selection and 'creamed off' the top 20% of the secondary school population in Redbridge, Waltham Forest and Newham. It was a 'hothouse' of learning, but still had some very poor teachers who should have been pensioned off a long time ago. The Religious Instruction master gave 100% to over half of his classes at examination times, *pour encourager les autres* he said, tongue in cheek. Nothing was done about him. I enjoyed teaching the sixth form and was actually providing them with work of first degree standard, because they were so avid to learn. I also tried to make the subject come alive by taking them to such operas as *Le Barbier de Seville* and *Carmen*.

The question of what to do with my money solved itself one day quite simply. The occasion presented itself when Valmai called in from work one evening and mentioned a friend who owned a cottage in France, in the Dordogne, who wanted to sell up quickly. She and I decided to fly to Bordeaux, hire a car and spend the weekend in the area to take a look at it. I was so excited that I forgot to take my driving licence with me and we had to cool our heels in Bordeaux until a copy could be faxed to us. On the way to Hautefort, the nearest small town to the cottage and famous for its medieval fortress perched high above, we passed groves of cork-oak trees planted in neat rectangles, for this was truffle country. The trees along the route were slowly deepening into their autumn colours of rich amber and russet-red and the air was perfumed with wood smoke, which curled up into the clear blue sky in hazy blue tendrils. The cottage was built of honey-coloured stone, with a red-tiled roof, which glinted warmly in the autumn sunshine as we drove towards it. It was architecturally a 'long house' built in the nineteenth century or possibly earlier since it was constructed before there were any written records. It was called *L'Aqueduc* after the well which was situated in the front garden. This well was so deep that one could not see the bottom of it. From it, pure, crystal-clear water could be pumped up for use in the garden. It was one of many such wells and springs in the area where the water table is very high. French neighbours would drink from the springs, but I never chanced it. In the local records of the cottage was the proviso that the owner must allow any other farmers in the neighbourhood to take water from it in time of drought, so it was an important asset. The cottage consisted of a large main room, attached to which were a barn and an area for the cattle in winter. Once upon a time, this main room had served as kitchen, living and sleeping area for a whole family. It still had the stone sink in one corner where all the ablutions took place. The present owner had spent quite a bit of money on it, installing a new septic tank and organising mains water and telephone, but the ancient charm of the place remained. Upstairs was the attic area, one half of which was originally used to dry out the walnuts collected from the walnut grove belonging to the property and the other half used for storing hay. I fell in love with the house and with the wide-open space around. It stood quite alone on a slight hill. The next property was a twenty-minute walk away, also owned by an English couple who lived there permanently. Since neither of them spoke any French, I was impressed by their courage. On the night of our arrival, we stayed at *La Mule Blanche,* a hotel at the bottom of the hill and enjoyed a fine French meal. I was woken up during the night by the sound of the church bells, informing the villagers of the passing hours, but they had a comforting sound and I went back to sleep smiling happily. The view of the village seen from my hotel window the next morning warmed my heart. It was a typical French scene with its ancient church spire towering proudly above the red-roofed houses grouped protectively around it. At breakfast, Valmai and I discussed the pros and cons of buying the property, but my mind was already made up. This was France, *la France profonde,* just as Francois Mauriac had described it and I wanted to be part of it. We went to the owner to tell him of our decision and then hastened to the *notaire* to pay the deposit. He was most courteous and said he hoped we would be happy with our new purchase. Then it was back in haste to London to start reading about buying properties in France and planning all the alterations I had already envisaged. I had to get plans drawn up to send to the *Mairie* for permission to be granted and then fill in endless forms, but it was a pleasurable task.

Weeks went by and finally I persuaded my brother-in-law, Roy, to come back with me to France for two weeks to arrange all that was necessary. He is a countryman at heart and leaped at the chance. We decided to stay in the house because as well as a double bed-settee in the living area, there was a single bed in the room next door which had been roughly turned into an extra bedroom. First we had to get the water, electricity and telephone put back on. My academic French was not so helpful when I was dealing with subjects such as plumbing, pipes and currents, but I acquired a trade dictionary, which saw me through. The telephone company was in Périgueux, the capital of the area, which impressed me with its Byzantine-domed cathedral. The first major problem when we arrived back at the house was how to open the front door. It had a triple lock, the mechanism of which floored us for half an hour. But the shock when we finally managed to open it and go inside the house! In the short space of time that it had been empty, the spiders had come into their own. The walls were covered in cobwebs and the silt, that had come through the gaps in the beams, lay everywhere. An even greater shock awaited us at night-time. The main living room had been reasonably renovated and furnished with its *coin cuisine*, but the small room had had no renovation. Once in bed, I could no longer communicate with Roy unless I went into the front garden and through the main door, something I didn't fancy in the pitch blackness of the night. Who knows what was lurking around? As soon as my head hit the pillow, I fell into an exhausted sleep after all the travails of the daytime, intellectual and manual. Suddenly I was woken up by something. I strained my ears to hear what it was, but the room was as silent as the grave. I fell back asleep and then was woken up again by something but again could hear nothing. I realised the sound that had woken me must be of mice or rats and was terrified. Images of all the creatures that populate the rural night flitted through my head. I buried myself under the bedclothes and bathed in sweat, fell back to sleep again.

This happened several more times and I could not wait for morning to come. It dawned, sunny and breathtakingly beautiful. I ran outside to speak to Roy and found that he had had the same experience. In his case it was the mice scurrying across the large expanse of the attic, which had kept him awake. Every night that we stayed in the cottage the mice were out in force but all was forgotten in the morning as we contemplated the exquisite beauty of the scene laid out before us in the early-morning mist; vivid-green trees silhouetted against the corn-gold fields, interspersed with the copper-red roofs of the houses. The Dordogne has often been compared to England's fresh, green countryside and it is similar, which is why so many English feel at home there. A whole column of the local paper is devoted to English concerns, written in English by an 'ex-pat'. But it is more lush, more abundant and blessed with warm, sunnier weather. Fortunately, our house was on the northern edge of the Dordogne and with the exception of my neighbour, there were few English around. That first time we were there, I noticed a lone figure working in the fields around, a dark, solitary figure on a tractor, like an ant scurrying across the landscape. He came nearer until, one day, he came into the neighbouring field and introduced himself. This was Raymond; a small, slight, wiry man with a bronzed, wrinkled apple of a face, usually bright red with exertion. He owned a farm some few kilometres away and lived there with his wife Madame Bourget, her very old mother and a daughter of about thirty who had crippling rheumatoid arthritis. He was not a typical stolid peasant; he had a very quick wit and a singular sense of humour. He returned often after our first encounter, curious to see what we were doing and providing us with practical help and suggestions. He became such a frequent visitor that Roy grumbled somewhat about him, but I really enjoyed talking to him in French. Once when the telephone wasn't working (it happened often because we were at the end of the line), he came in and announced, "If *faut arroser la ligne*". I looked at him to see if he was joking. "Water the line?" What did he mean? But he was in deadly earnest, took me outside to show me where the line was connected and repeated, "Il faut l'arroser." I duly watered the plastic-covered telephone line, feeling like Alice in Wonderland and sure enough, the telephone worked! I reasoned out the explanation later; the water must have helped the chalky, clay soil to stick closer to the line. We had a good laugh about that together.

Back in England, I decided that my first priority was to make a door between the main room and the rest of the cottage, so that communication could be maintained, then to renovate the attic into three bedrooms and bathroom so that we were no longer pestered with mice, and make the small room where I slept into another shower room and a wash-house for all the washing, what the French call a *buanderie*. My first mistake was being persuaded to let Timmy undertake the renovation. He had acquired a basic certificate as an electrician and had a builder friend, Ron. I did not know this builder but I saw the house he had built for himself and it looked good. I was rather distrustful of Timmy, but reasoned that as my son-in-law, he would protect my property. Of course, with hindsight, I could see that they were woefully inadequate to tackle the task ahead of them, since neither of them spoke any French and would have difficulty ordering materials and communicating with traders. At first all was well. I had regular telephone calls from the cottage detailing progress made. They had managed to find a local English tiler who could help them. There was a constant demand for money, even though I insisted on seeing all the invoices and receipts. Three months into the development, the bad news started to come through. Ron decided he was not going to sleep in the cottage with Timmy any more because, "He is doing my head in." Further enquiries elicited the information that Timmy was worried about Valmai who had chosen this time to consider divorcing him. Timmy, left alone with only the mice for company, drank too much, started having nightmares and was unable to work properly. Within weeks of this news, he announced to Valmai that he was returning to England, "I've had enough." Predictably, soon afterwards Ron decided he couldn't cope any more and followed him. The cottage was now left abandoned and only partially renovated. I was distraught and couldn't sleep for worry. Then came some apparently good news. The tiler who had befriended them said he could continue the work with others, but since he could not give me a precise figure for the renovation, that he should be paid on a daily basis. I should have suspected something. I had to wait until the school holidays, since I was still part-time teaching, to go to see this man for myself. He seemed genuine and reasonably intelligent. The problem was that he and his men seemed to think that work should only be done between 10 a.m. and 4 p.m. with the southern French custom of two hours for lunch. Progress was alarmingly slow and my money was disappearing rapidly. I realised he was taking advantage of me, and as soon as the cottage was slightly more habitable, I sacked him. He never forgave me. The French Government insists that all workmen have to have some form of qualification, the snag being that in this area, one had to deal with all different specialisms, so I had to employ, separately, a French carpenter, a decorator and a plumber. Eventually, after several years of money draining out of my retirement settlement like water from a sieve, we had a lovely home. Valmai and I enjoyed buying all the furniture needed for it and I hoped for a quieter life. The problem of the mice remained, however. No longer able to inhabit the erstwhile attic, they popped up everywhere, mainly because the building was uninhabited for long periods and there were many nooks and crannies in the walls that they could get through. I called in a pest control firm whose only solution was to put down huge amounts of poison around the walls outside. Their price for doing this was extortionate, so I terminated their contract and made it my business to put down poison myself every time I was 'in situ'. My English neighbour was also plagued with mice, particularly at harvest time, but seemed much less concerned. Distributing poison became one of my chores as well as making sure that the local dustmen came once a week to take away the rubbish. The problem was that I had to inform the local council in writing every time I was coming to the cottage and say how long I intended to stay, because the dustmen, in their wisdom, reasoned that it was not worth their while coming to my cottage, situated at the top of the hill, to check whether we had left any rubbish out. I had many a colourful exchange of language with the local *maire* on this subject.

The travel to and from the cottage when it was finally habitable was not without its dangers and excitement. Brakes that failed, tyres that burst, a clutch decided to give up the ghost on the long, empty roads of Limousin. Most of the time, we tried to economise by staying in one of the very cheap stopover hotel chains such as Formule 1 and Bonsai which offered three-bedroomed rooms with shower and television for less than £15 in those days. The only trouble was that they tended to be in the industrial or commercial areas on the outskirts of the big towns. The reception office usually closed at 10 p.m. Anyone arriving after that time, had to tap in a code into the entrance mechanism or insert a credit card. Our first attempt was quite funny. The ingenuity shown by the architect of the hotel to cram three beds, a TV and a shower in a very small space has my admiration. A bunk bed straddled the two lower beds and to get into it involved some quite complicated manoeuvres. The TV had to be viewed lying down on the bed which made for comfort but proved tricky when we wanted to turn it off. The shower cubicle consisted of a loo and a shower nozzle which projected from the wall allowing one the pleasure of having a pee and a shower at the same time.

    A much more serious incident occurred on another trip when I was taking my grandson, Leigh and his friend with me. I made the mistake of catching the late ferry at Portsmouth, thus arriving in Le Havre as darkness fell. As I drove through the silent countryside, with only the lights of the car breaking through the inky blackness, I missed the turning for the hotel, and landed up in the next town of Louviers. The only sign of life there at this time of night was a ramshackle cabin and two patrol pumps standing like sentinels in the shadowy light. We were sent back the way we had come with further instructions and finally found the necessary turn-off. It appeared to be a wasteland, but I learned later that it was the beginning of a building site. A vague shape gleaming palely in the distance was obviously the hotel. The eerie stillness and dense blackness had finally silenced my grandson, Leigh and his friend. Suddenly, I noticed the headlights of a car behind me. Realising that I was driving slowly, I pulled on to the gravel to allow it to pass. When I looked again in the rear-view mirror, to my horror the car had pulled in behind me. With a sudden lurch of the stomach, I was aware that we could be in trouble. I was galvanised into action. Shrieking at the boys to lock all the doors, I wrenched the car back on to the road and drove furiously forward, my tyres skidding on the road. Images flashed through my mind of what could happen as I put my foot on the accelerator. What followed was like a re-run of the 'Keystone Kops' but without the humour. I drove really fast, hotly pursued by this maniac behind me. I was unable to see properly for the waves of panic sweeping over me, my heart beating sickeningly. Twisting, turning, onto narrower and narrower roads, I reached dead-ends, braked viciously, and reversed rapidly thanking God for the new power-assisted steering. The black car behind followed tenaciously, like the black dog of fate. After what seemed hours but was only minutes, the driver must have finally tired of chasing me, overtook me and stopped right in front of us. By this time the children were on the floor, cowering with fear. I was sickeningly aware that I was completely lost in this dark wasteland. There was a tense, portentous silence and then a young man emerged from the car, strode purposefully towards us, stopped halfway as if he had forgotten something, returned to the car to fetch some object. Leigh said it was a stick or a gun. I saw nothing in my terror. We were mesmerised by the glare of his headlights. He peered into the car as we sat there frozen with fear and shouted: "*Ça alors!*" a phrase, meaning, "Well?" or "Well!" I was too shaken to infer the meaning. Was he saying that he had finally cornered us? Or expressed astonishment at the chase? Or at the occupants of the car? Whatever, those few moments of silence had given me the courage to set off again. Reversing madly over some rough stones, I flung the car once more back into the night and this time, thank God, he didn't follow us. He must have decided to give up once he saw that we were not the prosperous tourists he had expected. I eventually found the main road that we had left only a short time before, and careered onto it, driving on the left in my panic until the dazzling lights and shrieking horns of an oncoming car warned me to swerve over to the right. The 'gendarmerie' in the next village was shut, nor could we find any hotels open. We drove on to Evreux a biggish town about twenty km away, but it was the same story. Everything was shut, no one wanted to open up after midnight. A disembodied voice in one hotel shouted out, "*Complet!*" another threw up his window and repeated the same message with some colourful additions, the rest remained locked in silence. I began to wonder if I would have to drive all through the night until morning, when, on the outskirts of the town, a palatial four-star hotel which still showed signs of life, loomed up before us; some customers were still enjoying a late-night drink. The receptionist clucked sympathetically at our story and said: "*Ça arrive toujours*," and within minutes we were safe in a luxurious bedroom. The cheap overnight stop proved to be very costly, not only was there the bill in this hotel but I had to pay for the one we had not been able to find.

My family enjoyed many pleasant holidays at the cottage, relishing the beautiful sunshine and the food and wine. The men enjoyed the heavy meat-based diet, the typical Perigordian cuisine being basically peasant food, heavily dependent on pork in all its guises. It was also the area for foie gras, especially goose and duck foie gras. The farms employed the time-honoured traditional way of fattening them by the process of *gavage*, where the birds are force-fed for a period of weeks to fatten up their livers. This was also truffle country, although a dish containing the strong, earthy taste of truffles was still expensive. The local wine was a pleasant, full-bodied Bergerac, but we were on the doorstop of the great Bordeaux wine area and learned much about wine and its cultivation when we visited the great chateaux of St Emilion, Pommerel and others. The area's greatest claim to fame was the prehistoric site of Lascaux with its astonishing cave paintings. What the tourist sees are not the original caves, since to open them to hordes of visitors would damage the paintings, but one visits a splendid copy of them, a magnificent technological representation of the caves. Looking at the dark, skilfully outlined shapes of the prehistoric animals drawn on the rough walls of the caves, with their ochre, red and black colouring, I tried to imagine what life was like for these cave-dwelling families, who still found time to use their imagination, but we are too distant from them in time and I could only conjure up television images of life at that time. We visited Périgueux often, especially on Saturdays when the market was on. This was a big, bustling, colourful market with an astonishing array of fresh fish and meat and the ubiquitous cheeses. The town is very pretty, with its historic medieval quarter, a rabbit warren of narrow, cobbled streets opening out onto colourful *places* and a breathtaking Byzantine-style cathedral. Roy and I spent many a pleasant lunch in the small restaurants lining the squares.

The cottage also boasted a walnut grove, whose perfume would waft over one as one walked among the trees. At harvest time, the area was galvanised into action with all the farmers and their families out collecting the walnuts which fell into the strategically placed nets previously put down. It was an onerous time for them and back-breaking work picking up the walnuts preparatory to drying them and selling them. The families worked from daylight until dusk and the scene displayed before my eyes, resembled nothing so much as a scene from the medieval 'Book of Hours' as the peasants toiled in the vast groves. Our grove was small in comparison, but all the family undertook the task of collecting the walnuts and then Raymond offered to dry them in his *séchoir*. Some I managed to bring home and sell occasionally at a local market. Raymond would invite us regularly to his farmhouse to try out his homemade wine and liqueurs. I stuck to whisky. He wanted us to stay for dinner but we declined since the hygiene in his small farmhouse left a lot to be desired. His long-suffering wife not only did all the cooking, but made all her own pâtés and rillettes and foie gras, which she sold. She also tended all the animals and worked in the fields and vegetable garden.

Raymond liked the company of women and was prolific in his compliments about our dress whenever we went to see him. He was probably quite astonished at my transformation in the evenings, since most of the time while at the cottage, I was as bowed down as the peasants with all the work I did and so I wore my oldest clothes. On one occasion, only Doreen came with me to the cottage, and we were duly invited to take an *apéritif* with him and his family. That evening, he was in flirtatious mode, eying both Doreen and me quite amorously. We stayed rather longer than usual, becoming merrier by the minute as we drank. Eventually, I stirred myself to say we had to go, feeling quite woozy and thankful that we had only a short drive in the car to reach home. Raymond insisted on seeing us home in spite of our protests. I had a vague idea of his intentions. He followed us in his car through the black night. It was so dark that, in my inebriated state, I missed the entrance to the cottage and drove on until we were nearly in the next village. Realising my mistake, I reversed and arriving in front of the cottage, found Raymond standing on the lawn quite perplexed as to what had happened to us. More laughter and convivial chatter followed. Raymond was now even more fulsomely complimentary, especially to me since I was the only one to speak French. He came near me and started to embrace me, speaking of my *belle poitrine* and attempting to stroke me. Whereupon Doreen decided she would retire for the night. I held her back knowing what was likely to happen. But she disappeared and Raymond became even more pressing. I found the situation so excruciatingly funny that I couldn't stop laughing. My cheeks ached with laughter and I could hardly stand up. He proceeded to caress my breasts (he was obviously a 'breasts' man) murmuring endearments in French, which sounded so romantic. For one fleeting moment, I toyed with the idea of letting him come to bed with me, but commonsense and the thought of the state of his underwear deterred me. I finally pushed him off gently and went inside, in high good humour at our evening.

Some newcomers to the cottage one year were some baby barn owls. We had seen the apertures in the walls just under the attic where owls had previously been hatched but we had never seen any until this year. They made their presence felt by their constant chirping and squeaking. We only ever saw the mother late in the evening as she came swooping back, circling the cottage to ensure that the kestrel hovering around, that had seen the chicks, was not in the vicinity. With the coast clear, she would then alight on the ledge and enter the nest. Gradually we could see the young ones poking their tiny heads out of the aperture, grey-white and open-mouthed, with immense saucer eyes. As they grew older they became more adventurous, stepping hesitantly out onto the ledge. One or two fell out of the nest and could not fly well enough to get back, so Roy had to pick them up tenderly and put them back. One warm summer's afternoon, we had both gone for a siesta after all our labours, Roy on the settee in the living room and I to my bed. When I woke up and walked into the living room, there calmly and silently sitting on Roy's chest was a young barn owl. It must have fallen out of the nest and hopped into the room. It turned its head placidly from side to side oblivious of any danger. I whispered to him, "Roy! Wake up! There's an owl sitting on you." He had been so tired that he was in a deep sleep, but then opened his eyes and the two of them stared in amazement at each other. He softly caught hold of it and took it back to the nest. It was a magical moment.

We had another brush with the fauna of the area later. Early mornings at *L'Aquéduc* were the most pleasurable times for me, when the early morning mist was dispersed by the warm sun, promising a fine day. I would walk behind the cottage taking stock of my property, revelling in its beauty. One morning, Roy joined me in my walk. The silence of the early morning lay lightly over the golden cornfields but was broken by a call from a figure on the skyline. It was Raymond, just beginning his day's work. Our pleasantries about the lovely weather and scene were distracted by a sudden, fleeting movement behind a stook of corn. There, quivering by the stook was a small creature with dark brown fur, not much bigger than a rabbit. It was transfixed with fear at our arrival. I turned to Roy to marvel with him at its beauty, when with a sudden, lunging rush, it moved silently towards us, and disappeared up Raymond's trouser leg. I registered only the shock on his face before he reacted instinctively, chopping his hand brutally against his knee. The beautiful animal dropped like a stone to the ground, bloodstained and lifeless. I could not believe that such a beautiful, wild creature could suddenly be dead. I was about to remonstrate to Raymond when he told me about the animal. It was a ferret. These animals were somehow programmed to like exploring tunnels, particularly rabbit tunnels. But although sometimes kept as pets from birth, the ones who live in the wild can bite savagely, even humans and when they do they hang on grimly, sucking the saliva from the flesh. It had reacted automatically to the tunnel of Raymond's trousers. If he had not acted so fast and so effectively, it could have hurt him seriously. He explained that one of the stories about ferrets is that they can catch a frog, bite through its brain, 'leucotomising' it so that it is paralysed but still alive and kept in the nest for future feeding. I shivered and was suddenly aware that to a 'townie' like me, the countryside is not all beauty. Other mornings were more pleasurable. It was the custom for my family to breakfast on fresh croissants and bread from the local baker, and freshly brewed coffee, sitting around the large table on the lawn in the glorious sunshine, with the smell of wood-smoke still lingering on the morning air. I would look round at them enjoying the food and air and sun, and breathe a sigh of contentment. The evenings were also very pleasant. On one occasion, David and Valmai sat with me in front of the bonfire we had lit in the adjacent field. Its vaporous wood-smoke smelled of resin and curled in spirals upwards towards the dark shapes of the walnut trees. The night was deeply silent and the sky was sable velvet except for the stars shining brilliantly above. This was the evening when Halley's comet flashed blazing across the sky in all its rapid, shooting brilliance and because of the absence of any artificial light in the sky, we saw it so clearly. That was another night to remember.

Such pleasure could not last and so it proved. The final nail in the coffin of my house-purchase experiment and one which finally laid it to earth, was something quite unexpected. *L'Aquéduc* lay back from a small country road which meandered from the big, china-manufacturing town of Limoges to Sarlat-le-Canéda, one of the most populous of tourist areas in the Dordogne. Most of the traffic was local tractors and agricultural merchants' vans with the occasional fast tourist car navigating the dangerous bends in the road. After five pleasurable years in *L'Aqueduc* we learned that the new autoroute, the A20 named *L'Aquitaine* which would run from Paris to Bordeaux, had finally passed its planning stage and was now in the process of being built. One of its exits would be Limoges and our road was to be upgraded to allow tourists an alternative non-autoroute way to the Dordogne. This meant that the road outside our cottage was to have all of its bends straightened out so that it could become a three-lane highway. The planners arrived in force, armed with compulsory purchase documents. Land was commandeered either side of the existing road and this included most of my walnut grove. They even wanted to reduce the frontage of my garden, which would include felling the ancient bay tree, home to numerous birds. I protested strongly and was for once successful. The road would be widened beyond my stretch of lawn. But when finally the new road was built, the tranquillity and peace of the area was destroyed. Our final summer there was endured rather than enjoyed as the manic drivers raced along the smooth, new road and huge, lumbering lorries belching smoke and pollution followed them. My idyll was shattered, my romantic dreams of country life gone forever. The march of progress had destroyed them. I sold *L'Aqueduc* soon after.

Conclusion

Voltaire's dictum, "*Il faut cultiver son jardin*", seemed a wise path to pursue after the sorry saga of the cottage. There will be no more house-buying adventures for me. But the memories remain. When deciding to write these memoirs which *Le Figaro* newspaper thinks of as "*une exploration nombrilique*", some people expressed surprise that I chose a traditional chronological approach. It was instinctive, but I was reassured in my decision by A. S. Byatt's comment in her book *On Histories and Stories*, that "We are narrative beings because we live in biological time. Whether we like it or not, our lives have beginnings, middles and ends". I wanted to record the chronology of my life to try to understand it better and I wanted to 'unlock my word-hoard' as *Beowulf* said. The time seemed appropriate, since I am no longer involved in any form of teaching. Writing it, I have gained a clearer insight into myself and others, allowing me to be more understanding of their actions and motives. The predominant characteristic I have is a strong will. Schopenhauer spoke of the will as being an active but irrational force in human nature and looking back on my early life I can see how strong my will was. I would pester my father continually for money for sweets and he always finally gave in. So the will to succeed was already ingrained in me. This also showed itself in a strong quest for knowledge which I realised I could get from books, so I developed an strong desire to read and I read voraciously! The early books were all such *moral* stories which imbued me with a sense of middle-class morality. The time spent immersed in books may account for the fact that I have very few recollections of my early childhood, just vignettes of going to the library several times a week. My interest in reading must also have been an escape mechanism from the miseries of our daily existence. It provided me with an alternative universe, a window on another way of life that I aspired to. Books meant pushing the boundaries of the 'here and now', moving into the study of different civilisations and different lives. I am still in my element when I am in some class or other having my brain stimulated. And this knowledge of other worlds inevitably resulted in the desire for travel, to other countries and other societies. It was always beckoning me even when I was adult. It led me to an appreciation of architecture, particularly church architecture. And the cheap air flights now on offer have opened up to me all that wonderful architecture, in France and Germany, Austria and Hungary. I have grown to love the simplicity and austere beauty of the great Gothic cathedrals, their calm and their stillness. And, although my brain abhors the excesses of the German baroque, I can still admire the richness of its ornamentation, the sensual pleasure it must have given to so many believers.

My travels took me to the village of Oberammergau, to the passion play put on every ten years. It was a very emotional experience for me, with the passion of Christ played out by the local population to the backdrop of fine church music. I hasten to add that it was not the religious aspect of the story which moved me; rather it was its historical aspect. I am now immune to religion. After years of wrestling mentally with the problems of faith and belief, I am a confirmed atheist and accept what James Joyce called 'the soul's incurable loneliness'. The only label I can hang on myself now is that of 'humanist'. I appreciate human beings in all their complexities. I was for a time indelibly scarred by the rigid oppression of the Roman Catholic Church, made even more harsh by my mother's interpretation of it in her long-suffering life. We had it drummed into us for years; sex is for procreation purposes only, men only want to take advantage of you, don't give them opportunities to do so. This meant in practice, that my sisters and I were forbidden to wear make-up, we never received any love or even compliments, there was never any discussion of our awakening sexuality, and even more dangerous, no practical information about the changes that were occurring in our bodies.

I indulge in a wry smile when I read newspapers today describing how men are driven by the level of testosterone in their bodies. Isn't that simply another way of repeating what my mother warned us against? Not that I believe any of it. It simply suits the sex-permeated culture that we live in today to cast men in this role. Fortunately, the healthier, more relaxed attitude to sex that I found when living in France released me from this negative image of men. The landscape of my mind has changed, but vestiges remain of that old pernicious belief. I wear make-up and perfume only when I am going somewhere special, I wear no jewellery and pay little attention to my appearance except when socialising, and even then I breathe a sigh of relief when I can change back into my old clothes. My younger sister, Doreen is even more austere in her attitudes. Never having the desire or opportunity to live abroad, she is a pure product of my mother's teachings and confessed to me once that she had never had an orgasm, in spite of producing three children. My two daughters are totally different; they love wearing nice clothes, make-up and perfume and are great ones for socialising. Probably as a reaction to me!

My quest for knowledge meant that the teaching profession was probably a good career for me although at the beginning I did not think so, feeling totally overwhelmed by the fact that I had to stand in front of a class of over thirty, young teenagers. But young or not, these children learn very quickly to find one's weaknesses. Shirley and I often bemoaned the fact that teaching was really our only option apart from office work, because of the crass decisions made early on about our studies. I thought we would have been happier as librarians, surrounded by books. This was impossible at first because one needed a degree and a further period of study. Shirley disagreed, saying that we should both have become much more introverted. Teaching forced us to open up to others and gave us more confidence. I have come to believe that teaching is a truly honourable profession which offers great delights and satisfaction. In schools, every day is different, every child is different. The whole spectrum of personalities is on view. I developed an intense curiosity to see how people behave in certain situations, and am interested in their psychological make-up. I feel strongly that education is the window to opportunity and for working-class children particularly, an aspiration to a better, richer life.

The corollary to this need to escape was that I was totally unprepared for real life, especially in the form of marriage. I expected people to behave in a very moral way and was constantly let down when they didn't. We never learned how to behave socially. My elder sister Irene still complains about the fact that she was caught out once at a dinner table with inappropriate behaviour, that is, not knowing which cutlery to use! Even more serious, I never feel completely at ease in a large gathering, except when I am abroad. Then I am classless and can interact much better with foreigners. I have had to accept feelings of social inadequacy as part of my psychological make-up. I am now more aware of my extreme sensitivity to slights and hurts and possibly still see them where there are none. I understand now that this sensitivity and my heightened awareness of atmosphere is a result of the intense anxiety generated by my father's extreme behaviour in the home. We had to be constantly on our guard and keep out of his way in case we annoyed him. As a result, I am quite wary of life and my reaction to it. I am *méfiante* and slightly suspicious of people and their acts. Like a character in James Joyce's book, *The Dubliners*, "I have lived at a distance from my body, regarding my own acts with doubtful side-glances." I have learned that I cannot manage conflict easily. I still avoid confrontation like the plague. So I can see that in the past with Stanley, and others, I was accommodating when I shouldn't have been. Resentment would build up in me at being taken for granted and then, unable to control that festering resentment, I would explode, with all the fall-out that would occur afterwards. But I am more aware of the dangers now. I can also stand back and find some humour in the situation. Quoting *Beowulf* again, I have "wintered into wisdom" of a sort. The great French writer of the seventeenth century Michel de Montaigne wrote, "Every man carries in himself the complete pattern of human nature". He wrote copiously over the years of his own feelings about himself and about the world, noting each tiny change of attitude, each shift of perspective, each differing reaction to events. He said, "This is my teaching, this is my study – it's not a lesson for others, it is for me." But, of course, others have learned from him as a result of reading his work and I like to think that I have too.

What else to say after all this self-indulgence? I have forgiven Stanley for 'the long harrowing' he caused me. He lives alone now with his dog for company and I think he is happy like that. My children give me much pleasure. I tease my Welsh grandchildren by telling them that the word 'Welsh' is an English word and means the 'dark foreigner' who was chased out of England by the superior Anglo-Saxons. That sets them going! My epitaph will be the genes that I have handed down to my children; we are part of a long continuum of family, of which I become even more conscious as I research our genealogy.

I have decided that the last years of my life will be spent in what James Joyce calls 'the full glory of some passion'. I shall not 'fade and wither dismally with age'. My interest in life, in its constant changes, means that I shall never grow bored. The resilience and optimism I have always possessed, whether a product of my genes or my past, is still with me and will remain so until the end.